The English Semi-detached HOUSE

BY FINN JENSEN

HOW AND WHY THE SEMI BECAME BRITAIN'S
MOST POPULAR HOUSE-TYPE

an ovolo book

ovolo

Ovolo Publishing
1 The Granary
Brook Farm
Ellington
Huntingdon
Cambridgeshire
PE28 0AE

01480 891777

First edition published October 2007

Title and this edition © Ovolo Publishing Ltd 2007
Text © Finn Jensen 2007
ISBN: 978-0-9548674-3-0
Cover design: Gill Lockhart
Page design: Bounford.com

Printed in China

We can supply almost any book on housebuilding and related topics.
To browse or buy please visit **www.buildingbooksdirect.com** or call
01480 893833. To find out more about Ovolo titles
please visit www.ovolopublishing.co.uk

For Birgit

Acknowledgements

In the early stages of researching the topic of this book I owe special debts to my tutor at Liverpool John Moores University, Dr. Athanassios Migos, who as an architect showed professional interest in a subject that in general was considered undeserving of serious research. It is also thanks to Dr. Migos that I was introduced to the late Professor Quentin Hughes, who also with an open mind debated the enigma of the semi-detached house in Britain. My thanks go also to Dr. Migos' colleagues at the School for Architecture.

More broadly, I have received help and information from many anonymous estate agents, housing developers, librarians and archivists, all of whom have contributed to building up the history of the semi-detached house as it appears in these pages.

Thanks are due also to Lis Christensen MA, who carefully read the study as it evolved chapter by chapter and who helped me to improve the structure and language of the presentation. Considerable assistance in finding important statistics on the internet was given to me by Niels Jensen MA. It goes without saying that only I am responsible for any errors or omissions.

Finally, this work would not have been possible without the constant encouragement from my wife Birgit, who has coped most exceptionally with a husband who, for so long, has walked around with a far-away look in his eyes and his mind preoccupied with the English semi.

Contents

Preface

The semi-detached house has always, like the suburbs it represents, been a subject of ridicule and contempt among critics and architects. With one third of the population of England living in a semi today it is, however, the most common mode of housing in this country. Apparently we all take the semi so much for granted that hardly any real interest has been shown in its history and evolution from its humble beginnings in seventeenth century England. This study attempts to redress this situation by charting the rise and fall of this enduringly popular house type, which to many visitors is just as English as red pillar boxes and London taxi cabs.

The history of the semi-detached house is linked closely to the development of the suburbs. There is no single reason why semi-detached houses came to set their mark on the English suburbs in the way they do. It is not just a question of saving land and building costs or giving easy access to the rear of the property, although these factors are valid and important in themselves. But so would they be in any other country, and still you will not find semi-detached houses in, say, Rome, Paris or Copenhagen, in numbers to match those of an English suburb. There must be other factors peculiar to the English way of life that have promoted the semi-detached house to the prominence it displays in this country. While some of these factors are brought forward in this book and summarised in the final chapter, our fascination with the ubiquitous semi still needs to be studied more comprehensively.

The industrial revolution in the late eighteenth and early nineteenth century created a new, potent middle class eager to demonstrate its new-found wealth in its choice of dwelling. By the middle of the nineteenth century the semi-detached house had become an acceptable house style, due in part to new, prestigious estates in London with a significant proportion of semi-detached houses created by the architect John Nash and his contemporaries.

The first semi-detached town houses were intended for the more affluent sections of the middle class, such as bankers, city merchants, lawyers or doctors. As the manufacturing industries gained momentum through the nineteenth century, and more and more middle-class jobs were created, the speculative builders also turned their attention to building suburban estates for the growing population of office workers, managers, accountants, teachers, civil servants, etc. They, too, needed to segregate themselves from the working classes who were housed in more-or-less atrocious conditions in hastily erected terraced cottages. For the middle-class wage-earner, a semi-detached house in a suburb within striking distance of their city jobs became highly desirable. The improved bus, tram and train connections became all-important for a move to the suburbs.

The middle classes continued to grow in the first half of the twentieth century, and with the advent of cheap loans an increasing number of families were able to buy, rather than rent, their homes. An unprecedented number of semi-detached estates grew up around all major cities in the nineteen twenties and thirties. To this day, the suburbs of England are dominated by this housing boom. The 'Tudorbethan' semi with its mock timber gables can be found in every suburb in the country. It epitomizes the building style of the period. In fact, the style never really fell out of fashion, and it is still popular today in a slightly debilitated form in newly erected housing estates. A new surge of middle-class affluence in the second half of the twentieth century gave rise to new aspirations and the number of detached houses built annually eventually surpassed the number of semis.

New building regulations and legislation was brought in by the Government in the nineties to curb what was feared to become suburban sprawl and the erosion of the countryside by speculatively built estates. Plot sizes for housing were severely restricted, and some builders again turned their attention to offering middle-class buyers the semi-detached house as an attractive form of residence.

Finn Jensen, August 2007

Foreword

Semi-detached suburbia

The semi-detached house is a peculiar British compromise. Designed to appeal to a growing middle class, with their concerns for status, independence, and above all a desire to escape the teeming cities, the history of the semi-detached is the history of suburbia, and the battle between town and country.

It has taken a Dane, Finn Jensen, once again to research and tell the story of what makes British towns distinctive. And like his fellow Dane Steen Eiler Rasmussen, in London: the Unique City, or Stefan Muthesius in his account of the terraced house, he does it with great sympathy for the values and lifestyles the buildings supported and symbolised. The significance of the semi is brought out at the start in a contrast between the UK in 2003, where 33 per cent of the homes are semi-detached, and 28 per cent terraced, compared with a figure of 13 per cent for both types in Denmark.

The semi is a dying breed, because government density guidelines require the space that once allowed direct access to the back garden to be built over. Today many of the neighbourhoods that once were so treasured look neglected as cars sprawl over what were the front gardens and as local shops close, sometimes to be replaced by takeaways, but rarely providing the hubs that once gave the community its identity and meeting place.

Finn Jensen shows how the roots of the semi go back to aristocratic inventions in the 17th century, and started to take off in the 19th, with a rich profusion of styles. By 1850, the middle class had grown to a third of the population, and used the new trams and suburban railways to escape the smoke. As the English largely declined to invest in tenements, preferring the simpler terrace, our cities sprawled as far as the public transport routes could extend.

The garden city provided a better model, and was one of Britain's greatest inventions to be exported around the world. Finn points out that Ebenezer Howard was 70 when work started on Welwyn, and the masterplan was produced in two months because of his burning desire to show what could be done. In all there were 20 garden cities before the First World War, which led on to the great drive to build Homes for Heroes.

The new arterial roads radiating from the cities provided serviced sites often close to modern new factories. Between the two great wars some 76,000 builders produced three million semis in a variety of styles, the greatest house-building boom England ever experienced. Pattern books were the equivalent of today's codes, and worked because they were very much simpler. Modernism did not suit Britain's climate or preference for 'make-believe'. The privet hedge and street trees gave the illusion of living in the country, as well as endless work cutting the hedge and mowing the lawn.

Today, semis with large gardens in prosperous suburbs are being bought up to
redevelop in a haphazard and typically English way. Journeys to work and shop
are overwhelmingly by car, and only dog walkers and joggers seem to use the
pavements. English Heritage has launched a campaign to Save our Streets, but the
real SOS call should be for our suburbs, whose charms are disappearing before
our eyes. The hundreds of pictures and plans in this book therefore provide an
important memorial to a fast vanishing way of life, one when there were always
crumpets for tea!

Nicholas Falk

Dr Nicholas Falk is the founder director of URBED
(Urban and Economic Development Group)
and co-author with David Rudlin of
Building the 21st Century Home.

Suburbs, suburbia and semis

"Oh look, daddy, the houses are glued together"
Seven-year-old on seeing a row of semis for the first time

To understand the evolution of semi-detached housing in England it is necessary to understand also the development of the English suburb. The two are closely linked. In fact, on explaining the essence of the suburbs, Willmott and Young do not hesitate to state that "… the semi-detached, pebble-dashed villas … are more than the symbol, they <u>are</u> the suburb" [1].

There are many different opinions on how to define a semi-detached house and how to define a suburb. For our purposes the definition of a semi-detached house given in *The Dictionary of Architecture and Landscape Architecture* is appropriate:

> A semi-detached house or double house is one of a pair, built simultaneously with a common or party wall between them, ie attached on one side [2].

It should be added that the "common or party wall" is one that separates living or dwelling areas of the two houses as it would in a terrace house; it is not just a wall, for example, that separates garages between the houses. Each semi-detached house has the advantage of giving access from the front to the back of the house without having to pass through the house itself.

The suburbs of today have their roots in the industrial revolution in the eighteenth and nineteenth centuries. In its wake followed the growth of a middle class of office workers, bank clerks, accountants, teachers, nurses, engineers, salesmen, and any number of new, respectable jobs created by the developing wealth of the nation. According to [2] the word suburb denotes

> an outlying built area or urban fringe to a town, in origin a middle-class residential expansion providing a village-like arcadian alternative to the urban environment.

Suburbs in England are typically made up of several smaller housing estates erected either by local authorities, or more commonly by speculative builders. Speculative building is a phrase used to denote building houses without a particular purchaser in mind. Nowadays, you may find housing estates also in outlying villages. These estates can hardly be called suburbs, but they bear the trademark of their city counterparts in their layout and housing style, and often also in the social background of their inhabitants. These estates, and the real suburbs, constitute England's suburbia, a word first used in the 1890s[1] [3].

   Suburbia and suburban have, rightly or wrongly, received a derogative implication. The Oxford English Reference Dictionary tells us that suburban may mean either just the characteristics of suburbs, or it may mean "provincial, narrow-minded, uncultural, or naive" [5]. As approximately 50 per cent of the population in this country live in the suburbs this is a somewhat frightening interpretation. Indeed, modern housing research places no less than 86 per cent of the population in suburban, suburban/urban or suburban/rural areas [4]. Writing in 1923, Hughes and Lamborn expressed the sentiments of their age:

> Contemplation of our cities in the second half of the eighteenth century led Cowper to express the opinion that 'God made the country and man made the town'; it has been suggested that if he had lived to comment on the most characteristic results of the architectural activities of the following century he would have been moved to add: 'and the Devil ran up the suburbs'. [6]

---

1. Recent studies concerned with the suburban renaissance (see Chapter 12) have introduced a subdivision of suburbs in six typologies [4]. However, for the purpose of our story the simple definition given above is totally adequate.

This was written even before the mass influx of semi-detached suburban homes in the nineteen twenties and thirties.

The inhabitants of the suburbs are conscious of their privacy and their community and are, in general, suspicious of newcomers and strangers. Anyone venturing to stroll through a suburb on a Sunday morning is sure to be greeted by a householder or his wife asking if they might help in any way. If you do not belong, you must not expect a friendly remark from a hedge-clipping gardener or a husband washing the car in the driveway. You are, in essence, unwanted. The influx of ethnic groups, especially around London, has changed the traditional social uniformity of the pre-Second World War suburbs and has to a certain extent, but not wholly, brought about a more relaxed attitude. The solid middle class stability of the suburbs that had been taken for granted in the first part of the twentieth century has in some areas been challenged by such changes.

With the dominant role played by suburbia in the life of so many inhabitants of this country, it cannot come as a surprise that the ways of suburbia have drawn the attention of writers and artists. It was especially in the years just before and after the Second World War, when the suburbs as we know them now were well and truly established, that the social aspects of living in the suburbs became evident. The speculative estates created during the first part of the century might have had clean air, schools, and transportation, but the words boredom and isolation soon came to be used to describe the feelings of all too many of the new inhabitants, especially the wives.

The picture of a middle class leaning towards extreme uniformity of living and life style was illustrated in George Orwell's 1936 novel *Keep the Aspidistra Flying* [7]. In the closing pages of the book the advertising artist abandons his bohemian, down-and-out existence and re-enters his earlier middle class environment. The novel places him and his pregnant wife in a flat off Edgware Road in London, but the 1997 film adaptation [8] shows the couple in a massive 1930s estate of Art Deco style semi-detached homes. The choice of Art Deco rather than mock-Tudor style housing captures the image of a modern, 'artsy' individual, whereas the uniformity of the estate expresses the ideal of middle class living.

The pattern of a household in suburbia in those years would typically be a married couple with one or two children. The husband travelled to work every morning and came back in the evening, often quite late. His wife stayed at home minding the house (not the garden, which was a man's job), the children, the washing, the shopping, and in general keeping up appearances, often with little personal contact with even her closest neighbours. The plight of many a housewife in suburbia is told chillingly in a short story by Elizabeth Bowen [9]. She describes the frustrations of a wife, who, with a husband and two children, has recently moved into a semi-detached house in a newly built, and not yet completed, estate. However: "No sooner were the Watsons settled in their new home than Mrs Watson was overcome by melancholy." The melancholy turns to near-depression, and it is only through one of her children, the daughter, that she finally gets to talk to a neighbour, a Mrs Dawkins from 'Kosy Kot', and takes on the new realities of life in the suburbs. Mrs Dawkins is very likely close to the truth by observing: "Gentlemen, being out so much, don't feel it the same way."

The theme of boredom in suburbia seems to have persisted, even as family and living patterns changed. To the hippie generation of the nineteen sixties, being forced to live in a suburb was considered the ultimate punishment. The title of a Manfred Mann single from this period positively spits out the words "Semi-detached suburban Mr. James." In an illustrated book of Beatles' lyrics (1969) a typical speculative semi-detached house is used to illustrate their song 'She's Leaving Home'.

Until fairly recently the suburbs and suburbia of Britain have been largely neglected in serious architectural studies. It has not been deemed acceptable for the professional architect to be involved with a style of dwelling so far removed from the ideals of Le Corbusier or Frank Lloyd Wright. When the elite did venture to comment, it would invariably be to criticise. The cartoonist Osbert Lancaster [10], [11] and the poet John Betjeman [12] both with a life-long passion for architecture, were among those who, in the nineteen thirties, expressed their opinion of the British suburbs, concluding that a speedy demolition would be the best way of dealing with these estates, destined otherwise to become the slums of the future. Betjeman spoke of "the deep pit of speculative building" [13]. There is, still, a tendency to ridicule much about suburbia, the house styles and the way of life found there, but it must be acknowledged that the pattern of speculative building laid down in the early part of the twentieth century has been extremely resilient. The estates that are being built today can be criticised every bit as much as the earlier suburban developments, but for a variety of reasons that we will touch upon later, it is the kind of living that is chosen, and indeed preferred, by a very substantial proportion of families in this country.

It is interesting to observe that criticism of suburban estates seems to come mainly from those who do not themselves inhabit them. The architect Ian Davis, writing about his first day in a school of architecture in 1953, humorously recounts that the tutor (on learning that the new student lived in Edgware) "gave me a probing stare, followed by 'I take it that you live in one of Edgware's semi-detached houses?' My affirmative prompted the observation that I should make early plans to move to a more civilised address, such as Camden Town" [14].

The suburbs of Britain are in many respects unique to this country. Nowhere else in Europe will you find suburbs that are so totally dominated by semi-detached speculative housing, see a typical example in Fig. 1.1. In general, the homes in suburbia will be terraced, semi-detached, detached, or, more rarely, flats. It goes without saying that the detached houses are the only dwellings that realistically would have been commissioned by individuals with the intention of making them their homes. However, some detached houses in the housing estates were built as detached speculative building. The number was small in the early part of the twentieth century and detached houses were usually built whenever an odd corner or a neighbouring development limited the size of the available building plot. These houses were basically a 'half semi' with exactly the same interior layout as the surrounding semis.

Fig. 1.1. Nineteen thirties semi-detached houses in West Derby (2002).

The number of detached houses in the speculative building estates grew substantially as the century wore on. Nevertheless, at the turn of the new millennium about one third of the housing stock was semi-detached.

It can be interesting to briefly compare housing statistics from the UK with those of Denmark, a country that by and large has a social structure similar to that of Britain, see Fig. 1.2 and Fig. 1.3. These figures refer to the countries as a whole, not just the suburbs. The 2003 statistics from the UK show 28 per cent terraced houses, 33 per cent semi-detached, 21 per cent detached, and 17 per cent flats (www.housing.odpm.gov.uk). The Danish figures from 2005 show that terrace houses and semis combined account for only 13 per cent of all dwellings, 46 per cent are detached, and no less than 39 per cent are flats. The Danish statistics do not distinguish between terraces and semi-detached houses. The rest of the housing stock in the Danish statistics seems to be divided between farmhouses, residential homes, college accommodation, etc. With such a significant difference, especially in the proportion of terrace and semi-detached housing, it is no wonder that there is a visible impact when going from an English to a Danish suburb, as is indeed the case.

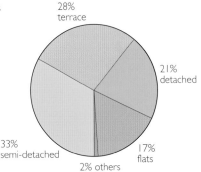

Fig. 1.2. Distribution of housing types in the UK.

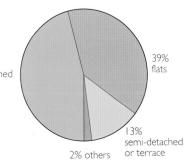

Fig. 1.3. Distribution of housing types in Denmark.

Suburban growth

The phenomenal growth of English suburbs took place in the twentieth century. Two examples of suburban growth are shown below. The most dramatic expansion was in the first half of the century, especially between the wars. Suburban growth continued vigorously, however, also in the latter part of the century, although at a somewhat less frenetic pace.

The first example is from the London suburb of Edgware, which has been the focus of quite a few writings on suburban development [14], [15] and [16]. The other example is from West Derby, a suburb of Liverpool [17]. In both cases the new housing estates were developed in what were then rural areas within easy reach of the city centres. In the early part of the century Edgware was served by a branch line of the GNR, the Great Northern Railway, but service from King's Cross was poor, involved at least one change of carriage, and took about forty-five minutes. The London Underground had extended its Northern Line to Edgware in 1924 at a time when green fields still dominated the surroundings of the tiny village.

The expansion of the underground to rural areas was a courageous policy. Profits would await first the erection of dwellings, invariably in the form of speculative housing estates, and second, the population of these estates by primarily middle-class workers with jobs in London, all requiring to travel to and from the town on a daily basis.

The policy was, however, one that had paid off earlier, when the then Charing Cross, Euston & Hampstead Railway in 1907 had opened an electrified line beyond Hampstead to the largely uninhabited pastures of Golders Green, see the early poster illustrated in Fig. 1.4. The line was under the control of the American entrepreneur C.T. Yerkes, of Chicago, who had been heavily involved in the American tramway industry. In spite of opposition to the planned extension, Yerkes persevered and was so confident of the success of the venture that he provided the purpose-built carriages with strap-hangers in anticipation of the

Fig.1.4. Early London Underground poster for Golders Green (London Transport Museum).

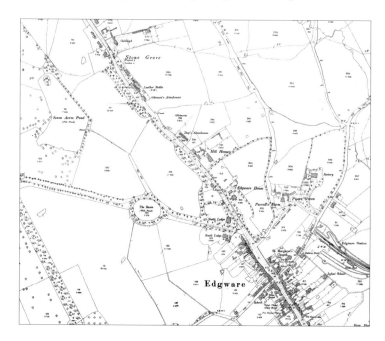

Fig.1.5. Edgware in 1895.

rush hour traffic to and from the city.

An excellent way of following the development of an area is through contemporary maps and aerial photographs, whenever such can be found. In the case of Edgware, for example, Ordnance Survey (OS) maps from 1895 and 1911 are available. The rural nature of Edgware is evident from the section of the 1895 map shown in Fig. 1.5. The village itself is clustered around St. Margaret's Church and hugs the old Roman Road of Watling Street, now the A5. Northwards from the station is open countryside. A single pair of semi-detached houses, in large grounds, may be found just north of the station to the east of Church Lane.

Some housing development had taken place by the time the map was revised in 1911 (Fig. 1.6), consisting mainly of blocks of terrace houses on either side of Watling Street. A few semi-detached houses appear on its west side going north to Stone Grove. Also, seven semi-detached pairs have been strewn, somewhat haphazardly it seems, north of Hale Lane, well removed from the village itself. They were advertised for sale in 1906 at £490 leasehold, a princely sum in those days, with four bedrooms, 300 ft gardens, and "room for motor" [16]. As the motor car was still a reserve of the very wealthy, these Edwardian villas must indeed have been exclusive, albeit semi-detached.

The First World War effectively put a stop to building private homes,

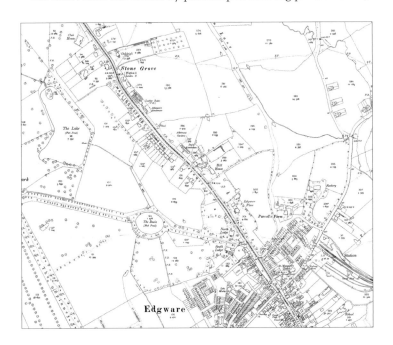

Fig.1.6. Edgware in 1911.

and precious little had changed in Edgware by 1923, but the London Underground was at that time in the final stages of constructing its terminal for the Northern Line. With the opening of the line the following year the speculative builders had moved in and vast estates of predominantly semi-detached houses marked the beginning of a suburb that soon covered the former hay-fields of rural Edgware. Fig. 1.7 shows a poster from the period illustrating the hive of building activity around one of the stations on the Northern Line, in this case Brent station, later to be renamed Brent Cross.

In 1924, London Underground issued a poster, an unusually

Fig. 1.7. Speculative builders at work close to the London Underground station of Brent, later Brent Cross, seen in the background. Poster 1923 (London Transport Museum).

gloomy poster, see Fig. 1.8, encouraging the move away from the dismal, grey, tightly packed semi-detached housing in the upper part of the poster to the green, open countryside around Edgware. 'Move to Edgware' it suggests. Critics might maintain that it only took a few years before suburban Edgware itself became a victim of its success and took on a cloak of monotonous mediocrity.

By 2001, the area had definitely taken on a tired look. It no longer had the look of a reasonably prosperous middle-class environment. There was a distinct lack of pride and maintenance, and an apparent lack of respect for a housing community that, without exhibiting the dignity of a Georgian estate, nevertheless had demonstrated a calm if uninteresting frontage to the world. Not so any longer. The front gardens had been concreted over to give standing space for one or two cars, many windows had been replaced by large area double glazing, and the nineteen thirties porches had had their solid, green doors discarded and replaced by doors of white PVC in an incompatible, Georgian look-alike style. Some householders had chosen to paint the lower brickwork of the house in a gaudy, blue colour, sometimes even underlining the painful effect by picking out the pointing in white.

The second example is the village of West Derby a few miles east of the centre of Liverpool. West Derby was mentioned in the Domesday Book of 1086 and was at that time more important than Liverpool, then only a small fishing settlement on the River Mersey. This changed as early as in the thirteenth century, and today West Derby is a typical suburb of Liverpool.

The nineteenth and twentieth centuries saw a massive growth in the population around Liverpool. As Liverpool grew in importance as a major shipping port in England, second only to London, the wealthy merchants and shipowners placed their villas well outside the noise and grime of the big city. Some built mansions on the Wirral on the other side of the Mersey, but some chose to settle with their families in West Derby, at the time described as "a quiet and secluded place of residence suitable for people of refinement and taste" in the text on an Ordnance Survey reprint of the 1906 map. No less than 60 large mansions were built here in the nineteenth century to house the influential owners. Extra housing for the servants and their families contributed to the growth of the village. In 1906, for example, the occupants of Hartington Road, a street consisting of mainly terraced houses still to be seen today, included a steward, two butlers, two coachmen, a gardener, and two labourers, as well as a number of artisans and municipal employees, not forgetting Mr. Albert Haskins of No.1, who was a 'professional golfer'.

A map from 1906, Fig. 1.9, shows the Cheshire Lines Railway dividing West Derby. The larger mansions can be found mainly to the west of the railway line, while a number of terraced estates, including

Fig. 1.8. London Underground poster 1924 (London Transport Museum).

Fig. 1.9. Map of West Derby 1906.

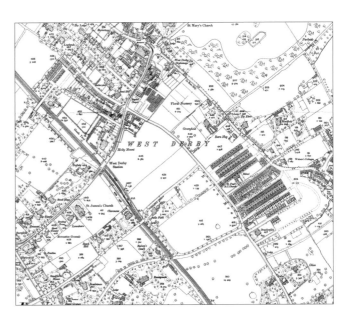

Fig. 1.10. Aerial photograph of West Derby in the nineteen thirties [17].

Hartington Road, lie to the east of the line around Eaton Road. A small number of semi-detached houses may be seen near the centre of the village. Otherwise, as with Edgware, the surrounding area is still agricultural land.

By the nineteen thirties the quiet and secluded place of residence has changed nearly beyond recognition with a massive influx of speculative building of semi-detached houses, see Fig. 1.10 [17]. In this photograph the Cheshire Lines Railway still runs in the cutting to the far left in the picture. The railway continued to carry passengers until 1950 and goods traffic till 1976. It is now a pedestrian and cycle way. In the bottom left-hand corner of Fig. 1.11 from around 1990 is the Alder Hey Children's Hospital with Eaton Road running north [17]. The new estates have filled in

Fig. 1.11. West Derby around 1990 [17].

the land to the east of Eaton Road and have joined the old Victorian terrace estates in the upper half of the picture. The suburban sprawl has continued north, west and east, but a few green areas do survive. The golfing green so prominent on the nineteen thirties picture can also be found in the most recent photograph (centre right), which would probably have pleased Mr. Albert Haskins.

The rise and fall of the semi-detached

Some of the characteristics of English suburbs have been touched upon in the preceding paragraphs. In the cases of Edgware and West Derby, the housing estates built in the nineteen twenties and thirties were dominated by semi-detached buildings, but a broader view is called upon to follow the course of the semi-detached through the twentieth century. One way of doing this is by looking at official national (and regional) housing statistics. A very useful source in this particular case is a House of Commons Library reference [18] showing summary housing statistics since the year 1900.

The authors show a profile of housing stock in the UK from 1900 through 1991, see Fig. 1.12. The columns show the number of dwellings built in the periods indicated on the bottom line. Housing is subdivided into

1. Flats and apartments
2. Bungalows
3. Detached houses
4. Semi-detached houses
5. Terraced houses

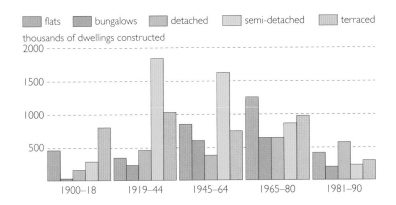

Fig. 1.12. Housing construction in the UK 1900-1990 [18].

In Fig. 1.13 the columns have been rearranged slightly to show the percentage of terraced, semi-detached and detached houses built in each of the periods shown. It demonstrates quite clearly the rise and fall of semi-detached building in the UK. As the population in England accounts for well over 80% of the total population in the UK it is reasonable to adopt this figure to illustrate the profile also of English housing over the same period.

The boom years for the semi-detached were in the inter-war period. This is very evident when one visits any English suburb today, where the majority of the semi-detached homes are characteristically from the nineteen thirties. Fig. 1.13 reflects the aspirations of the English people through the twentieth century, with respect to their preferred type of dwelling. Naturally, the broader economic structure of housing in England is also part of the equation.

Fig. 1.13. Houses built in the UK 1900–90. This graph is based on the information in Fig. 1.12. The columns show the number of houses built as a percentage of all houses built in that period. Flats and bungalows are not shown. However, it should be noted that a fair number of bungalows were built as semi-detached.

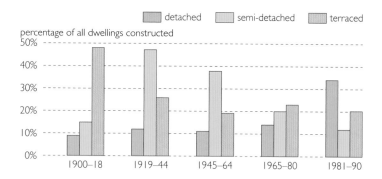

It is interesting to compare the decline in the construction of semi-detached dwellings with the rise in detached housing from 1945 onwards. The two trends are nearly a mirror image of each other. Also noteworthy is the nearly constant influx, percentage-wise, of terraced housing since 1919. It is a reflection of several centuries of building terrace houses in England coupled with the conservatism of the average home owner.

Of course, regional variations can be significant. For example, in 1996, in London there were 32 per cent terraced houses, 16 per cent semis, 5 per cent detached, and no less than 47 per cent flats, whereas the corresponding figures in the Yorkshire and Humber region were 30 per cent, 40 per cent, 15 per cent, and 15 per cent.

Clearly, with the overall pattern of housing being as it is, you would expect this to be visible, somehow, in many aspects of day-to-day living, such as in the books and journals, in television coverage, etc. If you work out the housing statistics in real numbers, you will find close to 25 million dwellings in England. Of these around 7 million are terraced properties and 8 million are semi-detached. Assume now that there are two adults per household. This gives a population of 30 million adult persons living in either a terraced or a semi-detached house. You would think that this should give a firm basis for, say, a periodical or a television series on semi-detached homes or the English terrace house. Alas, no. At the local newsagent there will be a large selection of magazines on homes and gardens, but not a single publication with either semi-detached or terrace in the title. This does not mean that the housing journals are totally devoid of articles addressing these most common of all dwellings, but you are going to be hard pushed to find them. Terraced houses are in a sense more acceptable than semis to the media. Both the popular TV soaps Coronation Street and Eastenders feature terraced houses to underline the working-class environments of the series.

Fig. 1.14. A cottage in the country. Model in ceramics for purely decorative purposes.

Another possible experiment by which you might gauge the pattern of housing types in England is to look at the range of miniature models of houses found in shops all over the country. They are usually made of pottery and intended for mantelpiece display in the home. Most of these models are of detached cottages of the 'chocolate box cover' type. They have thatched roofs, leaded windows and an abundance of roses, wisteria, hollyhocks or other colourful plants. They are usually olde worlde cottages of a nondescript era, but appealing to the Englishman's dream of a cottage in the country, see Fig. 1.14. Clearly, they do not reflect the way in which most of us live.

On a similar track it could be useful to investigate the range of scale models developed for scenic effects on model railways, especially for the most common and popular 00-gauge layouts. The models available are totally different from the romanticized ceramic miniatures. For the railway modeller there is quite a choice of terraced houses, typically from the Victorian era, either with or without the bay windows so much favored by Victorian builders. You may also find Victorian semi-detached houses as well more modern semi-detached dwellings, such as the council house semis shown in Fig. 1.15. You can also find the odd modern estate-

Fig. 1.15. Model of post-second world war council-built semis. Notice the lack of chimneys.

type detached house among the models on offer.

However, noticeable by its absence is the typical semi-detached pair of speculative houses from the nineteen thirties that so dominates English suburbs. There can be several reasons for this. One simple explanation is that space for scenic work on a model layout is usually very restricted, and there is just not room for semi-detached houses with surrounding plots, certainly not if the modeller wishes to convey the impression of a suburban estate. Another reason, of course, can be that even to the modelling fraternity the nineteen thirties semi-detached is not considered worthy of reproduction. Even the scenic backgrounds produced for wall mounting avoid suburbia. They will show rolling green hills, a village with its church, pub and post office, thatched cottages and even a busy industrial scene with factories, cranes, fork-trucks and lorries. You may choose the dream of the countryside and village life or you may choose the bustle associated with industries and railways. Semi-detached estates do not, it seems, capture the interest of the model-maker.

There can be interesting exceptions. One such exception is a model of an archetypal 1930s semi-detached pair of houses complete with mock-Tudor gables. The model was designed for the much smaller N-gauge, where even a small space would be able to accommodate much more generous scenic effects than 00-gauge layouts. Fig. 1.16 shows this diminutive, but realistically reproduced model.

Media and modelling aside, the fact remains that the period between the wars saw the strongest increase in semi-detached houses ever experienced in this country. In the latter part of the century the semi gradually lost ground to the detached house in the new speculative estates. The reasons for the changing pattern of housing are interesting. The following chapters will seek to unravel some of the parameters that have resulted in the present housing distribution in England. Not surprisingly, there are both social, architectural, legislative and local transport inputs to the development of the English suburbs and suburbia. Maybe most significant, and most difficult to quantify, are the more emotional factors commonly associated with the middle classes, such as class-consciousness, the idea that the Englishman's home is his castle, and an in-bred reluctance to live in high-rise flats.

Fig. 1.16. Plastic N-gauge model of a typical English semi-detached pair.

References

1   P. Willmott and M. Young, *Family and Class in a London Suburb*, Routledge & Kegan Paul, London 1960, p.11.

2   *Dictionary of Architecture and Landscape Architecture*, Penguin Reference (Fifth edition), London 1999.

3   Helen Long, *The Edwardian House*, Manchester University Press, Manchester and New York 1993, p.11.

4   Hampshire County Council, *In Suburbia*, Hampshire 2002, p.3.

5   *Oxford English Reference Dictionary*, Second edition, Oxford University Press 1996.

6   T.H. Hughes and E.A.G. Lamborn, *Towns and Town Planning, Ancient and Modern*, Oxford 1923, p.35.

7   George Orwell, *Keep the Aspidistra Flying*, 1936

8   Overseas Filmgroup, Inc., Keep the Aspidistra Flying, film adapted from George Orwell's novel, shown on BBC2, 1997

9   Elizabeth Bowen, *Attractive Modern Homes*, first published 1941. Reprinted in the *Collected Stories of Elizabeth Bowen*, Penguin, London 1983.

10 Osbert Lancaster, *Pillar to Post*, London 1938.

11 Osbert Lancaster, *A Cartoon History of Architecture*, John Murray, London 1975.

12 John Betjeman, Slough, poem 1937, reprinted in *Collected Poems*, John Murray (Publishers), London, Paperback Edition 2003, p.20.

13 John Betjeman, *Ghastly Good Taste*, first published 1933, reprinted by Century, London 1986, p.108-09.

14 Paul Oliver et al., *Dunroamin, the Suburban Semi and its Enemies,* Barrie and Jenkins, London 1981, p.27

15 Steen Eiler Rasmussen, *London: the Unique City*, Pelican Books, London 1960.

16 Alan Jackson, *Semi-detached London*, Second edition, Wild Swan Publications Ltd, Didcot 1991, p.205-222.

17 Colin Wilkinson, *Liverpool From the Air*, The Bluecoat Press, Liverpool 1999, p.58-59.

18 Joe Hicks and Grahame Allen, A Century of Change: Trends in UK Statistics since 1900, Research Paper 99/111, House of Commons Library, 21 December 1999.

2

From the Restoration to the end of the Georgian era (1660-1830)

"Ah, to build, to build! That is the noblest of all the arts"
Henry Wadsworth Longfellow (1807-82)

Rural beginnings

Although we in general associate semi-detached houses with suburbs, it seems likely that such dwellings appeared first in rural areas. It has been suggested that semi-detached cottages were not seen before the late seventeenth century [1]. However, one of the earliest references to what we today would call a semi-detached cottage is reportedly given by Haworth in 1623, when he describes "those two Houses or Cottages standing both under one Rooff" [2]. Quite possibly, the first semi-detached cottages were built to house different generations of the same family [3], which could have been common practice in many farming communities. A mid-to-late seventeenth-century semi-detached cottage, nicknamed Eyebrow Cottage, may still be seen on High Street in Sale near Manchester, although it has now been converted to a single dwelling.

One of the earliest examples of an estate of rural semi-detached cottages is at Chippenham, Cambridgeshire. These cottages were built as a result of 'emparking', an expression used to imply the enclosing of a park. The landowners would build a splendid mansion for themselves in the park, but an untidy village might spoil the view. Such villages were simply demolished, and an orderly village was designed instead, often as an entrance to the park to give visitors just a slight taste of the splendours to come in the form of the owner's Palladian manor. The Chippenham estate was erected by Lord Orford in this way for his farm labourers in the last years of the seventeenth century. A few of the cottages are still standing on New Street in the centre of the village. In 1712, Lord Orford commissioned a survey of his estate, and a magnificent illustrated map was produced by Heber Lands, see Fig. 2.1. New Street is the main village street running north-south. It is not possible, however, to identify on the map with certainty which cottages are semi-detached and which are detached.

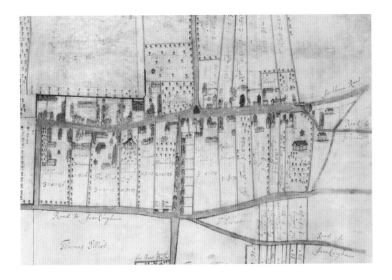

Fig. 2.1. The 1712 map of the Chippenham estate. Copyright Cambridgeshire County Council.

The practice of building houses for labourers was continued by wealthy landowners in the eighteenth century. On the one hand there was the practical aspect of ensuring reasonable living accommodation for the farm workers, and on the other there was an inclination to display one's own wealth and good taste to neighbouring estate owners. A particularly good example of this may be found at Houghton Hall in Norfolk. Houghton Hall itself is probably one of the grandest surviving Palladian houses in England. Built in the 1720s by Britain's first prime minister, Sir Robert Walpole, it soon became the centre of lavish entertainment for Sir Robert's political cronies and neighbours of standing. He swept away the original village, although the church still stands, and in 1729 laid the foundations to a new village lining the road leading up to the main entrance gates. Most of

2

the white painted cottages are semi-detached, back-to-back cottages with two rooms below and two upstairs. The cottages have been well maintained and still offer an impressive foreplay to the grandeur of Houghton Hall and its park, see Fig. 2.2.

Estate villages with a mixture of semi-detached houses and terraced houses were laid out early in the eighteenth century [4]. As an example, Houghton Village has some short terraces in addition to the semi-detached cottages. It is worth speculating that there would be a class divide between the labourers inhabiting the terraced houses and those living in the semi-detached cottages, when both housing types

Fig. 2.2. The Houghton Village semi-detached cottages built c.1730 (photo 2004).

existed on the same estate. There is ample evidence of such a housing hierarchy in later mining villages and in the garden villages built by benevolent factory owners in the nineteenth century.

Examples of early semi-detached cottages can be found in villages or townships over most of the country on what previously would have been agricultural land, or they may be situated in what at the time was an out-of-town development [5]. The cottages from 1793 illustrated in Fig. 2.3 are in Holbeach Clough [6]. Figs. 2.4-2.6 illustrate examples of semi-detached cottages from West Yorkshire from the period 1734 to around 1800. The three cottages illustrated, as well as those from Lincolnshire, are often termed 'mirror image' cottages, as they are mirrored around the vertical centre plane or party wall of the cottages. This strict symmetry was a hallmark of much Georgian architecture from the highest to the lowest ranks of society.

Fig. 2.3. Labourers', cottages in Holbeach Clough, Lincolnshire, 1793 [6].

Fig. 2.4 Semi-detached cottage dated 1734 in Heaton, West Yorkshire (2004).

Fig. 2.5 Semi-detached cottage dated 1779 in Queensberry, West Yorkshire (2004).

One of the best known rural estates of semi-detached houses or cottages from the late eighteenth century was created by the Earl of Dorchester at the Dorset village of Milton Abbas. From his mansion he looked down towards the existing village, a view that awoke his extreme displeasure. In keeping with the then established process of emparking, he had the village demolished and re-housed his labourers in a new village over the hill, out of view. Using Capability Brown (1715-83) as his landscaper and Sir William Chambers (1726-96) as his architect, he built around 40 semi-detached houses for his labourers over the period 1771-90. The white, thatched cottages looked out onto a curving village street. Originally, the space between the cottages was planted with chestnut trees, but these were done away with in the late twentieth century due to the darkness and dampness created by the massive trees. With the chestnut trees gone, much of the charm of the village was lost. A photo of the village as it appeared in 2006 is shown in Fig. 2.7.

Fig. 2.6 18th century semi-detached cottage in Riddlesden, West Yorkshire (2004).

The semi-detached pairs of Milton Abbas had been purposely designed to look like single dwellings. The single entrance door in the centre of the building was shared by the inhabitants. The notion of creating a design that made two houses appear as one was to be repeated over the next two hundred years in nearly all semi-detached buildings erected in this country. New variations on the theme were introduced by the speculative builders of the late twentieth century. Whereas the buildings in Milton

Fig. 2.7 Milton Abbas as the village appeared in 2006 (courtesy of F. Meno).

Abbas were designed this way for purely aesthetic reasons, many semi-detached properties now being built to look like individual villas have no longer the pleasing symmetrical aspect of the Milton Abbas houses. When modern semi-detached houses are built with strict symmetry, acknowledging that they are semi-detached rather than detached, they seem to lack the unpretentious calmness of the early estate villages.

In the village of Chippenham, Cambridgeshire, a further row of eight semi-detached cottages was built for labourers in 1791-1802. Named New Row, the cottages were laid out just outside the gates to the park in the north-west corner of the village to supplement the earlier cottages in the village centre. The simple cottages, one storey with dormers, were modernised in the 1950s, 1980s and 1990s.

LONDON: THE EARLIEST SEMIS

Semi-detached houses were not seen in cities and townships in any significant numbers before the industrial revolution was well under way in the late eighteenth century. Interestingly, however, Jackson in his book *Semi-detached London* does include the following statement in a footnote [7]:

> Semi-detached houses were first seen in London just before the opening of the eighteenth century, but for the following 200 years or so they remained the exception rather than the rule.

Fig. 2.8. The Rosary and The Hollies, Richmond (2003).

The semi-detached houses that Jackson refers to are possibly the pair named The Rosary and The Hollies in Ormond Road in Richmond. The pair was built by a local building speculator c. 1699-1700. They are built back-to-back with five bays on each front and three side bays towards the street. Bow windows were added to both houses at a later date. Fig. 2.8 shows a view of the pair as they appear today.

The Grove in Highgate is another example of very early London semi-detached pairs built as an investment around 1688 as part of a fund-raising venture for a charity school [8]. Three pairs of spacious semi-detached houses were built in the grounds of a former mansion, Dorchester House. The poet and critic Samuel Coleridge (1772-1834) lived in one of the houses, as did later the novelist, essayist and playwright J.B. Priestley (1894-1984). The houses and the area are still very attractive. A plan of one of these early semis, Fig. 2.9, shows the location of the staircases between the front and the back rooms, and the corner fireplaces, an arrangement that was used extensively by pre-Georgian builders.

There are many other instances [8], [9], [10], but several early pairs have since been converted to a single house, and the original pair can best be traced through historical archives.

Summerson [11] refers to a pair of semi-detached houses in Hampstead, London, dated 1702, Nos. 22 and 24 Rosslyn Hill. Today the houses are hiding behind tall brick walls and massive wooden gates, and only the uppermost parts can be glimpsed. Even in the heat of a summer's day the address looks a little foreboding, rather like Miss Havisham's house in *Great Expectations*, Manor House. As with Miss Havisham's house some of the windows on the Rosslyn Hill property have been bricked in. It is impossible from the road to see the complete house or pair of houses, and indeed their history is somewhat clouded; it has also been suggested that the house began as a mid-eighteenth century mansion, but was rebuilt as two houses in the mid-nineteenth century [12].

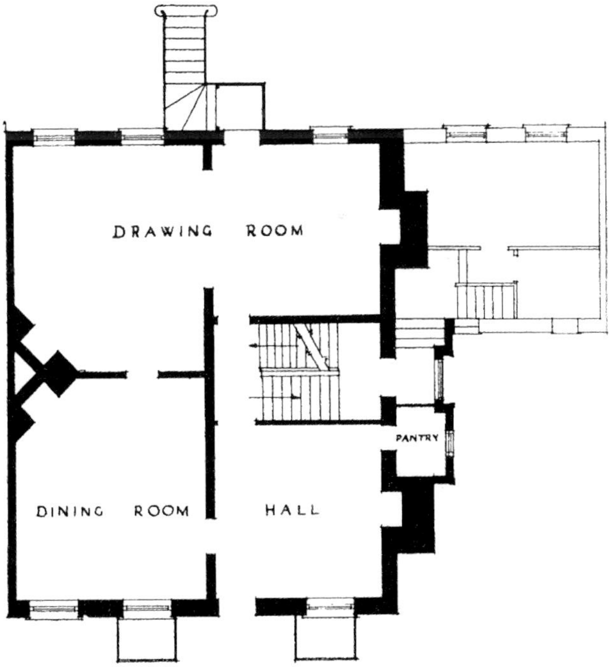

Fig. 2.9. Ground-floor plan of a semi-detached house in the Grove, Highgate, c.1688 [8].

The Bodleian Library holds plans of a layout for semi-detached homes at Westminster, dated 1720 [13]. The plans are for a small estate of semi-detached houses in the area of what was then known as Totthill Fields and the Horse Ferry Road, which today runs

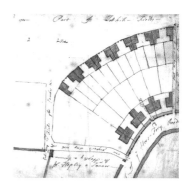

Fig. 2.10. Plan of Totthill Fields estate, Westminster, 1720. The map on the left shows the estate laid out as terraced houses in August of that year, whilst the map on the right the shows the estate laid out as semi-detached houses in October of the same year.

Fig. 2.11. Mid-eighteenth century semi-detached house on Sydenham Road, Lewisham, London.

down to Lambeth Bridge. A plan from August of that year shows the area laid out with terraced houses, but just two months later the plan was changed to that of a semi-detached configuration. Fig. 2.10 shows the two plans. It is unlikely that the houses were ever built, as a map drawn by John Rocque and published in 1746 does not show any buildings in that bend on Horse Ferry Road [14].

A craze developed in the eighteenth century for the well-heeled to take the waters at one of the many spas, either in one of the fashionable spa towns such as Cheltenham, Buxton or Harrogate, or in and around London. One of the minor London spas was at Sydenham, south of the Thames, and a mid-eighteenth century semi-detached house may still be seen on Sydenham Road, Nos. 32/34 (Lewisham), see Fig. 2.11. The pair displays classical door surrounds and weatherboarded sides. The use of weatherboarding of cottages was once a characteristic of the area. It is quite feasible that such fairly large houses were built as out-of-town residences for the use of wealthy Londoners attending the spas.

In general, the evolution of the semi-detached house and its

acceptance in cities or town communities came off to a slow start. It is not before we reach the end of the eighteenth and beginning of the nineteenth century that semi-detached housing in towns appears more frequently, especially in and around London.

LONDON: SOUTHWARK

The late eighteenth century developed a new building style, which we now identify as the 'quasi-semi-detached'. To give some individuality to the Georgian terraces many builders took to recessing the buildings at the party walls or lowering the height

Fig. 2.12. Three types of town and suburban housing in the late eighteenth century: a) linked terraces; b) semi-detached houses; c) quasi-semi-detached houses.

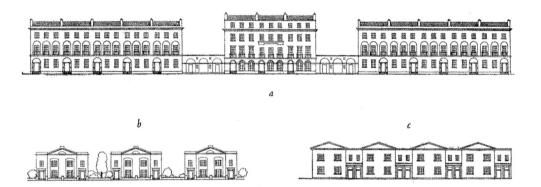

a

b   *c*

of the building over the main entrance. These techniques gave the impression of the houses being semi-detached rather than being just part of a terrace. Fig. 2.12 shows three types of housing developments in use at this time. The terraced configuration in its various forms still dominated speculative building in towns and their suburbs, but the semi-detached, and not least the quasi-semi-detached, were on the rise. Excellent examples of quasi-semi-detached housing from this period can be found in Camberwell Grove, Southwark, in South London, built in the 1770s, see Fig. 2.13. The large houses from the same period in Kennington Park Road, also in Southwark, illustrate the same technique, see Fig. 2.14.

To make the dwellings appear as detached houses, the builders took the visual illusion one step further by spanning each semi-detached pair with a pediment. The quasi-semi-detached and the use of conspicuous pediments became extremely popular in the late Georgian period. The Paragon in Blackheath and the houses on the Lloyd Baker estate, both mentioned later in this chapter, are typical examples of these building styles.

Fig. 2.13. Camberwell Grove, Southwark, c.1770 (2003).

Fig. 2.14. Kennington Park Road, Southwark, 1773-75 (2003).

LONDON: PARK VILLAGE AND THE EYRE ESTATE

The wealth of the nation created by the industrial revolution in England brought even greater riches to the upper classes, but it also created a new, wealthy middle class, eager to demonstrate its new-found prosperity.

The Georgian terrace houses dominated much of the more affluent parts of London in the late eighteenth century. There was, however, a growing call for a proper garden, a private rear garden with easy access to the street. It was part of a movement towards the picturesque, which despite (or perhaps because of) the wars in Europe had caught the imagination of the upper classes, impressed by the lifestyle of the royals and the successful landscapes created by Capability Brown. Terrace houses were not able to give passage from the street to the rear gardens. A detached house would be ideal, but in a limited space and at a cost that was within the means of the *nouveau riches*, the semi-detached plan, or maybe the quasi-semi-detached, offered an attractive alternative.

It was John Nash (1752-1835), the architect of Regent Street and protégé of the Prince Regent, who in 1824 created the first piece of London suburbia in an enclave on the eastern side of Regent's Park. Nash planned to have a branch of the Regent's Canal lead to Cumberland Basin, which was intended to replace the original Haymarket as a market for bringing in hay to the city. This branch of the canal is now filled in, but the canal bed can be seen from the Gloucester Road bridge, which previously spanned the canal. Nash took up the leases to the pieces of land on either side of the canal and built two villages, Park Village East and Park Village West. He evidently had in mind his 1810 development in Gloucestershire,

Blaise Hamlet, when he recalled his designs "in another part of the Kingdom" [15]. Most houses were planned as pairs, created to give the appearance of a single villa, but there were also detached houses and a short terrace. Fig. 2.15 shows a re-constructed site plan of the Park Villages, east and west, taken from contemporary maps [16].

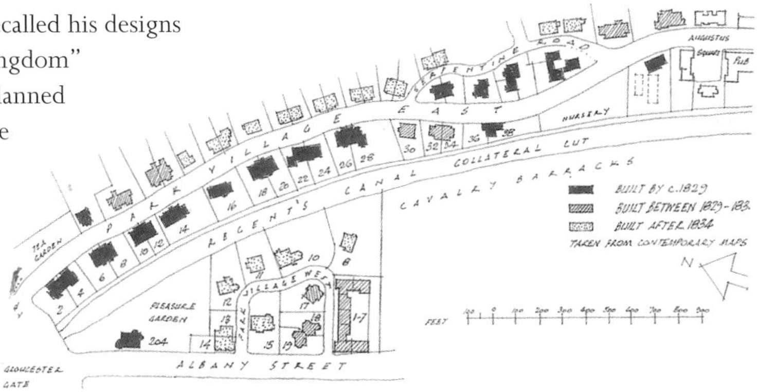

Fig. 2.15 Plan of Nash's Park Villages [16].

Part of Park Village East was demolished when the main line London and North Western Railway (LNWR) into Euston required a cutting through the area. However, most of the houses with back gardens leading down to Regent's Canal (now in-filled in this area) and the western part of the estate, Park Village West, remain intact. Both Park Villages are pleasant estates with handsome, white-painted, stuccoed buildings with an Italianate flavour, although with contributions from several different styles. Fig. 2.16 shows one of the semi-detached villas in Park Village East.

Although Nash may have been thinking about his Blaise Hamlet village when planning the Park Villages, the two designs have seemingly little in common. Blaise Hamlet was the epitome of the picturesque movement. The cottages were in a bombastic style, with dormers and thatched roofs and massive, eye-catching chimney stacks, elaborately executed. The cottages were ornamental to say the least, and the style was popularised as the *cottage ornee*. The buildings of the Park Villages were in a sense romantic and picturesque, but unlike the cottages in Blaise Hamlet they were elegantly unobtrusive, as one would expect of Regency architecture.

Fig. 2.16. Semi-detached villa in Park Village East (photo 2004).

At about the same time there were plans to establish London's first real suburb at St. John's Wood. It fell to the firm of auctioneers, Spurrier and Phipps, to lay out plans for a semi-detached estate in this area. The plans for the so-called Eyre estate were ready in 1794,

2

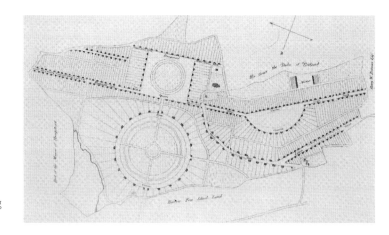

Fig. 2.17. Planned layout of the Eyre estate according to Spurrier and Phipps.

but the war with France effectively stopped its development, and it was not until the 1830s and 40s that the estate got under way to a slightly modified design. The new plans included detached as well as semi-detached houses. Fig. 2.17 shows the original plan of the estate, and Fig. 2.18 shows one of the semi-detached houses as it appeared in 2003.

Fig. 2.18. Houses on the Eyre estate, St. Johns Wood, London (2003).

LONDON: BLACKHEATH AND ISLINGTON

Another early speculative estate was developed south of the Thames in Blackheath around the same time as the Eyre estate plans were drawn up. The building of this estate, the Paragon, did in fact get under way even during the conflict with France, although only a few houses were built before credit restrictions delayed its completion.

The building of these large, semi-detached houses, or 'house-pairs', was initiated by a rich timber merchant, John Cator, using Michael Searles as his surveyor and builder. An earlier estate, also called the Paragon, had been laid out by Searles in the New Kent Road, but these buildings were demolished in 1898 [17]. The word paragon stands for a model of excellence, and The Paragon in Blackheath certainly does justice to this definition. The houses are laid out in an imposing crescent open to the Heath, the individual pairs of semis linked to their neighbours with a Tuscan colonnade incorporating the main entrances, see Fig. 2.19. In a sense, this estate represents a smooth transition from the Georgian terrace over the quasi-semi-detached houses to the pure semi-detached house style that was soon to gather momentum.

The first design by Searles had had an imposing classical centre building of two storeys with a pediment spanning four columns. An intermediate design added a storey and did away with the tall colonnade, but kept the pediment. The final design is the one that we see today. Each semi-detached house is huge. In its day it boasted two drawing rooms, a library, a gentleman's room, eight family bedrooms, dressing rooms and boudoirs, a cellar, a dairy, and a coach house. The inhabitants were, not surprisingly, citizens of some standing. According to the rate books, the lessees were bankers, City merchants, ship owners, lawyers, surgeons, architects, an art historian, and London's first health officer, Sir John Simon. Blackheath could now compare itself with Richmond or Hampstead as a desirable address for the wealthy new middle class.

Nevertheless, there were initially some problems of attracting the right sort of clientele. Many hesitated to make the move, maybe

because of the recurring stories of highwaymen and robberies on the Heath. Also, the respectability of The Paragon suffered an early snub, when two young ladies, Eliza Robertson and Charlotte Sharp, in 1800 took up a lease and began to spend extravagantly on furnishings and decorating, always demanding credit with the local shop owners. The youngest, Eliza, let it be known that she was to be married to a rich colonel, but the couple were discovered to be lesbians, and with a debt of £20,000 they fled the area.

Fig. 2.19. The Paragon, Blackheath (2003).

Some of the attractiveness of the crescent faded in the first half of the twentieth century, when a private hotel opened at two of the addresses in The Paragon, and The Paragon's Schools of Equitation and Ballroom Dancing established itself in No.7 [18]. Several of the houses suffered severe bombing during the Second World War. Following a dedicated programme of restoration and re-building after the war, the houses were converted into 100 flats, but outwardly the estate retained its inherent air of opulence and architectural splendour.

Other spacious semi-detached villas from the early eighteen hundreds, also developed by John Cator, can be found in the Cator Estate south of The Paragon.

Michel Searles' semi-detached houses linked with broad entrances behind classic columns seem to have been the inspiration for a smaller group of houses built 1809-13 in Hackney, North London. The three-storey buildings, on Paragon Road incidentally, are pleasant enough, but lack the breath-taking grandeur of the Michael Searles development. The most interesting feature is the unusual ogee-arched fanlights over the entrance doors.

Blackheath also boasts further smaller groups of less flamboyant semis, all from around the same period [19]. One such development may be seen at Eliot Place built between 1792 and 1805 [20]. This is an attractive assembly of houses, semi-detached, detached, and terraced, looking out onto Blackheath, see Fig. 2.20. The semi-detached pairs are the three four-bay houses to the right of the picture centre. The wings are later additions. The white building to the far right is a detached house from the same period, while a semi-detached Edwardian house is hiding behind a large conifer in the centre, and a house from the Modern Movement of the nineteen thirties is seen on the far left.

Islington, North London, had become fashionable in the late seventeenth century after the discovery of mineral springs at Sadler's Wells. It remained mostly agricultural land until the late eighteenth century, when John Dawes, a stockbroker, developed a small estate of very grand houses at Highbury Fields in the

Fig. 2.20. Eliot Place seen from Blackheath (2003).

northern part of the parish. The houses, 39 in all, consisted of three semi-detached pairs (six dwellings), balanced at either end by fine Georgian terraces. John Nelson, in writing about Highbury Place in his *History of Islington from 1811*, had high praise for the development:

> Highbury Place is one of the finest rows of houses in the environs of the Metropolis; it is inhabited by eminent merchants, and other persons of opulence and respectability. The prospect on both sides is very fine, and the situation remarkably healthy. It consists of 39 houses, built on a large scale, but varying in size; they have all good gardens behind, and allotments of meadow ground in front: to some of the houses there are coach-houses, in a line with the front of the dwellings, others have the same convenience, with stabling, &c. at the back of the premises, to which there is a convenient carriage way extending behind the whole of the houses. The road in front is private, being frequented only by the carriages passing to and from the several dwellings, between the village and Highbury-house [21].

A map of 1805-06 shows the small estate, see Fig. 2.21, as well as the later terraced estate, Highbury Terrace, in the north-west corner of Highbury Fields. The cartographer has shown formal gardens extending along the back of the terraced properties in both estates. The first Ordnance Survey map of the area from 1871 (Fig. 2.22) shows a significant change in the layout of the gardens, more appropriate to the Victorian age, with each individual terrace house having its own, narrow garden extending to Highbury Mews at the back.

Fig. 2.21. Highbury Fields 1805-06 showing Highbury Place and Highbury Terrace.

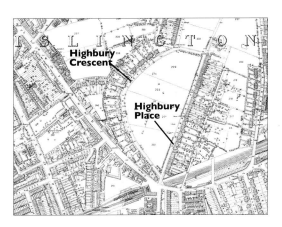

Fig. 2.22. Highbury Fields 1871, the first Ordnance Survey map. This is before the opening of Calabria Road, and the semi-detached houses in Highbury Place are still intact. Highbury Crescent on the western boundary of the field was built in 1844-50.

Fig. 2.23. Opulence and respectability in a watercolour of Nos. 38 and 39 Highbury Place (1807). These are the end houses in the northern part of the terrace. The builder of the estate, John Spiller, lived in No.39. Reproduced with the kind permission of the Islington Library Local History Section.

The actual building of the estate was in the hands of John Spiller, a speculative builder, who himself chose to live in the end house, No.39. Several famous people have at one time or another dwelt at Highbury Place, including the evangelist John Wesley (1703-91), Abraham Newland (1730-1807), the Chief Cashier of the Bank of England for nearly sixty years, and the statesman Joseph Chamberlain (1836-1914).

An impression of the opulence and respectability associated with this development is demonstrated in the aquatint from 1807, see Fig. 2.23. A much later view on a 1910 postcard shows one of the large semi-detached villas and its gabled coach house (Fig. 2.24).

Fig. 2.24. Highbury Place seen from the south, 1910. The main house in the picture is the southern-most of the originally three semi-detached pairs in the John Dawes development of 1787. In the centre of the picture leading off to the right is Calabria Road, which together with the building of the tunnel for the Great Northern Railway, ruined the balance of the Georgian terraces pivoted around the semi-detached villas.

Highbury Place

This particular pair is in fact the only one that remains today in its nearly original form, see Fig. 2.25. Of the other two pairs, one was demolished when the Great Northern Railway (GNR) ran a tunnel below Highbury Fields between Drayton Park and Canonbury stations, and the other was changed so as to become unrecognisable as a semi-detached villa following the opening of Calabria Road in the late 1880s [22].

Fig. 2.25. Highbury Place Nos. 10 and 11. The same view as on the 1910 postcard (left). The villa and coach-houses are little changed, but building has taken place to the left of the picture towards Calabria Road (2003).

Closer to the City centre, in Finsbury, a small, but impressive development of semi-detached (in reality quasi-semi-detached) houses was begun in 1818. The combination of recessing the party walls and, in this case, incorporating quite massive pediments to span each semi-detached pair completes the illusion of standing in front of an attractive, detached dwelling, see Fig. 2.26. At the time, however, the estate was considered fairly unpretentious. The residents were typically respectable tradesmen, merchants, craftsmen and moderately successful professionals.

The surrounding streets, nearly all part of the Lloyd Baker estate, are dominated by semis of the same basic design, varying only in size and in the details of the front elevations.

Fig. 2.26. Lloyd Square, Finsbury, 1818 (2003).

Architects and pattern books

The estates of Milton Abbas, Park Village and St. John's Wood were all designed by architects, John Nash being probably the best known and most prolific. However, engaging the services of an architect for the design of a domestic building was the prerogative of only the very rich. The professional architect was essentially a product of the second half of the eighteenth century. The profession's standing in society was underlined by a group of London architects forming a dining club in 1791, the very exclusive Architects' Club.

In general, though, the design and construction of domestic buildings were not managed by architects, but by surveyors, master-builders, and craftsmen, as was, for example, The Paragon estate. Surveyors had been known since Tudor times. They were trained professionals with the remit of surveying, measuring and pricing the land for building purposes, as well as administering the actual building work. A year after the Architects' Club was formed the surveyors, not to be outdone, founded their own club, the Surveyors' Club. This club still exists, whereas the Architects' Club at some point vanished without trace. It may seem curious that the surveyors found the need to imitate the architects as, at that time, there was no strict distinction between the two professions. The reason is very likely the elite nature of the Architects' Club, to which could be elected only persons who belonged to the Royal Academy or had comparable qualifications.

Below the architects and surveyors in the social hierarchy stood the master-builder. He had probably trained as a craftsman, either a stonemason, bricklayer or carpenter, and he was the person most closely involved with the actual construction of housing for the speculative market. He hired and organised the necessary craftsmen for any particular development. He was, as it were, the speculative builder of the period.

There were two developments in the eighteenth century that were to influence the building of domestic housing for many years to come. One was the building requirements dictated by the 1774 London Building Act. This document and its predecessors arose out of the Great Fire of London in 1666. It was to affect building practices not only in London, but throughout the country. Although primarily designed to set building guidelines that would curb the spread of fire, the act was in part responsible also for the extensive standardisation that dominated domestic building in the late Georgian and Regency period (1774-1830). The Georgian houses, not least the many terraces that came to set their mark on politically and commercially influential cities like London and Bath, demonstrated to the onlooker an orderly and well proportioned façade. The standardised buildings might easily have been criticised as being monotonous, but they managed to display an elegance and tranquillity that has rarely, if ever, been surpassed.

The second important feature of this period was the printing of the first pattern books. These pattern books became, as it were, the bibles of the master-builders and craftsmen alike. When only the barest of instructions regarding the development of a new house or housing estate were given, these books provided the builders with all the necessary information about layout, structures, materials and even decoration.

The first well-known pattern book was published in 1762 by William Pain, who called himself 'Architect and Joiner'. The book was titled *The Builder's Companion* and subtitled *Workman's General Assistant: Demonstrating, after the most easy and practical Method, all the Principal Rules of Architecture, from the Plan to the Ornamental Finish* [23] (Fig. 2.27). It was soon to be followed in 1767 by Langley's *The Builder's Jewel*, in 1825 by Nicholson's *Builder's and Workman's New Directory*, and in 1846 by Loudon's *Cottage, Farm, and Villa Architecture*.

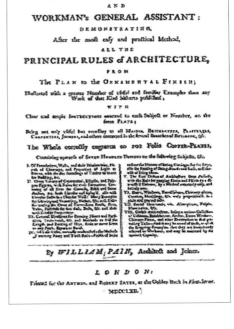

Fig. 2.27. Frontispiece to *The Builders' Companion*, 1762.

These titles represent only a small selection of the growing number of pattern books that came to be published in the eighteenth and, especially, the nineteenth century. In *Victorian Houses and their Details* (2002), Helen Long gives a quite detailed discussion of the pattern books over the period 1720-1920, including also architectural

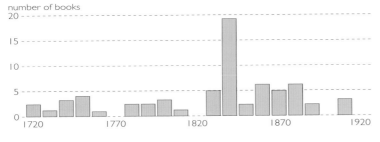

Fig. 2.28. Number of pattern books and manuals published 1720-1920. Based on [25].

2

manuals [24]. An overall picture of the publishing activity in this period is shown in Fig. 2.28, based on the material in Long's book. Clearly, there was a production boom in the 1840s. This reflects not only the increased interest in buildings and architecture in general, but also the advances in printing and illustration techniques developed since the mid-eighteenth century. Machine typecasting and the introduction of machine-made paper, which reduced the paper cost in a book from around 20 per cent to less than 10 per cent at the end of the nineteenth century, both contributed to lowering the cost of book production, as did improved distribution channels. Considering that the print run of architectural books at the end of the eighteenth century was typically less than 250 copies, any measures to keep the production costs down were welcomed by the publishers.

The end of an epoch

At the end of the Regency period the Georgian tradition was still in evidence in the building of not only sumptuous villas for the extremely wealthy, but also in the speculatively built estates designed to house the rising middle class. The late eighteenth and early nineteenth century had in England been the glorious period of neo-classicism, with architecture finding inspiration in the Classical Greek, Hellenistic and Roman excavations of the period, and in the knowledge and sketches brought back by the more talented of the young aristocrats on their Grand Tours. Many of the buildings from the Georgian period borrowed freely, and usually very successfully, from the architecture of Classical Antiquity.

John Nash and his contemporary Sir John Soane (1753-1837) were the great architects of English neo-classicism, but it was John Nash, especially, who made his mark with the *nouveau riches*, as we have seen in his villas in the Park Village estates at Regent's Park, see Fig. 2.29. It is to Nash, perhaps more than to any other single person, that we owe the socially successful career of the semi-detached house.

At the time of Nash the term villa was used to describe a house that had the stamp of gentility, but with very little land attached. It would typically be the secondary house of a nobleman, within comfortable driving distance by carriage from Westminster. Also industrialists, merchants, lawyers and other well-to-do citizens now aspired to having a villa in the London area. The semi-detached pairs built by Nash and others in the first quarter of the nineteenth century were also called villas,

Fig. 2.29. A Nash villa. A semi-detached Pair on a corner plot in Park Village West, London (2003).

and it was not long before the word was being applied also
to each semi-detached house in a pair. This implied a stamp of
social respectability to each individual half, and the future of the
semi-detached house as an acceptable, even desirable mode of
dwelling was assured.

Architecture in Britain was, however, at a water-shed. In his
seminal book *Architecture in Britain 1530-1830* (1993) John Summerson
has even suggested that architecture in this country more or
less ground to a halt around 1830, when he states that English
architecture was "at no moment so feeble, so deficient in genius, so
poor in promise" [25].

The latter part of the Georgian regime was a tumultuous period.
The industrial revolution was well under way, the wars with France
dominated the political and military scene, and the emerging middle
class in English society was making an impact on the social life of
the times. Architects now needed to cater not only to the aristocracy,
the church, and the state, but also to the bourgeoisie. Writing in his
third edition of *Treatise on Civil Architecture* (1791) Sir William Chambers
(1723-1796) could not help remarking, apparently with some
disdain, that "even men of inferior rank now aspire to taste in the
fine arts" [26]. He is here referring to the new generation of middle
class industrialists, professionals and artisans, who were to become
the main patrons of the architects and builders of private houses in
the nineteenth century – men with standards far removed from the
classical upbringing of England's ruling classes.

The growth of a prosperous middle class was one important
factor that was to influence the change in building style soon to set
its mark on domestic housing. Another factor was the prevailing
romanticism of the age. This mood was reflected clearly in the
extremely popular works of Walter Scott (1771-1832), and novels
such as *Ivanhoe* (1819) and *Kenilworth* (1821) whetted the appetite
of the general public for medieval romance. The taste for all things
Gothic had already been present in the eighteenth century, and
architecture in a Gothic Revival style was fairly widespread, but only
for castles and country houses for the extremely rich. Now, Gothic
romanticism caught the fancy of middle class patrons, and buildings
based on an eclectic mixture of neo-classicism, Georgian, Gothic,
Italianate, and many other styles were about to shape Victorian
domestic architecture.

A contributing factor to the change in building practices was the
presence of new building materials. Coade stone, an artificial stone,
cast iron, and new stucco materials were being eagerly adopted

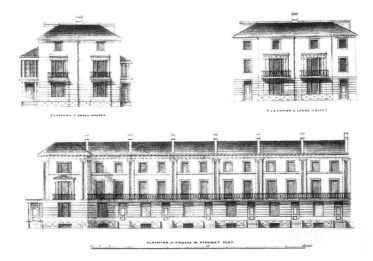

Fig. 2.30. Papworth's 1829 design for semi-detached villas and a terrace [26].

by architects and builders to cater for middle class tastes. Different constructional techniques and different decorative effects were being put into use. Architecture was definitely in a transitional period. The Georgian style was still popular, but architects were more adventurous in their use of materials and ornamental effects. Examples of designs from this period of change are the 1829 semi-detached villas executed by J.B.Papworth (1775-1847) illustrated in Fig. 2.30 [27]. The buildings show a lingering Georgian style, but a new fussiness can be seen, for example in the window surrounds and balconies.

Looking slightly ahead to the early Victorian period, a semi-detached house of c.1840 is shown in Fig. 2.31. The three-storey house favoured by the Georgians has become a two-storey house with equal dimensions to the windows at both levels, and the artificial stone surrounds for the windows and doors show off the trend of new materials.

Fig. 2.31. Semi-detached pair c.1840 [27].

Although both illustrations show houses still in the Georgian mould, to most people they do not exhibit the understated grandeur which was once a defining feature of much Georgian architecture. The houses are very plain, even boring, and they do not forewarn of the extremes of the Gothic Revival shortly to appear in early and mid-Victorian domestic architecture.

References

1   David Iredale and John Barrett, *Discovering your Old House*, Shire Publications Ltd, Princes Risborough, 2002, p.64.

2   George Sheeran, *Good Houses Built of Stone*, Allanwood Books, Pudsey 1986, p.65.

3   B.Greysmith, *Tracing the History of your House*, Hodder & Stoughton, London 1994.

4   David Iredale and John Barrett, *Discovering your Old House*, Shire Publications Ltd, Princes Risborough, 2002, p.63.

5   M.W.Barley, *The English Farmhouse and Cottage*, Alan Sutton, Gloucester 1987.

6   John Woodforde, *The Truth about Cottages*, Routledge & Kegan Paul, London 1969, p.104.

7   Alan A.Jackson, *Semi-detached London*, Second edition, Wild Swan Publications Ltd, Didcot 1991, p.129.

8   Bridget Cherry and Nikolaus Pevsner, *The Buildings of England, London 4: North*, Penguin Books, London 1998, p.24.

9   Bridget Cherry and Nikolaus Pevsner, *The Buildings of England, London 2: South*, Penguin Books, London 1983.

10 Andrew Saint et al., *London Suburbs*, Merrell Holberton Publishers, London 1999.

11 John Summerson, *Architecture in Britain 1530-1830*, Yale University Press, 9th edition, New Haven and London 1993, p.494.

12 C.Wade, *The Streets of Hampstead*, Campden History Society, 2000.

13 Gough Maps 41 G4, Bodleian Library, Oxford.

14 John Rocque, *Plan of the Cities of London and Westminster and Borough of Southwark*, London 1746, Map 18.

15 Michael Mansbridge, *John Nash, A Complete Catalogue*, Phaidon Press Limited, London 2004 (paperback edition), p.256.

16 *Ibid.*, p.257.

17 F.Barker, *Greenwich and Blackheath Past*, Historical Publications Ltd, London 1993, p.70.

18 *Ibid.*, p.71.

19 Andrew Saint et al., *London Suburbs*, Merrell Holberton Publishers, London 1999, p.49.

20 Bridget Cherry and Nikolaus Pevsner, *The Buildings of England, London 2: South*, Penguin Books, London 1983, p.422.

21 John Nelson, *History of Islington*, 1811.

22 Mary Cosh, *The Squares of Islington – Part II*, Islington Archaeology & History Society 1993, p.104.

23 William Pain, *The Builders' Companion*, London 1762.

24 Helen Long, *Victorian Houses and their Details*, Architectural Press, Oxford 2002, pp.21-70.

25 John Summerson, *Architecture in Britain 1530-1830*, Yale University Press, 9th edition, New Haven and London 1993, p.496.

26 *Ibid.*(quoted).

27 Robin Guild, *The Complete Victorian House Book*, Sidgwick & Jackson, London 1989, p.30.

3

The early and the high Victorian era (1830-75)

"Oh, Aunt Sarah! You don't mean that you expect me to live in a semi-detached house?"
Emily Eden, *The Semi-detached House*, 1859

Population growth and the middle classes

The expanding industries of the early nineteenth century created new jobs at all levels and substantial numbers of workers moved from their agricultural background into the cities. It goes without saying that the house-building industry experienced a very active period in order to keep up with demand, making the building industry the second largest employer of labour in the first half of the century, second only to agriculture.

In the first quarter of the nineteenth century a fair number of semi-detached houses existed in rural areas and in London, especially, but they were at opposite ends of the social scale. This is not surprising, considering that English society did not at that time have a middle layer population of any real significance.

The creation of new jobs and a reasonably prosperous middle class, a development that had started in the Georgian era, now took on a new dimension as the need for bankers, shippers, insurers, engineers and designers went hand-in-hand with the industrial expansion. In its wake came also a call for more architects, surveyors, master builders, doctors, dentists, teachers and office workers. These white-collar workers were distinct from the landed gentry above them in social status, and from the labouring masses below them. They were to become the great English middle class, which was far from being a well-defined, homogeneous group.

At the top end, the upper middle class, were found persons with incomes comparable to those of the landed gentry. They might be factory or mill owners, merchants, bankers, or shipping magnates. Below them, in the centre tier, were the members of the professions, for example, the doctors, lawyers, engineers, and architects, as well as owners of smaller factories. At the bottom end, the lower middle class, were the shopkeepers, apothecaries, small tradesmen, secretaries and teachers. Around 1850 it is estimated that about 6-700,000 income receivers in England and Wales would have been bracketed as middle class [1]. If the wives and families were counted as well, about three million people, or one sixth of the total population, could be termed middle class. This was the new social group that the speculative builders were to target. The middle classes were typically insecure as far as their status in society was concerned, but they had aspirations, and they were eager to disassociate themselves from the labouring classes. Their choice of housing became a visible expression of these aspirations – and the semi-detached house offered an attractive compromise between the villas of the rich and the basic terraced accommodation of the workers. The elevation of the semi-detached house to the villa status promoted by John Nash and others in the first part of the century had given the semi-detached a maybe unexpected aura of respectability. Even so, the idea of sharing a party wall with neighbours not of your own choosing could unnerve the middle class inhabitants as described vividly in Emily Eden's novel, *The Semi-detached House*, from the middle of the century. The same sentiments can be found today.

Victorian values

In order to follow the development of the semi-detached house in the Victorian period, it is necessary to have some impression of how the middle classes of Victorian society functioned. The houses and estates erected by the speculative builders of the period naturally reflected the attitudes and values of their middle-class clients.

For the most wealthy of the Victorian middle-class society the road to social recognition was the ownership of a house in the country. This was not always achievable by the first generation of the newly rich, but maybe for their sons or grandsons who were sent to Eton

and Harrow for an education worthy of a gentleman. If their abilities stretched to becoming involved on the political arena, the sought after status was within reach. As an example, Sir Robert Peel (1788-1850), son of a Lancashire cotton manufacturer, became Tory Prime Minister. William Gladstone (1809-98) was born in Liverpool the son of a slave trader. He became Liberal Prime Minister and acquired Hawarden Castle in Flintshire. These careers were exceptional, of course, and most middle-class Victorians happily settled for less, without ever losing sight of the ultimate goal of a country residence.

Throughout the Victorian period most houses were rented. This was the case for all tiers of society. The poorest paid weekly, the middle classes could take on leases of a quarter, six months, a year, or even seven years [2]. Historians have estimated that no more than 10 per cent of the population owned the houses they lived in [3]. Renting suited the middle-class households quite well. They were restless, socially upwardly mobile, and they did not necessarily wish to put down firm geographical roots. This situation changed towards the end of the century, when building societies were able to lend money for home ownership.

To middle class Victorians, their homes and families were the focus of existence. A veritable deluge of magazines was published incorporating the words home or family in their titles: *The Home Circle*, *The Home Companion*, *The Home Friend*, *Family Friend*, *Family Treasure*, *Family Record*, and many others. At the same time a strong current of religious fervour, primarily Christian, came to influence the daily lives of middle-class families. A Christian attitude to love and charity was expected to reside in the home between all family members and between family and servants. To the outside world the home was to be seen as an ideal society in miniature, a society in harmony with itself.

Within the family it was an undisputed fact in Victorian times that God had given his authority to the man. The husband dictated the agenda, and the task of the wife was to make sure that his wishes were followed through. She ruled the household, the children and the servants. It was her role in life to create an atmosphere of peace and comfort to please and protect the man returning home from his business in the harsh world outside. Books were published to help the woman create the ideal home. In *The Women of England: Their Social Duties and Domestic Habits*, Sarah Ellis, laid out the rules quite clearly:

> Not only must the house be neat and clean, but it must be
> so ordered as to suit the tastes of all … Not only must a

constant system of activity be established, but peace must
be preserved, or happiness will be destroyed [4].

It was important that members of a Victorian middle class household
were seen to be polite and to demonstrate Christian behaviour,
culture, and respectability. The house and its location were the visible
embodiments of these values.

The religious and social attitudes of middle-class England brought
about changes in living arrangements, which had a direct impact
on the layout and design of Victorian villas, including the semi-
detached villas, or double-villas as they were called in the beginning
of the period. In Georgian times, sleeping arrangements often
accommodated family members of different age groups and gender
in the same bedroom. Not only that, but servants or apprentices also
slept in the same rooms as the family [5]. This pattern was clearly no
longer acceptable to a virtuous Christian household.

The Victorians preferred to organize their homes so that babies
did not sleep in the same room as their parents; boys and girls slept
in separate rooms from an early age, and younger children did not
share the same bedroom as their elder brothers or sisters. Middle
class families were often large in spite of a high death-rate among
children. In 1850, out of every 1000 children born, 146 died within
one year of birth, and many more died before the age of five [1].
Even so, in the early stages of building up a family there could easily
be between three and nine children in the home at any one time.

If the household had live-in servants they were typically given
bedrooms under the roof. Two maids might share a bedroom, but
the cook would expect her own room. Any manservants would, of
course, have bedrooms of their own – above the coach-house, if the
income ran to a horse and carriage.

As servants were an intrinsic part of most middle-class households,
indeed a family's status was determined by the number of domestic
staff in residence, it is not surprising that houses of this period
needed a substantial number of rooms to ensure moral and social
standards could be upheld.

Additionally, there would need to be rooms in which to receive
callers, the drawing room or a morning room, and a dining
room. With also a parlour, nursery, study and maybe a library and
billiard room, it is no wonder that we today find many Victorian
villas enormous. A semi-detached house containing ten or more
rooms would not be unusual. With so many rooms and the firm
requirement of isolating the family from the servants, the layout of

even a moderately sized suburban house became a bewildering maze of small rooms, dark staircases and rambling passages.

However, even the Victorians had to compromise on their ambitions, and what was considered an ideal size for a house was far from always matched by the available income. For the lower tiers of the middle classes, rooms serving several purposes had to be accepted of necessity. In the smaller of the middle-class houses it was quite common for servants to sleep where they worked. The cook and the parlour maid might well have had to sleep in the back kitchen or scullery, and the smaller children would often sleep in their parents' bedroom. All in all, the living and sleeping arrangements in a Victorian household could be quite complex.

Housing the middle classes – architectural styles

The erection of homes for the expanding population in Queen Victoria's reign (1837-1901) changed the landscape of most towns and cities all over England and gave them the character that we see today. Massive estates of humble terraced houses were built to accommodate the seemingly ever-growing workforce of industrial Britain. Concurrently, suburbs sprang up on the outskirts of most cities, creating homes for the new monied classes, who had definite ideas of what they wanted in terms of space and neighbourhood, but, in spite of their energy and resourcefulness, were uncertain of what type and style of house would be appropriate to their status. Living in a world of social and technological changes, they sought something new and different also in the type of housing they were prepared to accept. The uniformity of the Georgian house style was slowly falling out of vogue.

The complexity of architectural development in the nineteenth century was indisputable. Victorian architects and builders borrowed freely from any and all of the known architectural styles, from Gothic to Tudor, from Palladian to Regency, from Dutch Renaissance to Venetian. Poking fun at the confusion of styles and at the self-important architects of the day, Robert Kerr, writing in 1871, relates a fictitious conversation between an architect and a wealthy client:

> *Architect*: "Sir, you are paymaster, and must therefore be pattern-master; you choose the style of your house just as you choose the build of your hat; – you can have Classical, columnar or non-columnar, arcuated or trabeated, rural or civil, or indeed palatial; you can have Elizabethan in

equal variety; Renaissance ditto; or, not to notice minor
modes, Medieval in any one of many periods and many
phases, – old English, French, German, Belgian, Italian,
and more."

Gentleman Client: "But really, I would much rather not.
I want a plain, substantial, comfortable Gentleman's
House ... I don't want any style at all." [6].

With Victorian architecture drawing on so many sources as it did, for
domestic housing as well as for monumental buildings, it is indeed
surprising that we today have mostly no hesitation in identifying
buildings as being Victorian.

In an effort to bring some kind of order to the chaos of Victorian
domestic architecture, and to present the development of the semi-
detached house in the decades following the end of the Regency
period, it is useful to consider three separate periods:

The first period, 1830-45:	The tail-end of the Georgian period (1830-45). The most influential architect, as far as housing is concerned, was J.C. Loudon (1783-1843).
The second period, 1845-75:	The Christian epoch associated with the architect A.W.N. Pugin (1812-52) and the critic John Ruskin (1819-1900). This period, the high Victorian era, is from 1845 till around 1875.
The third period, 1875-1901:	The secular epoch from 1875 and into the twentieth century. Main figures were the craftsman and poet William Morris (1834-96) and the architects Philip Webb (1831-1915), Norman Shaw (1831-1912) and C.F.A. Voysey (1857-1941).

The first two periods are dealt with in this Chapter, the third in
Chapter 4. There is, of course, no hard-and-fast dividing line
between these three periods and a considerable overlap of house
styles is only to be expected.

THE FIRST PERIOD, 1830-45
The architecture of the Regency period (1811-30) had popularised
the use of stucco on all but the most humble buildings. The pale

3

yellow façades created a new street picture in most major cities. Although architects often preferred to build in stone, especially Bath stone, this was out of the question for speculative building because of the expense. The *trompe l'oeil* substitute of stucco was readily accepted, and Regency style buildings continued to dominate the housing estates throughout the eighteen thirties and well into the forties. The stucco embellishment was typically used only up to first floor level.

The Park Villages in London designed by John Nash were begun in 1824, but not completed until the mid 1830s; they are a prime example of the stucco age. Although firmly rooted in the Georgian and classic traditions, the buildings nevertheless brought a freshness to upper middle-class houses with their eclectic use of styles borrowed from Italian, French, Greek, Tudor and Gothic architecture. The majority of the houses were semi-detached although designed to appear as single villas.

The same style of building may be found in the Rock Park estate on the Wirral, near Liverpool. Twelve wealthy Victorians purchased a plot of land facing the Mersey estuary and drew up an Articles of Agreement in 1836. Most of the houses that were built on the estate shortly after were semi-detached, as may be seen on the contemporary map in Fig. 3.1. The large semi-detached villas underlined the acceptance of this configuration as a desirable form of residence for the upper tiers of Victorian middle classes.

The covenants of the Rock Park agreement stated quite specifically that

> ... if two dwelling houses be built on any of such last mentioned lots containing 1300 or more superficial square yards therein, and in every such case each two dwelling houses shall be built adjoining each other so as to form in appearance one dwelling house, but in no case shall more than two dwelling houses adjoin each other, so that there may not

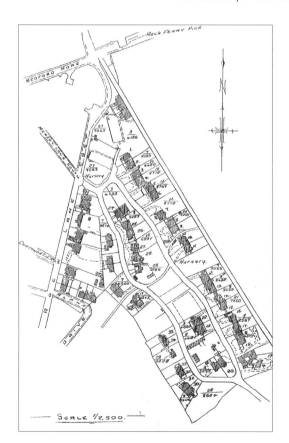

Fig. 3.1. Plan of the Rock Park estate near Liverpool. Late 1830s.

be any continuous line of more than two houses adjoining each other.

In other words, the semi-detached form – in the appearance of a single villa – was very much acceptable, but a terrace was strictly ruled out. It was further stipulated that "each dwelling house shall be built of stone, or be cemented, stuccoed, or roughcast." Brick façades had not yet returned to favour. An example of one of the semi-detached villas, incorporating a unifying balcony, is given in Fig. 3.2. Compare this villa with the very similar Nash villa of the same period in London, Fig. 2.16, where the unifying element is the wide pediment. Most of the houses in Rock Park are still standing and in good repair, but some have been demolished to give way to the Rock Ferry by-pass.[1]

The Eyre estate planned in the last decade of the eighteenth century, but not built before the 1840s, is another instance of Georgian architecture being applied successfully to large semi-detached houses, see Chapter 2.

While architects would be engaged to design detached villas for those who could afford it, most speculative building was created without their involvement. The architects' impact on the building styles would come from the builders' use of any of the numerous pattern books (see Chapter 2) that appeared in this period.

With a surge of interest in speculative middle-class housing, the publication of such pattern books, or copy-books, became an acceptable, and sometimes even lucrative way, for architects to influence building styles without themselves being involved with speculative projects. The books were usually eminently practical, designed to function as instruction manuals for master builders and craftsmen. One such book was *Original Designs for Cottages and Villas, in the Grecian, Gothic, and Italian Styles of Architecture* written by a London architect E.W. Trendall in 1831. It was important because it singularly addressed the design of smaller suburban houses rather than the palatial mansions that many pattern books had hitherto portrayed [7].

Arguably the most important contributions to the flow of pattern books at this time came from the Scottish-born landscape gardener and architect John Claudius Loudon, a prolific writer of books on

Fig. 3.2. A Rock Park semi-detached villa from the late 1830s.

---

1. I am most grateful to Dr. Athanassios Migos, Liverpool John Moores University and resident of the estate for giving me access to his documents on the Rock Park development.

3

horticulture and architecture who also founded and edited *The Gardener's Magazine*, 1826-43, and the short-lived *Architectural Magazine*, 1834.

Loudon's best-known pattern book was *Encyclopaedia of Cottage, Farm and Villa Architecture* [8]. First published in 1833, it ran to 14 editions and became a standard reference work for builders over the next 50 years. It was a unique piece of work of more than 1000 pages in small print, with more than 2000 wood engravings illustrating patterns for cottages, villas and farms in a multitude of styles, including Tudor, Greek, Italian and Swiss. The *Encyclopaedia* contained ideas and contributions from numerous specialists; working to bring the book together for publication was, according to Loudon himself, an enormous effort with never more than four hours' sleep and "drinking strong coffee to keep ourselves awake" (*The Architectural Magazine*, 1834). Its popularity was due not least to its very practical approach to the design of convenient and comfortable houses combined with an open eye for the domestic ideals of Victorian middle class society. Loudon was intent on bringing good design to the house-seeking public, and in doing so he accepted an eclecticism of styles, unlike Pugin's more single-minded approach some ten years later.

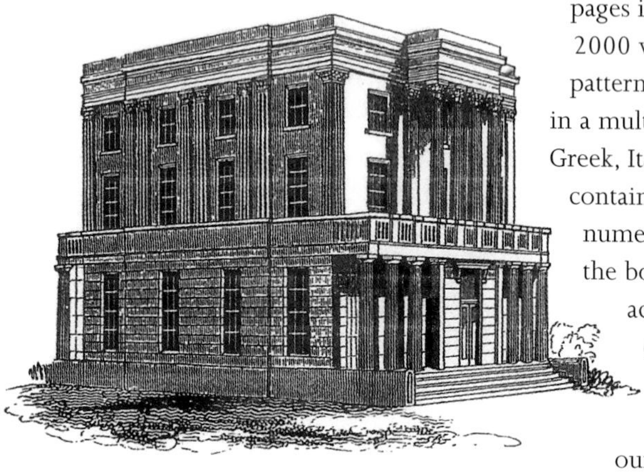

While Trendall had concentrated on the smaller houses, Loudon's designs spanned a wider range, from humble three-room cottages to magnificent mansions. A reproduction of one of his plans for a back-to-back semi-detached house in the Grecian style is shown in Fig. 3.3. Loudon introduces the design as "A Double Suburban Villa, adapted for a particular Situation in the Suburbs of Leicester." The broad flight of steps leading up to each house is "supposed to be covered with pots of plants in the summer

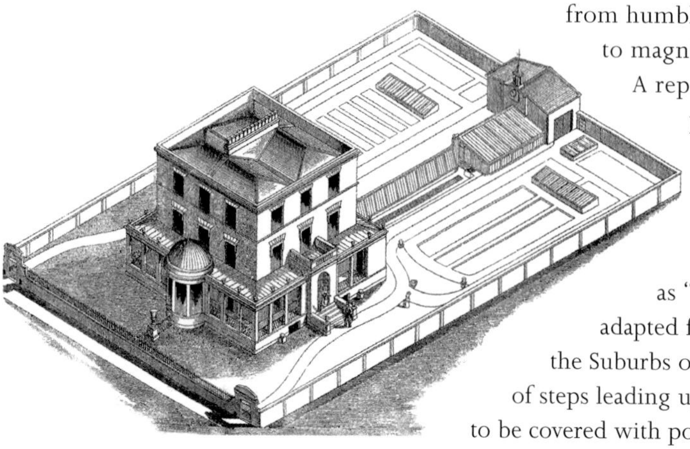

Fig. 3.3. Loudon's design for a large semi-detached villa in the suburbs of Leicester [9].

Fig. 3.4. Loudon's own semi-detached house in Porchester Terrace, London, completed 1823-25.

season," a subtle hint from an avid horticulturist.

Another important contribution from Loudon was *The Suburban Gardener and Villa Companion*, which appeared in 1838 [9]. This seems to be the first time the term suburban was used in the title of a book. In his manual, Loudon showed detailed designs for his own semi-detached house in Porchester Terrace, numbers 3-5, in Bayswater, London, see Figs. 3.4 and 3.5. This impressive private home strengthened the acceptance of the semi-detached house as a viable alternative to a detached mansion, also for the upper tiers of middle class Victorians.

Loudon was at the time experimenting with curvilinear forms in glazing, and he invented the curved wrought-iron glazing bars, which made it possible to produce the quite stunning, domed conservatory that he placed on the front of the house. The conservatory acts to disguise the fact that the house is semi-detached, and thus fulfils Loudon's aim "to build two small houses which should appear as one, and have some pretensions to architectural design." The house, which was expertly restored in 1972, still stands proudly, although it has been shamefully dwarfed by twentieth century high-rise buildings, and the back garden has been built over by new neighbours.

Fig. 3.5. Loudon's Porchester Terrace house as it appeared in 2004.

Though terraced houses were found undesirable on more exclusive estates, such as at Rock Park mentioned above, they were still being built in large numbers in major cities and their suburbs. They were built for all social classes, although small terrace houses for the working classes dominated the building activity. More and more, though, speculative developers saw fit to attract middle class clients with semi-detached and detached villas, sometimes modest in size, sometimes fairly grand. A good example of a small-scale 1830s development with a mixture of housing types may be found concentrated around Barnsbury Square, Islington, London.

Thomas Whowell, gentleman, acquired the land just north of the new Minerva Road in Islington with the intention of developing a number of villas around a central square. The first reference to Barnsbury Square occurs in 1834. The small estate was developed over the period 1834-47 and comprises terraces, semi-detached and detached villas. In 1836, the Rate Books record the quite substantial

3

house that Whowell had had commissioned, Mountford House, the first building to be erected on the square. Looking deceptively like a single, prosperous villa with five bays and a central entrance, it is nevertheless a semi-detached building. The 1844 map of the square, Fig. 3.6, shows the subdivision clearly. The individual semis are of unequal size. The entrance to the smaller part of the villa is on the south side of the house as may be seen on the photograph in Fig. 3.7. Built in an Italianate style with the deep stucco of Regency architecture and with elaborate shell mouldings crowning the first floor windows facing the square, Mountford House is easily the most imposing of the Barnsbury Square buildings.

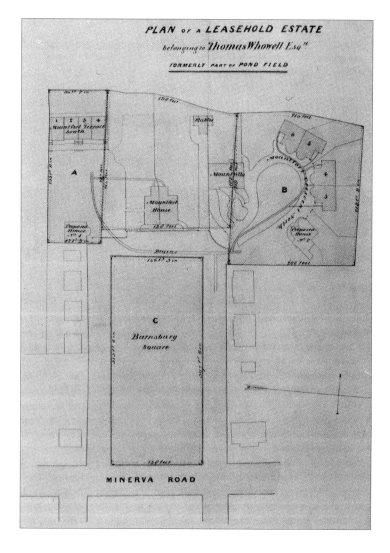

Fig. 3.6. Plan of Barnsbury Square 1844 [10].

The two semi-detached villas were initially let to two clergymen. According to the 1851 census the inhabitants of the square included a printer, a clerk of the admiralty, a commercial traveller, a medical student, a manufacturer, a furniture dealer, a fund holder, a ship broker, as well as several solicitors and merchants. Also an architect, a portrait painter, and a silk dyer are known to have lived in the square, and a celebrated Shakespearean actor had spent his childhood in the 1860s at Mountford House. The area, however, deteriorated towards the end of the century, and 1896-1914 Mountford House was run as a home for destitute boys.

Fig. 3.7. Mountford House in 2003.

The north-west corner of the square is laid out in a somewhat unusual loop, Mountford Crescent, serving two pairs of substantial semi-detached houses as well as a single detached villa. Overall, the crescent houses have a definite Regency feel to them, enhanced by their elegant bow frontages. They are the most handsome buildings on the estate.

Semi-detached houses were also placed on the south and the north sides of the square. These houses were much plainer, and much smaller. One of the southside houses is illustrated in Fig. 3.8. It bears a close resemblance to the anonymous pair of semis shown at the end of the previous chapter, in Fig. 2.31.

Apart from Mountford House, the houses on the square were not built for really large households. Nevertheless, the large number of clergy and professionals always living there gave the area an aura of respectability; it shared

Fig. 3.8. Small semi on Barnsbury Square (photo 2003). Compare with Fig. 2.31.

this attractiveness for middle-class Victorians with the Lloyd Baker estate south of Pentonville Road, with the much earlier Highbury Place properties north of the area, and indeed with much of the development in this part of London.

The shift of middle class taste in housing in the early part of Queen Victoria's reign can be studied no better than in the streets around Barnsbury Square. Preference shifted from the terraced house, through the quasi semi-detached, to the semi-detached, and ultimately to the detached house – for those who could afford it.

3

To most people today Georgian terraces seem well proportioned and elegant, although sometimes, it must be admitted, bland and monotonous as in Fig. 3.9. But the Victorian middle classes had definitely tired of Georgian terraces. They were, however, ready to accept the compromise offered by the semi-detached house, or semi-detached villa ('villa' had a ring of gentility to it), and even the quasi-semi-detached villa. This housing type had been introduced in the suburbs of south London around 1800 (Kennington and Blackheath, see Chapter 2), and it became very popular in the 1830s and 40s. The houses combined the pleasant uniformity of the terrace with the villa appearance of the semi-detached, but they shared with the terraced houses the problem of access to the back of the house.

Fig. 3.9. Georgian terrace, Islington, London (photo 2004).

This did not seem to bother the class-conscious occupants, who were more concerned with the location of the property and the number of rooms than with easy access to the rear and the prospect of sharing a party wall with their next-door-neighbours. The appearance of a 'villa' had visually been taken care of by the architect or builder: In the case of quasi-semi-detached buildings by using a wide pediment spanning both properties, and in the case of a semi-detached property by using either a pediment or by building back-to-back.

Numerous small speculative estates dominated by semi-detached and quasi-semi-detached villas were built in Islington over this period to cater for the Victorians move away from terraced accommodation. The architectural style was still basically Georgian, often stuccoed up to first-floor level, but typically now with wrought-iron or cast-iron balconies and more prominent window surrounds. Victorian households in this area of London were not yet large, and many of the houses were only moderately sized. A walk through the streets of Islington, today a much sought after location, will illustrate the variety of building styles in this transitional period. Figures 3.10 through 3.14 give an impression of the area, still middle class, but with many of the houses now divided into flats. Their outward appearance has thankfully been preserved.

3.10

North of Islington and Barnsbury lie Highbury Fields. The early semi-detached houses in Highbury Place on the east side of the fields were presented in Chapter 2. In 1840, the covenants restricting building opposite Highbury Place on the west side of Highbury Fields expired. James Wagstaffe, builder and surveyor, secured a 99-year building lease from Dawes's descendant and drew up a plan for a string of villas bordering the western boundary of Highbury Fields. The villas were mostly semi-detached and quite substantial, more in keeping with the sizes required by middle class families with live-in servants than the houses on the Barnsbury Square

3.11

3.12

3.13

3.14

Fig. 3.10-3.14. Examples of quasi-semi-detached (3.10) and semi-detached (3.11-3.14) houses in Islington from the second quarter of the nineteenth century (photo 2004).

3

estate and in the surrounding streets. The development, Highbury Crescent, comprised 25 houses erected over the years 1844-50 in a grand Italianate style, the central pairs incorporating low towers with pointed, pyramidal roofs. Fig. 3.15 shows a contemporary drawing of the crescent, and Fig. 3.16 shows part of the crescent as it appeared in 2004.

The Islington and Highbury developments shown in the previous paragraphs mark the tail end of Georgian and Regency architecture. Still firmly in the Georgian tradition, the buildings used additional architectural features borrowed from classical Grecian and Italian ideals. Italianate villas, such as Mountford House, favoured the shallow pitched roof with overhanging eaves supported on brackets and window cases capped by arched pediments. The use of prominently stuccoed quoins (cornerstones) as in the Highbury Crescent development and on some of the houses in the streets surrounding Barnsbury Square, is also influenced by classical Italian buildings. The towers of the semi-detached pairs in Highbury are undoubtedly inspired by the Italian campanile – a feature made popular by their prominence in Queen Victoria's and Prince Albert's retreat, Osborne House, on the Isle of Wight, see Fig. 3.17.

The crescent houses were let to respectable citizens such as solicitors, brokers and clerks. It was not unusual

Fig. 3.15. Highbury Crescent from a contemporary drawing, 1844 [11].

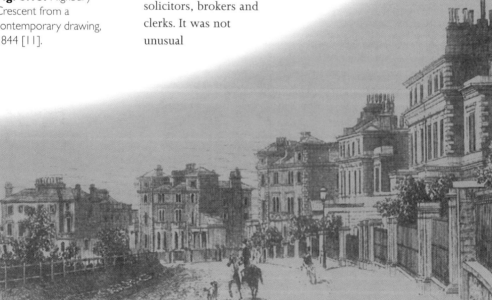

for up to 12 or even 14 people to live in one of the semi-detached houses. This number could include as many as five servants. Today the magnificent buildings have mostly been split into flats, with four or more flats being accommodated in each semi.

THE SECOND PERIOD, THE HIGH VICTORIAN ERA, 1845-75

In terms of housing styles the years between 1845 and 1875 are perhaps the most chaotic of the whole Victorian era. This was a period when a growing fascination with the Gothic architecture of the Middle Ages made itself strongly felt in the style adopted for public buildings of any importance; in time the Gothic spirit filtered down to middle-class suburbia, where it was to dominate both detached and semi-detached housing well into the 20th century. The diffusion of the style may be ascribed largely to the influence of two very different individuals: one a sophisticated, whimsical dilettante who belonged to the highest ranks of society in eighteenth-century England; the other a prolific nineteenth-century architect-designer, a Catholic convert who passionately believed that medieval Gothic was the true architecture of Christianity. Before returning to our subject proper it may be appropriate to say a little about these two men: Horace Walpole (1717-97), the son of Britain's first Prime Minister, and Augustus Welby N. Pugin (1812-52), the son of a French émigré architect.

HORACE WALPOLE

By the early nineteenth century a build-up to the Gothic influence had been under way for some time. The middle-class reading public had acquired a taste for medieval trappings, romanticism and melancholy through the popular literature of the eighteenth and early nineteenth century: Percy's *Reliques of Ancient English Poetry* (1765), for instance, and that best-selling novel of the 1790s, Mrs. Radcliffe's *The Mysteries of Udolpho* (1794) – not to mention the novels of Sir

Fig. 3.16. Semi-detached house in Highbury Crescent in 2004.

Fig. 3.17. Osborne House on the Isle of Wight, built 1845-51 [12].

3

Walter Scott (1771-1832). The more wealthy had had the time and the money to indulge in building romantic follies in their grounds or even to transform a modest house into a Gothic 'castle', as Horace Walpole did at Strawberry Hill in Twickenham.

Walpole also contributed to the medieval mood of the day with a spinechilling romance, *The Castle of Otranto* (1764). This 'Gothick story', as it was subtitled, inaugurated a seemingly endless stream of horror stories including Mary Shelley's *Frankenstein* (1818), and echoes of the book can still be seen more than two centuries later, for example in the novels of Stephen King.

It is chiefly for Strawberry Hill, however, that Walpole is remembered today. In 1750, a few years after buying the property, he confided to a friend that he was going to build a "little Gothick castle" there; the prospect was "delightful", he reported, but the house "very small," and till he added two or three rooms it was "scarce habitable" [www.richmond.gov.uk/localhistory]. With its pointed arches and fanvaulting and fretwork, its painted glass windows and papier

Fig. 3.18. Strawberry Hill. This house was the product of the first Gothic revival of the eighteenth century.

mache ornaments, the house he built became a foremost example of eighteenth-century Gothic – indeed, Strawberry Hill Gothic is an expression commonly used to describe the carefree, sometimes frippery use of medieval detail in similar buildings of the period. The house as it stands today is shown in Fig. 3.18.

Walpole did not create a popular taste for Gothic, but he did something just as important in the history of taste: to borrow the words of Kenneth Clark, "he did not so much popularise as aristocratise Gothic ... Walpole gave Gothic social standing" [13].

AUGUSTUS WELBY PUGIN

The major Gothic revival of the nineteenth century must be laid firmly at the doorstep of Augustus Pugin. In his all too short life – he died insane at the age of 40 – this extraordinary man designed 100 buildings including many churches, produced numerous designs for furniture and stained glass, and wrote eight books which he illustrated with his own delicate, often visionary drawings and etchings. The first major work that he was associated with was the Houses of Parliament, built over a period of 30 years to replace the Palace of Westminster that had been destroyed by fire in 1834 (see Fig. 3.19). The respected architect Charles Barry (1797-1860) was responsible for the overall design of the building, but it was Pugin who was entrusted with the exterior and interior details, even down to ink wells and hat stands.

Fig. 3.19. Engraving of the Houses of Parliament, while work was still under way [14].

Pugin's father had for a time worked in the office of John Nash and was an authority on Gothic design. Shortly after converting to Catholicism the younger Pugin published a little book that brought him fame and some notoriety: *Contrasts: or a parallel between the noble edifices of the fourteenth and fifteenth centuries and similar buildings of the present day; shewing the present decay of taste*, (1836), where he sought to demonstrate the superiority of building styles of the middle ages by comparing them with what he saw as the meanness of the classical buildings that so long had dominated English architecture[2].

There was an organic connection, he believed, between architecture and society, and there could be no true Christian architecture before society had recaptured the religious spirit and social commitment of the Middle Ages. If Walpole had given Gothic architecture an aura of fashion, Pugin thus supplied it with an element of morality. After his time Gothic was not only socially but also ethically acceptable.

In *The True Principles of Pointed or Christian Architecture* (1841), Pugin

---

2. The title of *Contrasts*, as it appears above, is taken from the title page of the first edition. Many later writers have shown slightly different wordings. Pugin himself apparently didn't bother too much. The front of the 1836 book for example bears the title *Contrasts or a parallel between the architecture of the 15th and 19th centuries*, and in the second edition from 1841 the title was changed to *Contrasts: or, a parallel between the noble edifices of the middle ages and corresponding buildings of the present day; shewing the present decay of taste*.

formulated two ideas that were to be of lasting importance [15]:

1. that there should be no features about a building which are not necessary for convenience, construction or propriety;
2. that all ornament should consist of enrichment of the essential construction of a building.

He later explains: "what I mean by propriety is this, that the external and internal appearance of an edifice should be illustrative of, and in accordance with, the purpose for which it is destined." Half a century later the American architect Louis Sullivan (1856-1924) revived this principle in his widely cited statement 'form follows function'. This is the philosophy of functionalism: that an object's purpose should be the prime determinant of its appearance. It was most famously expounded in the twentieth century by Le Corbusier (1887-1965) and other architects of the Modern Movement, but its roots lie with Augustus Welby Pugin. And yet in spite of a common denominator the resulting styles, Victorian Gothic on the one hand and the sparse style of the twentieth century modernists on the other, can hardly be less alike.

Today we associate Pugin's name chiefly with the extravagantly decorated public buildings of his day, but the two houses he built for himself were much more restrained in their ornamentation and could well have served as an inspiration for the suburban villas of contemporary pattern books.

THE GOTHIC REVIVAL AND THE SPECULATIVE BUILDERS

By the 1840s the Victorian middle classes were ready to take on medieval and ecclesiastical fantasies in their houses, and they longed for something which would be radically different from the insipid Georgian terrace, something which would be compatible with their position in society. However, although the middle classes had been pre-conditioned to everything Gothic, it took many years before architects, and more importantly speculative builders, accepted the style and began building Gothic revival houses for those tenants who were ready to demonstrate their wealth, as well as their Christianity, in their choice of housing.

There were several reasons why the new Gothic style was delayed in arriving at middle-class homes. The classic architecture of the Georgians was maybe on the wane, but pattern books still showed mostly derivatives of the Palladian style, with maybe variations in

Greek revival or Italianate styles. In fact, nearly all the well-known pattern books of the forties and fifties boasted an unparalleled eclecticism. Richard Brown's *Domestic Architecture* (1842), for example, included a Venetian summer residence, a Flemish-style chateau, a Chinese casino, and other dwellings in the Florentine, Swiss, Egyptian, Grecian, Roman, Persian, Morisco-Spanish, and Plantagenet styles [16]. It is no wonder that the expression "the battle of the styles" was applied to this period of domestic architectural history. Lamenting on the state of architecture in England in the mid-nineteenth century Tarbuck writes "... and architecture ceases to progress, continuing a mere scheme of copyism in its premature, second childhood, instead of flourishing with manly vigour" [17]. At this point the middle classes needed to see the acceptance by their superiors of Victorian Gothic as a style for family homes, and this came about only after Gothic had set its mark on public buildings such as the Houses of Parliament, on churches, colleges, and railway stations.

In the middle of the century Parliament passed a number of new bills that had a direct impact on the way in which new houses were built. The duty payable on bricks was abolished in 1850, the excise duty on glass was repealed in 1845, and the tax on windows was finally done away with in 1851. A growing awareness of hygiene and health led to Edwin Chadwick's report in 1842, *Report on the Sanitary Conditions of the Labouring Population*, and a general attempt at sanitary reform came with the Public Health Act of 1848.

In short, the speculative builders were confronted not only with new customer demands in terms of style, albeit somewhat uncertain demands, but also with new legislation, some of which would result in additional complications and expenses.

It was the speculative builders who were responsible for the vast majority of Victorian middle-class homes, as well as those for the labouring classes, and in order to survive they needed to judge the mood of their potential clients carefully. The middle classes might have wanted something different from a 'bland' Georgian terrace or semi, but they were not ready to break new ground without being absolutely certain that this would be considered respectable and Christian. There was, therefore, no immediate reappraisal in the 1840s either of house style or materials for a suburban middle-class dwelling, and many speculative houses built over the next two or three decades retained traces of the Georgian tradition. This is well demonstrated in an example from Battersea that shows a row of semi-detached houses erected in the 1860s, all with a classical face, but nevertheless recognizably Victorian by their bay windows, see

3

Fig. 3.20. A new kind of uniformity, different from the Georgian terraces, was creeping into the street picture, a pre-cursor to the 'bye-law streets' (see Chapter 4) soon to make their mark on speculative suburban estates all over the country.

Two pattern-book semi-detached houses in the Gothic revival style are shown in Figures 3.21 and 3.22. The first illustration shows a 'double suburban villa' from Richardson's *The Englishman's House from a Cottage to a Mansion* [19], a rambling mansion designed with a strong Gothic influence in its steep roofs and towers, and in general a pointed architecture that gives it a medieval appearance.

The second picture shows a pair of semi-detached Gothic villas from the pattern book *Suburban and Rural Architecture* [20]. The design is much more subdued than the one shown in the previous illustration, but the Gothic influence is apparent in the treatment of, for example, the entrance porch and roof finials.

Neither of the houses shown approach the elaborate Gothic style seen in many of the churches of the period or, say, in the Houses of Parliament. The eye-catching difference between the new Gothic of the churches and monumental buildings on the one hand, and that of the middle-class villas on the other, made one early twentieth-century writer comment that the Victorians had decided "that the architecture of Sundays and week days must be different" [21].

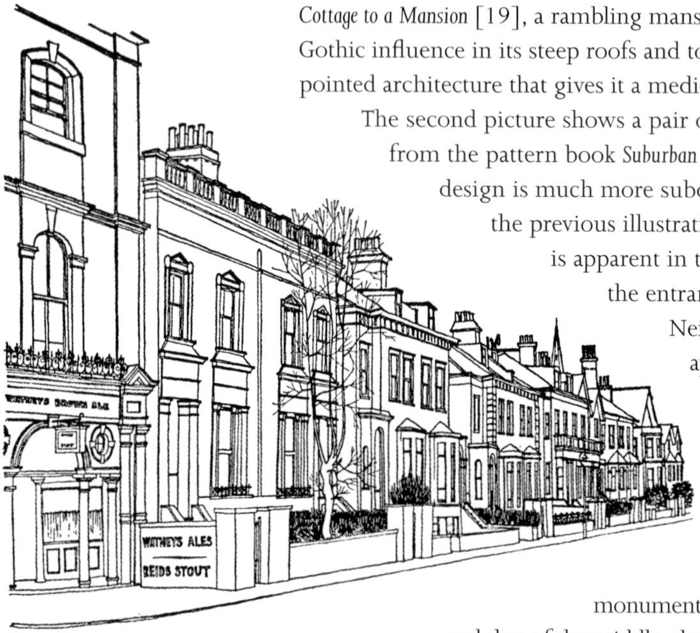

The reluctance of the speculative builders to engage in Pugin's Gothic revival style can be easily understood. The builders were conservative people, comfortable with a well-tried, moderate style of building based on Georgian housing styles and their derivatives. Not before a debilitated Gothic became accepted did suburban housing estates start appearing in the new style.

JOHN RUSKIN

Pugin did not live to see the fulfillment of his ideas in the speculative housing for the English middle classes. The transition to the new Gothic

Fig. 3.20. Semi-detached houses in Battersea, London, developed 1860-68 [18].

Fig. 3.21. A Gothic double suburban villa [19].

Fig. 3.22. A pair of semi-detached Gothic villas [20].

FRONT ELEVATION.

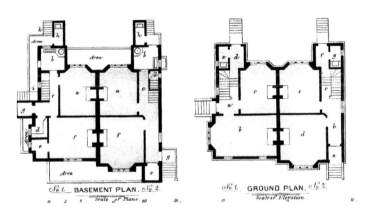

No.1 BASEMENT PLAN. No.2

Scale of Plans.

No.1 GROUND PLAN. No.2

Scale of Elevation.

style evolved only slowly in the 1850s and 60s, and it was probably the influence of John Ruskin (1819-1900) more than any other single person that finally brought about the changes.

Ruskin was the leading Victorian critic of art, whose voluminous output together with the moral fervour that informed his writings gave him an enormous prestige among his contemporaries (though his pronouncements are often self-contradictory, and he modified some of his views to a startling extent during his long life). Perhaps largely because of this prestige and the forceful manner in which he put forward his ideas, it is he rather than Pugin who is popularly remembered as the originator of the Gothic revival in the nineteenth century. In fact, Ruskin was quite in line with Pugin in respect of the close connection between architecture and society, which is the main tenet of his first important book, *The Seven Lamps of Architecture*

3

(1849) [22]. His initial enthusiasm was not for the eccentric Gothic revival buildings around him, but for the old Gothic of the cathedrals of England and Northern France, yet in the second edition of *Lamps* (1855) he was expressly recommending the use of Gothic in contemporary England. At some point he had become a Gothic revivalist. Ruskin was later to say: "In this style let us build the church, the palace and the cottage; but chiefly let us use it for civil and *domestic* buildings" [my emphasis] [23].

In *The Stones of Venice* (1851-53) Ruskin devoted a well-known chapter to the Nature of Gothic where he goes so far as to praise Gothic architecture, to the detriment of Greek, for its imperfections. Greek architecture, he maintained was made under the direction of a master-workman who could tolerate no imperfection; Gothic architecture was the work of individual, perhaps inferior, workmen who took pleasure in their work. "Accept this then for a universal law," he said, "that neither architecture nor any other noble work of man can be good unless it be imperfect" [24]. It is clear that Ruskin's admiration for Gothic buildings extended to the society that made such architecture possible, a society which respected the craftsman and manual labourer, as unlike the Victorian production-line society as possible. His criticism of architecture thus led him to a criticism of society, which was taken up notably by William Morris (see Chapter 4). Ruskin's ideas also reached out to the garden city philosophy of the late nineteenth century, and thus indirectly to the suburbs of the twentieth.

Fig. 3.23. Window in Oakham Castle drawn by John Ruskin [27].

THE RUSKINIAN FAÇADE
There are primarily three elements of Ruskin's teachings that were taken on by the architects and builders of his day which make buildings of that period recognizably Ruskinian:

1. The pointed arch
2. The polychromatic brickwork
3. The carved capitals on porch and window columns.

The pointed arch had, of course, already been introduced by Pugin in *The True Principles of Pointed or Christian Architecture* and employed extensively in churches and monumental buildings by himself and other architects of the period. A common criticism of Gothic architecture at the time was its structural complexity, especially as seen in relation to private houses. Ruskin, however, argued that medieval Gothic church architecture was "merely the perfect development of the common dwelling-house architecture of the period" [25]. He goes on to say that

> There is not the smallest necessity, because the arch is pointed, that the aperture should be so. The work of the arch is to sustain the building above; when this is once done securely, the pointed head may be filled in any way we choose … [26].

Fig. 3.23 demonstrates Ruskin's viewpoint in his drawing of a pointed window at Oakham Castle [27], and Fig. 3.24 shows the incorporation of a standard sash window within the pointed arches a Victorian private home in north Oxford.

Fig. 3.24. Ruskinian Gothic windows in a north Oxford suburb (2005).

The polychromatic brickwork of Venetian buildings was highly praised by Ruskin in *The Stones of Venice*. By the 1850s stucco was falling out of favour in England, and the tax on bricks had been abolished. Furthermore, the improved transport of goods made possible by the canal system established over the past half century, and the new railway network now being continuously extended, increased the availability of bricks in several colours at any given building site. At a very practical level this meant that the use of bricks now became an attractive alternative to stone and stucco, and Ruskin's dictum of multicoloured brickwork attracted the speculative builders and their clients.

Polychrome decoration using bands of contrasting coloured brick became popular. To take an example, alternating courses of red and yellow brick on facades was much used by the architect William Butterfield (1814-1900) on his churches. The effect soon appeared in speculative villas, and the overall picture gave rise to the colloquial expression "streaky bacon Gothic". Occasionally the builders went overboard and alternated red and yellow bricks in every course on the façade giving it a chequer-board appearance, see the semi-detached house from the early 1870s in Fig. 3.25.

Fig. 3.25. Semi-detached pair in Little Sutton, Cheshire, 1870s, with polychromatic brickwork

Also the carved capitals and in general the carved stonework framing windows and doors became a much used feature in high Victorian Gothic buildings. Ruskin had a preference for natural forms such

3

as the use of carved foliage. Although he again and again stressed that carvings should be worked by hand by dedicated craftsmen, there can be hardly any doubt that Victorian builders and manufacturers used their ingenuity to mass produce 'carved' ornamentation in artificial stone to keep the costs within reason. Manuals picturing carved ornamentation were readily available. Pugin had published *Floriated Ornament* in 1849, and Glazier had shown details of authentic Gothic carvings in his *A Manual of Historic Ornament* from which the illustration of Fig.3.26 is copied [28].

In short, the Gothic revival started by Pugin was now finally becoming a practical proposition. Ruskin had at one point written

> Do not be afraid of incongruities – do not think of unity of effect. Introduce your Gothic line by line and stone by stone … existing houses will be little the worse for having little bits of better work fitted to them … Remember that it is the glory of Gothic architecture that it can do anything [29].

Fig. 3.26. Illustration from Glazier showing original medieval carving on which architects and builders could base their designs [28].

This sounds as though builders were given the *carte blanche* to stick on any adornment that might catch their fancy (what the trade today would call 'gob-ons'). This was certainly not Ruskin's intention, but it became the reality in many of the lower middle-class and working-class houses that swamped the suburbs of the industrial cities in the high Victorian era. The historian and writer John Gloag may to some extent be excused, when he writes "… no previous civilisation had ever had so many citizens who combined high moral standards with deplorable taste" [30].

Notwithstanding the deplorable taste displayed by much Victorian domestic architecture, the maxims of Ruskin could, when handled with sensitivity, result in well proportioned and aesthetically pleasing dwellings, also when viewed with the eyes of a twenty-first century student of architecture. There are several examples among the many semi-detached houses in north Oxford, where St. John's College had embarked on a programme of housing development just north of The Parks in the 1860s and 70s with a view to meeting the needs of married dons and their families. An example is shown in Fig. 3.27. It was built in 1872 by the architect Frederick Codd as part of the St John's College estate. The pointed window arches and porches are very conspicuous, whereas the polychromatic brickwork is quite subdued. A detail of the bay windows and the entrance porches is shown in Fig. 3.28, where also the rather stumpy columns with carved capitals may be better seen.

Similar in general appearance to north Oxford is the north London suburb of Tufnell Park, which was laid out as a speculative estate in the late 1860s in the Gothic revival style with numerous semi-detached houses. Ruskin's influence can be found also on estates in south London, in Bath, Bristol, Northampton, Bradford, and most other towns of any industrial significance in the high Victorian period.

Ruskin was a man hard to please. His writings on architecture had inspired architects and builders, as had Pugin's publications, but he was not happy with the popular interpretations of his aesthetic philosophy. In March 1872 he wrote to the Pall Mall Gazette:

> I have had an indirect influence on nearly every cheap villa builder between Denmark Hill and Bromley; and there is scarcely a public house near the Crystal Palace but sells its gin and bitters under pseudo-Venetian capitals copied from the Church of Madonna of Health or of Miracles. And one of my principal notions for leaving my present house is that it is surrounded everywhere by the accursed Frankenstein monsters of, indirectly, my own making. [29]

The move Ruskin refers to here is to Brantwood, the property he had recently bought on the shore of Coniston Water in his beloved Lake District. This was where he died in 1900, far from his place of birth in the suburbs of what he called "loathsome London", where the houses "… are fastened in a Siamese-twin manner together by

Fig. 3.27. Semi-detached house on Woodstock Road, north Oxford, built 1872 (2005).

Fig. 3.28. Detail of the house in Fig. 3.27 (2005).

their sides, and each couple has a Greek or Gothic portico shared between them, with magnificent steps, and highly ornamented capitals" [31]. Ruskin could in his criticisms be fiercely acerbic.

The end of an era

Nearly forty years into the reign of Queen Victoria the picture of domestic housing was as confused as ever before. The extraordinary growth in the population and in the wealth of the nation as a whole had thrown the Victorians into a house building frenzy. The battle of the styles, primarily between the classicism of the Georgians and the Gothic revival of Pugin and Ruskin, had no outright winner. A cross-section of middle class houses from the sixties will show nearly equal measures of houses with a strong Georgian ancestry on the one hand, and houses with a decidedly Ruskinian Gothic influence on the other.

In all the architectural melee, the acceptance of the semi-detached house slipped quietly and unobtrusively through the battle lines as being a highly respectable mode of dwelling for middle-class Victorians. The large Victorian families with live-in servants needed roomy houses, and even the newfound wealth of many middle class householders could not stretch to the ultimately desirable detached villa. With the precedence given to the semi-detached house by John Nash, Jack Loudon, and others in the first half of the century, the Victorian pater familias happily settled his household in a semi-detached, as long as it was in a good location and displayed a suitable degree of ostentation.

The last quarter of the nineteenth century was to become as complex as the high Victorian era as far as the ethos of housing was concerned. The poet and artist William Morris (1834-96) was influenced by Ruskin's philosophy on the revival of craftsmanship in an age where anything machine made normally would fetch the highest accolade. He was instrumental in a revival of craftsmanship in all aspects of house building and decoration and also in introducing a new attitude to design in domestic architecture, which began even before the Gothic revival had reached its peak. The new spirit in housing design has since been called the Domestic Revival, and it created some of England's most outstanding vernacular houses thanks to a handful of brilliant late nineteenth century architects.

References

1   John Burnett, *A Social History of Housing 1815-1970*, Methuen, Newton Abbot 1978, p.95;99.

2   Judith Flanders, *The Victorian House*, Harper Perennial, London 2003, p.xxxix.

3   *Ibid.*

4   Sarah Ellis, *The Women of England; Their Social Duties and Domestic Habits*, 1839, quoted in John Burnett, *A Social History of Housing 1815-1970*, Methuen, Newton Abbot 1978, p.193.

5   Judith Flanders, *The Victorian House*, Harper Perennial, London 2003, p.xxv.

6   Robert Kerr, *The Gentleman's House*, John Murray, London 1871, Third edition, p.341.

7   E.W.Trendall, *Original Designs for Cottages and Villas, in the Grecian, Gothic and Italian Styles of Architecture*, London 1831.

8   John Claudius Loudon, *Encyclopaedia of Cottage, Farm and Villa Architecture*, Longmans, London 1833.

9   John Claudius Loudon, *The Suburban Gardener and Villa Companion*, Longmans, London 1838.

10 Mary Cosh, *The Squares of Islington – Part II*, Islington Archaeology & Historic Society, London 1993, p.29.

11 *Ibid.* p.99.

12 Helen Long, *Victorian Houses and their details*, Architectural Press, Oxford 2002, p.33.

13 Kenneth Clark, *The Gothic Revival*, John Murray, London1962, pp. 61-62.

14 Helena Barrett and John Phillips, *Suburban Style*, Macdonald & Co (Publishers), London 1987, p.52.

15 Augustus Welby Pugin, *The True Principles of Pointed or Christian Architecture*, John Weale, London 1841.

16 Richard Brown, *Domestic Architecture*, 1842. Quoted in Helen Long, *Victorian Houses and their Details*, Architectural Press, Oxford 2002, p.41.

17 E.L.Tarbuck, *The Builder's Practical Director*, Hagger, London 1855-8, p.77.

18   John Gloag, *Victorian Comfort*, Adam and Charles Black, London 1961, p.24.

19 C.J.Richardson, *The Englishman's Home from a Cottage to a Mansion*, London 1870, p.192.

20 E.L.Blackburne and E.F.S.A.Arch, *Suburban and Rural Architecture*, James Hagger, London 1867, p.95.

21 T.D.Atkinson, *English Architecture*, Methuen & Co Ltd, London 1928, ninth edition, p.194.

22 John Ruskin, *The Seven Lamps of Architecture*, first published 1849, George Allen & Sons, London 1907.

23 Cited in [13], p.199.

24 John Ruskin, *The Stones of Venice*, first published 1851-53. Consulted edition c. 1900 (no date given) in three volumes, George Routledge & Sons, London, vol.II, p.188.

25 Rebecca Daniel and Geoff Brandwood (editors), *Ruskin and Architecture*, Spire Books Ltd, Reading 2003, p.100.

26 *Ibid.*, p.101.

27 *Ibid.*

28 R. Glazier, *A Manual of Historic Ornament.* Reproduced in Linda Osband, *Victorian Gothic House Style*, David & Charles, Newton Abbot 2003, p.25.

29 Rebecca Daniel and Geoff Brandwood (editors), *Ruskin and Architecture*, Spire Books Ltd, Reading 2003, p.102;109.

30 John Gloag, *Victorian Comfort*, Adam and Charles Black, London 1961, p.30.

31 John Ruskin, letter 29, *Fors Clavigera*, 1873. Cited in Rebecca Daniel and Geoff Brandwood (editors), *Ruskin and Architecture*, Spire Books Ltd, Reading 2003, p.99.

4

Bye-law housing, the Domestic Revival and model villages of the late Victorian era (1875-1901)

"… to build houses in which our work-people will be able to live and be comfortable. Semi-detached houses, with gardens back and front …"

William Lever at the inauguration of Port Sunlight in 1888

As we move into the last quarter of the nineteenth century suburban housing was to undergo some quite radical changes. There were, however, two quite separate trends. On the one hand, speculative building continued in a style that paid homage to the Georgian tradition while including a sprinkling of Gothic revival embellishments so beloved by the Victorians. On the other hand, the Domestic Revival, discussed later in this chapter, was about to transform middle-class housing nearly beyond recognition.

Legislation and bye-law housing[1]

The high Victorian house style, had after a slow, start become the

---

1. Bye-law or by-law is an expression stemming from Viking times. The Danish word for town is "by" and a by-law means a law applying to a particular town or village.

favourite of the speculative builders. The semi-detached plan was now a firmly established and popular housing type in middle-class estates. An 1871 map of lslington, for example, shows a housing density per square mile (in round figures) of:

Detached houses: 25
Semi-detached houses: 400 (200 pairs)
Terraced houses: 3000

The detached and semi-detached houses naturally tend to dominate the more salubrious, outermost areas of this early London suburb, mainly towards the north-east, whereas the terrace houses cluster in the working class areas closer to the city centre. The proportion of semi-detached houses is nowhere near what it was to become in the outer suburbs, but it is still quite significant and underlines the overall favourable reception given to the semi-detached house by the Victorian middle classes.

In the last half of the nineteenth century Parliament passed a number of laws that were to have a profound impact on the way houses were constructed, and indirectly an impact on the outward appearance of whole streets of speculative housing. To put this statement in some perspective, it is useful to have a brief look at the history of building acts in this country.

In London, the Great Fire of 1666 was the major reason for several building acts designed to assure, especially, fire-proofing and structural stability. The 1774 London Building Act already mentioned in Chapter 2 became the one most often referred to. Buildings were divided into four major classes after their size and building costs. The main distinction between the classes in terms of building practices was in the thickness of the walls, class I being the most robust with walls two or more bricks thick. No restrictions were placed, for example, on the height of the buildings or on the width of the streets, and nothing was said about sanitary arrangements [1]. Several other acts followed, for London as well as for the provinces, but it wasn't until a rising concern for the health of a vigorously expanding population made itself felt that building legislation included requirements concerning sanitary matters. Outbreaks of cholera in the 1830s, 40s and 50s finally prompted local authorities to legislate regarding housing sanitation, drainage and sewage disposal. In the 1840s, health acts were passed in London, Liverpool, Manchester and Nottingham. In 1848, Parliament consolidated such local acts in the first Public Health Act, primarily designed to

improve sanitary arrangements. The municipalities were now given the freedom to pass their own bye-laws, respecting the statutory Public Health Act, and most local authorities used their powers to issue building bye-laws regulating, for example, the areas of open space about houses and the width of streets in order to provide better ventilation and lighting for the inhabitants.

Several revisions of the 1848 Act were passed before the advent of the Public Health Act of 1875, which was a landmark in nineteenth century social legislation. Apart from encouraging local authorities to produce their own bye-laws, the act introduced general rules concerning building-lines and required the appointment of local surveyors. The 1875 Act was supplemented in 1877 by Government producing a set of Model Bye-laws for the guidance of local authorities. For the first time housing developers were required to submit plans for a proposed development, and if the houses upon inspection did not live up to building regulations the authorities could require that they should be altered or even demolished.

Bye-laws could be quite specific: New houses needed to have access to at least 150 square feet of open space at the rear, the windows of houses had to be at least 10 per cent of the floor space, the distance to the next building had to be a minimum of 10 feet, or 15 feet in the case of a two-storey building, and carriage streets over 100 feet long were to be at least 36 feet wide. The bye-laws also regulated the provision of satisfactory drainage, and they required access to privies which would allow removal of their contents without the receptacle being carried through the house.

Most municipalities adopted the suggestions of the Model Bye-laws, although they were only permissive, not mandatory. The legislation provided by the bye-laws coincided with a major building boom in the 1880s. The terms bye-law housing and bye-law streets came to denote the characterless estates of terraced and semi-detached housing that were built on the outskirts of most cities to house factory labourers (terraces) and middle-class, white-collar workers (semis). These must have been the houses Oscar Wilde referred to in a lecture to art students, when he expressed:

> Art is very difficult in this unlovely town of ours, where, as you go to work in the mornings, or return from it at eventide, you have to pass through street after street of the most foolish and stupid architecture that the world has ever seen; architecture … reducing three-fourths of the London houses to being, merely, like square boxes of the vilest proportions,

Fig. 4.1. Bye-law terraced housing in Birkenhead, 2005.

Fig. 4.2. Bye-law semi-detached housing in Birkenhead, 2005.

as gaunt as they are grimy, and as poor as they are pretentious [2].

The photographs in Figs. 4.1 and 4.2 show typical bye-law streets of respectively terraced houses and semi-detached houses from the last quarter of the nineteenth century.

The ground plan of one of the semis is shown in Fig. 4.3. Notice the restricted size of the back yard, not a garden in any sense, and that the kitchen, wash house, etc. are located in a back-extension to the main part of the building. The back-extension on these houses is two storeys high, thus providing space for a bathroom and two small extra bedrooms on the first floor. The full height back-extension does, however, block out much of the light to the back of the houses, especially when, as here, the pairs were placed very close together. The semi-darkness has given rise to the expression 'tunnel-backs' for this type of housing.[2]

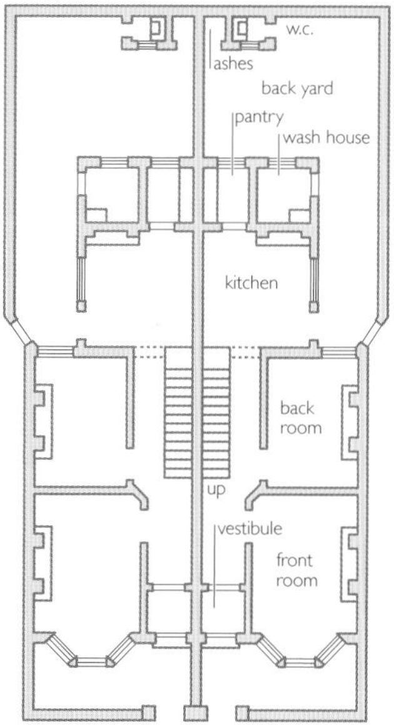

The bye-law housing of the period 1880-1914 has been much derided in the twentieth and twenty-first centuries on account of its rigid precision and monotony, but the houses themselves represented an enormous advance in living conditions for the working classes and the lower middle class. The streets were lighter, the houses more solidly built and sanitation was vastly improved in comparison with the conditions offered to those classes

Fig. 4.3. Ground plan of a pair of semi-detached houses in Hawarden Avenue, Birkenhead, 1899.

2. Housing historians have given the term tunnel-back two interpretations. One explanation is the one just given. The other refers to the tunnels or through-ways that were created in the terraces for every block of four or six dwellings. These lead to the back-lanes ('ginnels' in the north of England), giving access to the coal sheds, ash-pits and privies.

in the first part of the century. That so many of these houses stand inhabited today is indeed a testimony to the competence of their builders.

The bye-laws did not, in fact, impose the regimented layout of streets that came to typify the estates of the period. They insisted only that the streets should be of a certain width. Nor did they require that the houses be identical, only that they were built to minimum standards. However, the speculative builders were building for profit, and they, not surprisingly, used proven, simple prototype models out of well-worn pattern books to maximize their return on investment, and a rectangular grid of streets was for them the most cost-effective layout. Aesthetic values did not enter into the equation.

Even so, some bye-law districts are not without their special appeal in those areas where the streets and their houses have been maintained to reasonable standards. It is often a lack of overall maintenance, combined with later incongruous additions of porches, PVC doors, dormers or stone cladding of a façade that today detracts from what could have been a desirable urban or suburban environment.

The Domestic Revival

Bye-law housing was the speculative builder's paradise. Terrace after terrace and semi after semi were put up in regimented rows on a scale never seen before. The bye-law houses from the late nineteenth century are what most people today think of as Victorian houses. They still dominate vast areas of the suburban landscape close to major towns and cities in this country.

However, while the builders were erecting pattern-book houses by the thousand, some totally different developments were taking place at the upper levels of middle-class society. New forms of middle-class housing designs were being proposed by late Victorian architects, wealthy industrialists were building model estates for their workers and managers, and around the turn of the century the garden city movement was creating a new type of suburb. The semi-detached house played an important part in all these developments.

The term Domestic Revival is probably the one that best describes the trend in housing styles in the last quarter of the century, styles that were radically different from the uniformity of the bye-law houses. The term itself is quite ubiquitous and will be discussed in more detail below. In a historical perspective the domestic revival created the suburban villas that are recognisably Edwardian and it determined many of the visual features of the massive inter-war speculative estates.

New middle-class aspirations
ARTS AND CRAFTS AND THE RED HOUSE AT BEXLEYHEATH

The first generation of the newly rich middle classes had looked to the gentry to define a mode of behaviour they believed would be appropriate to their social position. Their efforts centred on acquiring a respectable house in a respectable neighbourhood, maintaining a suitable vestige of Christianity, and employing domestic help to allow the lady of the house to keep up the all-important appearance of a family in harmony with itself – everything guided by the unquestioned superiority of the head of the family. The etiquette expected of middle-class families was published in a plethora of books and journals that appeared on the subject throughout the Victorian age.

By the time we reach the last quarter of the century things had changed slightly. The middle classes had by and large mastered the social technicalities of being middle class in a comfortable suburban environment. Many, though, were still restless in society and sought new aspirations in which to channel their energies. To Christianity and 'refined' behaviour was now added a new element: the artistic. Under the headings of sweetness and light, Matthew Arnold (1822-88) had promoted the appreciation of beauty (sweetness) and a desire for knowledge (light). His ideas were embraced by the Victorian middle classes, and an Aesthetic Movement was born, which encouraged the practical introduction of art and beauty in every home. The movement was concerned mainly with interior decoration, but it soon became ridiculed, as ferns, aspidistras, Japanese fans, Flemish beer-jugs and peacock feathers began to clutter up the homes.

The Aesthetic Movement is mentioned here mainly because it had many ideas in common with another philosophy of the period, the Arts and Crafts Movement, which was to have a lasting impact on not only interior design, but also on the design of middle-class houses in general. This movement, its designers and architects laid the foundations for the Domestic Revival.

Probably the most simple way in which to explain the style of the revival is to say that it takes its inspiration from ordinary family dwellings from before the Industrial Revolution. These buildings were invariably made from local materials and thus represented

4

the vernacular tradition of the area. Brunskill introduced the term 'domestic vernacular architecture' to describe such unpretentious buildings, designed for living in [3]. The Domestic Revival is essentially a revival of the vernacular style.

It is sometimes maintained that the first exponent of the Domestic Revival is one particular house, the Red House near Bexleyheath in Kent [4], see Fig. 4.4, although some place the birth of the Domestic Revival in the *picturesque* style of the early nineteenth century [5]. The Red House was built for William Morris, the leading figure in the Arts and Crafts Movement.

Morris possessed an extraordinary range of talents: designer, poet, craftsman, painter, architect, entrepreneur and political activist. He was also blessed with wealthy parents and was all his life with independent means. With Ruskin he shared a scorn for machine-made products, and he campaigned tirelessly for a return to the principles of medieval craftsmanship.

Together with a few friends, Morris founded a firm that put his ideas into practice by producing hand-crafted articles for everyday use such as chairs, wallpaper, fabrics, carpets, plus, not least, the printing of beautiful books – what he called the lesser arts. The group of friends and the company, which later became Morris & Co, sowed the

Fig. 4.4. The Red House at Bexleyheath (2005).

seeds of what we today know as the Arts and Crafts Movement.

One of Morris's friends was the architect Philip Webb (1831-1915). They had met at the offices of the well-known architect George Street (1824-81), where Morris had spent a year as an architect apprentice. Street's practice was firmly anchored in the Gothic Revival style. Whilst Morris and Webb both respected the Gothic spirit in architecture, Morris decided for his own house to commission Philip Webb in 1859 to design a house totally different from the reigning styles, for example, the Gothic Revival on the one hand, and Italianate classicism on the other. They found what they wanted in the ordinary buildings in villages and townships around the country, traditional houses built of local materials, England's 'vernacular' buildings.

The Red House[3] had an enormous influence on domestic architecture in this country, and if the house appears not all that different from our houses of the twentieth century, it is precisely because it became the prototype for generations of suburban villas. As may be seen from the illustration, the building is constructed of warm red brick under a steep, tiled roof, with an emphasis on natural materials – and not entirely devoid of a Gothic influence. In fact, Morris himself had stated that it was "in the style of the thirteenth century" [6]. A main feature of the façades is that the windows appear in a highly irregular fashion, at odds with the strict symmetry of classical architecture. The windows now relate to the interior room layout, which was unburdened by either Georgian or Victorian traditions.

The following decades added new elements to the Domestic Revival – and further confusion in architectural terminology by introducing for example, the Arts and Crafts style, the Queen Anne Revival style, the Vernacular Revival and the Old English style, all part of what we have chosen to call the Domestic Revival.

BEDFORD PARK AND NORMAN SHAW

In spite of its inherent qualities the immediate impact of the Red House on contemporary middle-class houses was minimal, and its status as an icon of domestic architecture was to come much later. Soon after the completion of the house, William Morris channelled his energy and talents into the Arts and Crafts design company. Webb was never a prolific architect, and it was left to other architects to practice the free style of architecture on a grander scale. One of these

---

3. The Red House is open to the public under the National Trust. Its original countryside isolation in an orchard of apple and cherry trees is difficult to picture today, where it is surrounded by vast estates of inter-war semi-detached houses.

was R. Norman Shaw (1831-1912), who also had trained in Street's offices and was acquainted with both Morris and Webb, although he was not one of the inner circle. Norman Shaw was to have an overwhelming influence on his contemporaries, and he probably did more than anyone else to popularise the styles of the Domestic Revival. With his associates in the 1870s he developed the vernacular architecture into a style peculiarly his own, the Queen Anne style.

Shaw had started his career as a Gothic revivalist, but he was soon building large country houses in a more romantic style. Inspired by journeys into Kent and Sussex with his architect friend W.E. Nesfield (1835-88) he devised a refreshing approach to domestic housing, using tile hangings on the walls, dominant hipped and tiled roofs, dormer windows, pargetting (an old East Anglian technique for decorative plasterwork). The use of red brick was very common. Other attributes were white stone dressings and white painted woodwork. Dutch gables and Elizabethan style windows with small panes were also part of his designs. Surprisingly, perhaps, the result looked both original and pleasing to the eye. It came to be known as the Queen Anne style, or Queen Anne Revival, although it did not strictly try to emulate the architecture of her short reign, 1702-14.

The style was quickly accepted by the middle classes, and even the speculative builders had to come to terms with the fact that the watered-down Gothic Revival style, so favoured by them in the bye-law estates, would no longer suffice for new generations of moderately prosperous middle-class clients looking for the most fashionable of detached or semi-detached houses.

For Shaw the first major opportunity to become involved in the design of a suburban estate using the Queen Anne style came with the layout of Bedford Park in Chiswick, London. The estate was the brainchild of one Jonathan Carr (1845-1915), cloth maker and speculator. His aim was to create a small community of 'artistic' houses, an estate for aesthetes who could afford a rent that would be fairly high for that part of west London. Carr purchased the land in 1875 and started the development immediately. The estate was to have its own shops, clubhouse, pub, and a church. Also planned was an Art School. Detached and semi-detached houses, and some terraces, would be set out in plots that respected the many groups of trees in the area.

Carr's first architect was E.W. Godwin (1833-86) who immediately had 18 semi-detached houses built to his standard designs. Carr was not happy with the results, however, and Shaw was employed to lead the project in 1877, first as estate architect and later as consultant. One of the significant innovations Shaw and his architects brought to the house designs was the elimination of basements. Kitchens were now placed on the ground floor,[4] and with plots much wider than commonly used, the typical Victorian back extensions could be eliminated – thus, in principle, spelling an end to the gloomy tunnel backs of so much speculative housing of the nineteenth century. At Bedford Park a pair of semi-detached houses would typically have a frontage of 50 ft. Rooms were now spacious and light, and Shaw included a bathroom and WC on the first floor, a novelty at the time.

An example of one of Norman Shaw's plans for a semi-detached house on the estate is shown in Fig. 4.5. Like many of the other houses in Bedford Park this one is quite substantial, with seven bedrooms. Note the balcony, a popular feature of the Queen Anne revival. They were described by a burglar at the time, it is said, as being "uncommon 'andy".

Fig. 4.5. Plan of one house of a pair of semi-detached houses on the Bedford Park estate to the design of Norman Shaw [7].

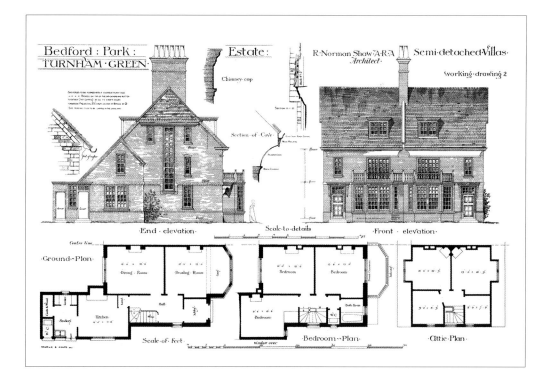

4. This was not entirely unheard of in the high Victorian era. Tarbuck in *The Builders Practical Director*, c.1855, shows plans for modest semi-detached houses with kitchens at ground level.

4

The community was a great success. The preservation of so many trees gave it a predominantly rural atmosphere, unique for a suburb at that time, and in this respect it heralded the Garden Suburb movement at the turn of the century. An 1896 map of the development is shown in Fig. 4.6. The inhabitants of the village included artists, journalists, academics, poets (W.B. Yeats live there for a number of years with his parents and sisters), playwrights, publishers, and a fair number of retired military men. Bedford Park was visited by the Architectural Association, its houses were described in The Building News, and it was even praised by William Morris as having "quaint and pretty architecture" [8].

A contemporary poet captured the mood of the estate in 'The Ballad of Bedford Park' published in the St. James Gazette of 17 December, 1881, from which the following verse is taken:

Here trees are green, and bricks are red,
And clean the face of man.
We'll build our houses here he said,
In style of good Queen Anne.[5]

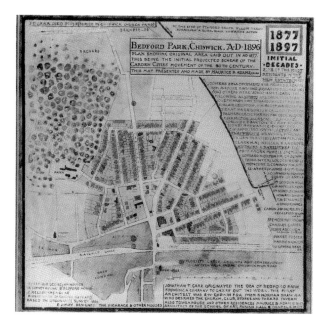

Fig. 4.6. Map of Bedford Park 1896.

An early prospect showing the style of the houses is illustrated in Fig. 4.7. This shows a publicity poster, which was widely displayed on London stations. The semi-detached house on the left in the illustration is by Norman Shaw (the plan and elevations are shown in Fig. 4.5). A house of this design photographed in 2005 is shown in Fig. 4.8. It is very nearly original, but many of the houses on the estate have suffered from extensions and alterations, which makes them appear incongruous and somewhat ostentatious. Altogether about 30 prototype house designs were drawn up for the estate, which by 1883 accommodated no less than 490 houses. Notice in Fig. 4.7 the emphasis on the closeness to Turnham Green Station. This was opened in 1869 by

---

5. The 23-verse ballad is quoted in full in [9].

Fig. 4.7. Semi-detached and detached houses at Bedford Park. Publicity poster shown in the Building News of 21 December 1877.

the London and South Western Railway and offered travel into the City of just 30 minutes. The station is now served by the London Underground.

By the late 1880s the Bedford Park estate was beginning to lose its novelty value. Aesthetic arbiters considered the buildings erected "by cheap builders possessed by the idea that red brick, a blue pot, and a fat sunflower in the window are all that is necessary to be fashionably aesthetic and Queen Anne" [10]. The Domestic Revival idiom was a dominant characteristic of suburban speculative estates in England, however, for generations to come. The style was often modified by using mock-Tudor gables (floor-board Tudor) and diamond-paned windows. Even today the legacy of Shaw and his fellow architects can be found in new housing developments all over the country.

Interestingly, a house of a different character appeared in the dominantly red-brick estate, when in 1891 the architect C.T.A. Voysey (1857-1941) introduced a rather

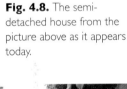

Fig. 4.8. The semi-detached house from the picture above as it appears today.

bleak, three-storey house in roughcast (see footnote 9) with a slate roof. Voysey, a disciple of John Ruskin and William Morris, came to have an impact on suburban house styles equal to that of Norman Shaw. His houses were strongly influenced by the Arts and Crafts Movement. They displayed accentuated gables, conspicuous chimney stacks and long sloping roofs – features copied by numerous semi-detached houses in the following decades, see Fig. 4.9.

Bedford Park was a fascinating and important experiment in housing, but it was definitely a piece of middle-class suburbia, totally out of reach of even the best-paid workers. Although income alone cannot define social classes, L.C.Money in the early twentieth century divided the total population into three categories: those earning less than £160 a year, mainly the working classes (£160 was the point where income tax started), those with incomes between £160 and £700 a year, the lower and middle middle-classes, and those with incomes above £700 a year, the upper middle classes and the landed gentry [11].

Fig. 4.9. Voysey-style semis from the inter-war period (photo 2005).

A fairly consistent housing pattern had become the norm in the last part of the nineteenth century, a pattern which is still found today with minor variations.

Factory workers and labourers were housed in terraced accommodation in the painfully dreary bye-law streets hurriedly erected on the outskirts of all cities of any industrial significance. Lower middle-class families tended to rent the most basic of the speculatively built semi-detached houses, often rubbing shoulders with the bye-law terraces. Mr. Pooter of *The Diary of a Nobody* fame, a clerk of 20 years standing in the City, would be the archetypal tenant of such a house, in this case in the not very attractive London suburb of Holloway. Pooter himself, however, was delighted with the location and proud of having moved into "'The Laurels', Brickfield Terrace, Holloway, – a nice six-roomed residence, not counting basement, with a front breakfast parlour" [12]. As drawn by Weedon Grossmith the house was a simple box of Georgian ancestry, but with some Gothic features. The main living area is ostentatiously raised above street level, so that the Pooters can feel elevated from the multitude.[6]

Higher up in the middle-class hierarchy, doctors, lawyers, civil servants, and lesser factory owners preferred to move to the outer, more 'leafy' suburbs, where the air was cleaner and more healthy. A semi-detached house with five or more bedrooms would in general be found very suitable. Also the upper middle classes moved easily to the outer suburbs, maybe to the desirable status of a detached house if they had the financial means, but often enough to a large semi-detached house in an area acceptable to their equals. Today the same sensibilities can be found in the 'post-code syndrome' of middle-class England. The location, the address of the house, is an all-important factor as far as desirability and price are concerned.

Model villages of the late nineteenth century: semi-detached housing for the working classes

The inhabitants of Pooterland considered themselves fortunate when they were able to occupy a semi-detached property; they could thus demonstrate their social superiority over the working classes, who were tightly packed in their ubiquitous two-up and two-down houses of the bye-law terraces. Most workers could never even dream of aspiring to a semi-detached house with a garden front and back. Only in exceptional circumstances did working class families approach a near-middle-class environment. In Victorian England such circumstances were invariably guided by the patronage of wealthy industrialists, who set up model villages to house their factory workers in conditions far superior to those of the average labourer. Although critics have been quick to point out that such villages were fuelled only by the self-interest and convenience of the employer to recruit and sustain his business workforce, it is likely that a Christian element of concern and social responsibility played just as great a role. In the 1850s men such as Edward Ackroyd, Titus Salt, and the Wilson brothers established housing estates for their workers. Later, and in the beginning of the twentieth century William Lever, George Cadbury and Joseph Rowntree built estates which in many ways set the scene for the later middle-class garden suburbs.

---

6. Several authors call The Laurels a semi-detached house [13], [14], although I have not been able to find this mentioned in The Diary. The drawing by Weedon Goldsmith is not conclusive. It looks like one half of a semi-detached house, with a front garden and a solid garden wall, but it may equally well be an end house in a terrace. Support for the latter interpretation would be in the street name Brickfield Terrace.

4

Ackroyd's village of Ackroydon outside Halifax and Salt's employee housing at Saltaire on the Leeds and Liverpool canal near Bradford were among the earliest model villages. They were mainly laid out as terraces, as was the later New Earswick development near York by Rowntree, whereas the villages founded by the other philanthropists mentioned above included also semi-detached houses. These model villages and their semi-detached houses are presented in the following sections.

BROMBOROUGH POOL VILLAGE

The Wilson brothers, James and George, were the managing directors of Price's Patent Candle Company with manufacturing facilities in Battersea, London. The main raw material needed by the company was West African palm oil, for which Liverpool had become an import centre. With the company expanding at the middle of the century, with outbreaks of cholera in London, and with the terrible housing conditions for the poorer classes, the Wilson brothers decided to move production closer to Liverpool and build not only a factory, but also a village for their employees. Their final choice was at Bromborough Pool on the Wirral. It was inexpensive agricultural land and had a small, natural harbour suitable for the company's barges, and it was on the Mersey directly across from Liverpool.

Fig. 4.10. Semi-detached pair for management personnel at Price's (photo 2005).

Plans for the first part of the village were drawn up in 1853 and key workers from London moved in the year after to train local workers for the factory. By 1858, the village had 76 houses (all with water-borne sanitation), a school, cricket-pitch and bowling green. At this time all houses for the workers were terrace houses, although quite large by the standards of the day, and they all had sizeable gardens. This was on the insistence of George Wilson, who was a keen horticulturist. Two imposing semi-detached pairs were built at the side of the cricket field. These were intended for the managerial staff. One of these handsome Georgian-style houses still stands and is shown in Fig. 4.10. The village soon came to be known as Price's Village and it is still known as such locally. Oddly enough, there had never been a Mr. Price involved in the company and the name remains, it seems, unexplained.

The company ran into financial problems in the late 1850s, and building in the village was stopped until 1872. A few years later new problems delayed the further expansion of the village, and it was not until 1896 that the company prospered again and new houses were erected. This time all the new houses were semi-detached. Nineteen pairs were built over the period 1896-1900. These were the last dwelling houses to be built, the fortunes of the company again declining after the turn of the century, when gas and electric lighting led to a diminishing demand for candles.

Fig. 4.11. A pair of Price's worker's semi-detached houses at Bromborough Pool Village (photo 2005).

The architects of the new houses had quite likely found inspiration in the buildings of Port Sunlight a few miles inland, for as with many of the Port Sunlight houses the new designs now used red Ruabon bricks, which were much in vogue at the time. Most of the semi-detached houses in Bromborough Pool were built facing the playing fields to the south of the village. A pair of these houses

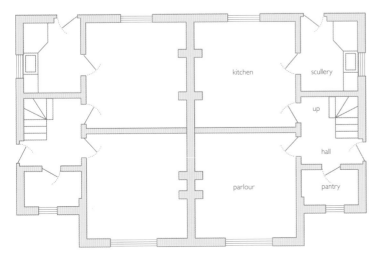

kitchen

scullery

up

hall

parlour

pantry

Fig. 4.12. Original downstairs layout of Price's semi-detached houses.

4

is shown in Fig. 4.11. Apart from the strikingly red bricks there is from the outside little to distinguish the houses from many estate houses being built today. The original downstairs layout is shown in Fig. 4.12. On an architect's 1998 drawing of the plan the parlour is renamed the living room, the kitchen is the dining area, the scullery is the kitchen, and the pantry is a storage cupboard. Upstairs there would originally have been two or three bedrooms. When the houses were built, the water closets would be in an outbuilding at the back of the house. Today most, if not all, houses now have a bathroom and toilet on the first floor.

Plans were proposed in the mid-1980s to demolish most of the existing village and build a new estate of semi-detached houses in a curious non-descript Gothic Revival style. The villagers protested and took their concerns to the local council, which declared the village a conservation area, and the plans were shelved.

PORT SUNLIGHT

Wealthy Victorian paternalism is seen nowhere better than at Port Sunlight Village, a close neighbour to Price's Village on the Wirral. According to Edwards the village was "probably the most elaborate piece of suburbia ever built" [15].

It was William Heskith Lever (1851-1925), the later Lord Leverhulme, who in 1887 realised that his soap factory in Warrington, Cheshire, needed more space, as production had risen from 20 to 450 tons a week and the factory could no longer meet the growing demand. He planned to build not only a new factory, but also a model village for his workers, and, as was the case with Price's candles, he was looking for a site with easy access to the river Mersey. His main product Sunlight soap was based on vegetable oils imported from Africa to Liverpool.

After looking at several sites he settled on an uncompromising site near Bromborough Pool. The land was marshy and scarred by tidal inlets from the Mersey, but it was cheap. Initially 56 acres were purchased, 32 of which were allocated to the village, which later came to cover no less than c.130 acres.[7] The name Port Sunlight was given to the village at an early stage, and in 1888 the ceremonial cutting of the first sod was performed by Mrs. Lever. At the following banquet Lever remarked: "It is my hope, and my brother's hope … to build houses in which our work-people will be able to live and be comfortable.

7. This figure is quoted in the official guide to Port Sunlight Village [16].

Semi-detached houses, with gardens back and front …".

William Lever himself had a strong interest in architecture, arts, and housing, and his plans for an estate for his employees were ambitious from the very beginning. With the Warrington architect William Owen (1846-1910) he planned to use the natural contours of the land to create a housing landscape which would be in complete contrast to the standard bye-law housing of the period. The village was for the workers what Bedford Park was for the middle classes.

Over the years Lever engaged no less than 30 architects to design the houses, which ranged from semi-detached to small terraces, or blocks, of three or more dwellings. Lever was not afraid of seeking out new talent, and the twenty-one-year-old Edwin Lutyens (1869-1944), who later was to win everlasting fame as one of the great English architects of his time, was commissioned to design a short terrace of four houses. Although there were many styles of houses at Port Sunlight, they all fall under the umbrella of the Domestic Revival – half-timbered gables, elaborate carvings and mouldings, tile hanging, and a wealth of details from nearly every period of English architecture; there were, however, no houses of Georgian extraction. The black and white timbering, the tiled roofs, and the small-paned windows gave the village an olde worlde feeling, which indeed had been the intention of Lever and his architects.

Only employees of the company could rent houses in the village, and the very low rents were taken off the workers' wages, which meant that rent arrears were practically unknown. The upkeep of the houses and the running of the many communal facilities were in the hands of an estate office and paid for out of the Lever company profits. Lever also built a village inn, but being very conscious of the ill effects of alcohol and a strict teetotaller himself (a trait he shared with many other leading industrialists of the Victorian era) it started life as a temperance hotel. Only after Lever reluctantly bowed to a vote among the residents to apply for a licence did he concede to the wishes of the majority, and the inn was granted the right to sell alcoholic beverages.

William Lever was a true philanthropist, although sometimes accused of being overly paternalistic, and he was quite prepared to channel profits from the company into the development of the very best houses that money could buy. There was one point, however, where he was forced to admit defeat. His vision to provide every worker with a semi-detached house had to be abandoned; the workforce had grown far beyond the first expectations and there was just not enough land to go around. He did succeed, though, in

4

keeping the housing density below the ten houses per acre that he had set himself and his architects as a target. The village now has around 900 houses, most of them arranged in terraces.

The question of resorting to housing his workers in flats never arose. In addressing an international housing conference in 1907 Lever categorically stated that "All tenement dwellings, flats, and such devices for crowding a maximum amount of humanity in a minimum amount of ground space are destructive of healthy life", and he continued "I am positive, from all statistics available, that the most healthy conditions of the human race are obtained where the home unit exists in a self-contained house, with the living rooms on the ground floor and the bedrooms on the floor immediately over" [17].

A small number of semi-detached houses were built around the turn of the century, nearly all of them fronting on to the New Chester Road on the eastern fringe of the village. Some of these semis as they appear today are shown in Fig. 4.13. There were two basic types of house erected at Port Sunlight. One was the 'kitchen type', which had a combined kitchen/living room downstairs and three bedrooms on the first floor. The other was the 'parlour type', which had a kitchen and a front parlour downstairs and four bedrooms upstairs. The semi-detached houses were all of the parlour type.

Fig. 4.13. Semi-detached houses at Port Sunlight on the Chester Road (2005).

The ground plan of a parlour-type semi was very similar to that of the semi-detached houses in Price's village at Bromborough Pool. The insistence on incorporating a parlour in the house, which elevates it from the more 'inferior' kitchen type houses, is a curious social phenomenon. Logically it is a waste of space to have a room set aside for the sole purpose of receiving visitors, a room for Sunday best. As Davison pointed out in his book on Port Sunlight: "Theoretically, one would perhaps like those who live in cottages to give up the fetish of the parlour and have one really ample living-room instead. But the inherent yearning for privacy is an English characteristic which closes the door of domestic affairs from the casual visitor" [18]. It is a fetish that is imbedded in the two-up and two-down house plan, and the parlour or front lounge remained in speculative building well into the second half of the twentieth century.

BOURNVILLE VILLAGE

Although Port Sunlight has been hailed as being the most exciting in terms of its layout and architecture, the contemporary development of Bournville near Birmingham by the Cadbury brothers was probably more influential on suburban housing in the twentieth century. It is certainly the most prolific in terms of semi-detached housing, and today it has much less of a museum atmosphere than Port Sunlight and is considered a very desirable residential area.

Fig. 4.14. A wrapper for Cadbury's plain chocolate – Bournville.

Richard and George Cadbury had re-vitalized their family's ailing cocoa and chocolate manufacturing company in the 1860s, and by 1870 the firm was outgrowing its city location in Birmingham. Belonging as they did to a Quaker family, they were appalled by the living conditions of the working classes, and they were convinced that their business would make greater profits if the workers were well paid and better housed. They decided to move their business out of Birmingham to a site in the country, where they would locate the factory itself and build a village around it. In 1878, they found a greenfield site some four miles south-west of Birmingham, a plot of land divided by the Bourn Brook. Although road connections were poor, the Birmingham West Suburban Railway ran along the eastern border of the site, parallel to the Birmingham and Worcester Canal, so access for people and goods was already available.[8]

The brothers named the new site Bournville. The French-sounding name was chosen because French chocolates were particularly esteemed at that time. The name Cadbury's Bournville was for many years used on the wrappers of their plain chocolate (Fig. 4.14). The new factory opened in 1879, but only 17 houses in the village had then been built. One of these was a detached house for the works manager. The other 16 were semi-detached houses for key workers. The houses themselves were very traditional Gothic Revival style houses with typical late Victorian terracotta embellishments on the façades. They have unfortunately not survived, as they were demolished in the 1930s to give way to an extension of the factory.

In the beginning the workers had to travel by train from

8. The Birmingham West Suburban Railway was shortly after to become part of the Midland Railway, and the Birmingham and Worcester Canal is now the Worcester and Birmingham Canal.

Birmingham, and special rates were negotiated with the railway company to allow them to travel as cheaply as possible to Bournville station. Not until 1893 did George Cadbury acquire an extra 120 acres of land adjacent to the factory. Shortly after, he wrote to a fellow Quaker, a surveyor, to ask for assistance in drawing up plans for the village [19]:

> Please let me know whether you would be likely to be able to give up some years carrying out a scheme I have in hand for laying out 120 acres in the neighbourhood of our works for cottages, each surrounded by their own garden, not more than six to the acre. I would not care for anyone to undertake it who did not enter into the spirit of the undertaking as a labour of the Lord.

Fig. 4.15. Garden plan of a semi-detached pair in Bournville. Schematic adapted from [21].

Plans for the village were duly drawn up, and in 1895 a young designer, William A. Harvey, then only 20 years old, was appointed architect to the estate. George Cadbury had a keen interest in gardening and stipulated that not more than a quarter of any given plot should be occupied by the house itself. Harvey later published a typical layout for a semi-detached house in its garden setting, see Fig. 4.15. The front garden was given over to flowers and small trees, whereas the back garden was intended to provide the household with vegetables and fruit from the trees (apple, plum, cherry and pear) that were planted at the bottom of the garden by the estate management (from 1900 part of the Bournville Village Trust) before the residents moved in.

George Cadbury considered the building of the village not as a form of industrial paternalism, but as an experiment in social reform. From the beginning the scheme was not restricted to Cadbury workers, but in general for "a superior class of quiet and respectable tenants" [25]. Although Cadbury wished to encourage a social mix in the community, it soon became apparent that the very poor could not afford the mortgages offered, even though the financing was on a non-profit basis. The trust admitted at one point that "it was difficult to ensure that the 'better class' did not take possession of Bournville," and that "every endeavour was made to give preference to bona fide working men" [20]. Nevertheless, only about 40 per cent of the tenants were Cadbury employees. The majority would typically be artisans and white-collar workers.

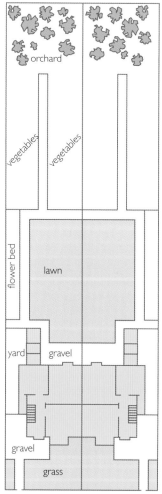

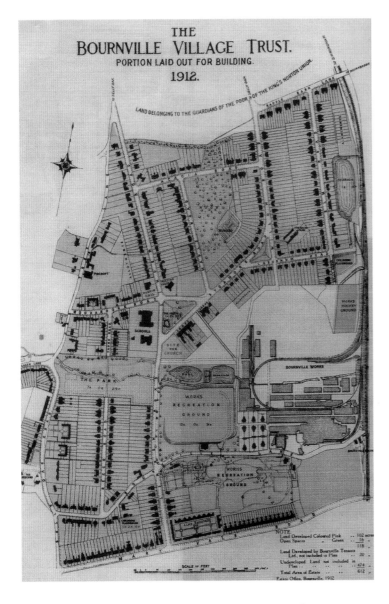

Fig. 4.16. 1912 map of Bournville Village [24].

In the planning of the estate as many as possible of the old trees on the site were left standing, and areas were given over to green parks, playgrounds, a village green, and men's and women's recreational areas. New trees were also planted to line the streets, and compared with Port Sunlight the overall impression is less austere and closer to the special charm that we often associate with old English villages.

By the turn of the century 370 houses had been built [22]. A

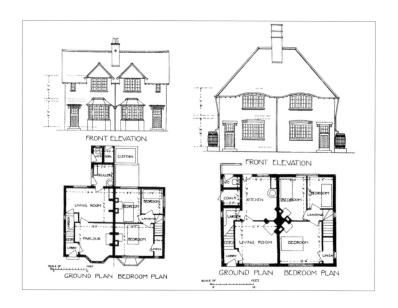

Fig. 4.17. Two early house plans by W.A.Harvey [25].

map of the village from 1912 shows around 570 houses, of which no less than 350 are individual semi-detached homes, making this estate the most semi-detached dominated model village in the country (Fig. 4.16).

Harvey was responsible for most of the buildings over a ten-year period. The houses have occasionally been accused of being dull [23], but although they are based on maybe just a few basic plans, they exhibit enough variation to give an overall pleasing aspect to the village. Harvey was influenced by the Arts and Crafts Movement, and he used a variety of façade finishes ranging from carvings, pargetting, and decorative brickwork to half timbering, pebble dash and rough-casting. [9] Some of his early designs had back extensions, but he soon changed his layouts to eliminate these, see for example the house plans illustrated in Fig. 4.17, one with a back extension, the other without. An 1899 Voysey-inspired pair of semi-detached houses may be seen on Mary Vale Road. Plans and elevations are shown in Fig. 4.18, and the house as it appears today is shown in Fig. 4.19.

It is interesting to note that viewpoints concerning a front parlour were given considerable attention in the design of the Bournville semis. Although Harvey's early houses nearly all had front parlours,

9. Roughcasting is an external wall-covering of cement and sand onto which a wet mixture of cement and small stones is thrown before the backing coat has dried. In a pebble dash finish small stones or pebbles are thrown on to the rendered wall without first being mixed with cement.

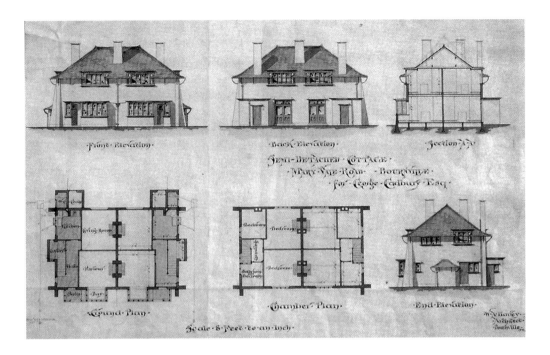

he soon came to favour the use of one spacious living room, preferably extending through the depth of the house and receiving light and air from two sides. Early in the new century he wrote that "the plan should be adopted freely, and the preference for the useless front room in small cottages discouraged" [27]. In this he

Fig. 4.18. Plans and elevations for Voysey-inspired house on Mary Vale Road. Drawn by W.A.Harvey, 1899 [26].

Fig. 4.19. The Voysey-inspired semi-detached house on Mary Vale Road as it stands today (photo 2005).

was in accordance with architectural reformers such as Parker and Unwin (see Chapter 5). As often happens, though, reformers can be far ahead of their time, and many residents did not agree. In 1913 the secretary to the Bournville Trust had to admit that "rightly or wrongly, there is a demand for a parlour, and this has been recognized at Bournville" [28].

Housing commentators were ready to join in the debate, and Whitehouse writing on the Bournville experiment in 1901 offered the following observation: "It is perhaps hardly necessary to remark that people who live in small houses usually use one inadequate room as a living room, keeping a spare room or parlour carefully shut up, which is used on rare occasions only. The result is doubly unfortunate; the parlour is a source of no pleasure or convenience, and its existence means that the living room is generally far too small to be even moderately healthy. The plan in question is an attempt, we believe, a wise and well-considered one, to get rid of an absurd convention. The parlour is abolished, and one large living room is substituted with the addition of a scullery and the usual outhouses" [29]. It was only after the middle of the twentieth century that the parlour, or front room in more modern terminology, finally lost its prominence in semi-detached houses.

Even at the beginning of the period covered by this chapter, the middle classes had accepted the semi-detached house as being a respectable form of housing for Christian families, as long as the setting was correct. Most of the early houses were in the Gothic Revival style, but the Domestic Revival slowly, very slowly, changed the face of middle-class suburbia from Ruskinian Gothic to a more vernacular, Old English style, such as first demonstrated in Bedford Park. The model villages also helped to popularize the trend in housing architecture, and the speculative builders soon used the same formula to create estates of detached and semi-detached houses for their middle-class clients. By the 1890s the Victorian era was on the wane, and middle-class housing quite naturally reflected the changing economic and social conditions. The style that we now recognize as Edwardian was the visible outcome of these changes. The Edwardian semi-detached and the concurrent development of the first garden cities and garden suburbs are discussed in the following chapter.

References

1   Peter Guillery, *The Small House in Eighteenth Century London*, Yale University Press, New Haven and London 2004, p.284.

2   Maria Leach, *The Wicked Wit of Oscar Wilde*, Michael O'Mara Publishing Limited, London 2000, p.64.

3   R.W.Brunskill, *Vernacular Architecture*, Faber and Faber, London 1978, second edition, p.20.

4   Helena Barrett and John Phillips, *Suburban Style*, Macdonald & Co (Publishers), London 1987, p.85.

5   Helen Long, *The Edwardian House*, Manchester University Press, Manchester 1993, p.33.

6   Bridget Cherry and Nikolaus Pevsner, *The Buildings of England, London 2: South*, Penguin Books, London 1983, p. 139.

7   *Building News*, 16 November 1877.

8   Bridget Cherry and Nikolaus Pevsner, *The Buildings of England, London 3: North West*, Penguin Books, London 1991, p.408.

9   M. Girouard, *Sweetness and Light: The Queen Anne Movement 1860-1900*, Yale University Press, New Haven and London 1977.

10   R.F.Foster, *W.B.Yeats, A Life*, Oxford University Press, Oxford 1997, p.60.

11   John Burnett, *A Social History of Housing 1815-1970*, Methuen, Newton Abbott 1978, p.185.

12   G. and W.Grossmith, *The Diary of a Nobody*, first published in bookform 1892, edition consulted is by Penguin Books, London 1999, p. 11.

13   John Burnett, *A Social History of Housing 1815-1970*, Methuen, Newton Abbott 1978, p.186.

14   John Gloag, *The Englishman's Castle*, Eyre & Spottiswoode, London 1944, p.154.

15   Arthur Edwards, *The Design of Suburbia*, Pembridge Press, London 1981, p.79.

16   E.Hubbard and M.Shippobottom, *A Guide to Port Sunlight Village*, Liverpool University Press, Liverpool 1988, p.12.

17   *Ibid.*, p.6.

18   T.Raffles Davison, *Port Sunlight – a Record of its Artistic and Pictorial Aspect*, BT Batsford, London 1916, p.27.

19   Michael Harrison, *Bournville: Model Village to Garden Suburb*, Phillimore, Chichester 1999, p. 36.

20   *Ibid.*, p.79.

21   *Ibid.*, p.60.

22   J.H.Whitehouse, 'Bournville: A Study in Housing Reform', in *The Studio*, XXIV, No.105, December 1901, pp.162-72.

23   Arthur Edwards, *The Design of Suburbia*, Pembridge Press, London 1981, p.82.

24   A.Vaughan and P. Jordan, *George Cadbury and Bournville*, Published by the Friends of Bournville Carillon, 2004, frontispiece.

25   Michael Harrison, *Bournville: Model Village to Garden Suburb*, Phillimore, Chichester 1999, p. 47; 40.

26   *Ibid.*, p.38.

27   *Ibid.*, p.57

28   *Ibid.*

29   J.H.Whitehouse, 'Bournville: A Study in Housing Reform', in *The Studio*, XXIV, No.105, December 1901, pp.168.

5

Suburbs and semis in Edwardian England 1901-1920

"Such basic and enduring middle-class conservatism called for houses which would communicate the respectability and values of their inhabitants to others"
Helen Long in *The Edwardian House*, 1993

The housing landscape at the turn of the century

When Queen Victoria died in 1901 the monarchy passed on to Edward VII. Edward was popular with the public and he epitomized the glamour and extravagance of the rich in early twentieth century England. Although the Edwardian era strictly speaking began with King Edward's ascension to the throne and ended with his death in 1910, the social and technological changes that influenced his short monarchy had started in the last quarter of the nineteenth century and the *zeitgeist* associated with his reign continued till well after the First World War of 1914-18.

Fig. 5.1. A simplified zonal configuration of a typical English city at the beginning of the twentieth century.

By the turn of the century, many English cities showed a pattern of zoning which was fairly uniform, although with regional variations dictated by the presence of commerce and industry specific to the area. A simplified picture of the zoning landscape is shown in Fig. 5.1.

Buildings in the centre of the city were inherited from previous generations and would be dominated by civic buildings, banks, offices and stores. The most genteel of terraces from the Georgian era would also have survived, still inhabited by persons of wealth.

Surrounding this core was a mixed zone, where you would expect to find previously superior Georgian terraces, now run-down and given over to multiple tenancy, interspersed with small industrial

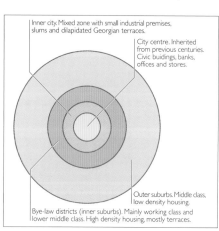

Inner city. Mixed zone with small industrial premises, slums and dilapidated Georgian terraces.

City centre. Inherited from previous centuries. Civic buidings, banks, offices and stores.

Outer suburbs. Middle class, low density housing.

Bye-law districts (inner suburbs). Mainly working class and lower middle class. High density housing, mostly terraces.

premises. The industries were often squalid and made the area very unattractive to live in. Typical industries could be breweries, distilleries, builders' yards, brick works, iron works, warehouses, gas works, and a sometimes massive and noisy presence of railway goods yards, not to mention more noxious industries such as slaughterers, soapboilers and grease and varnish manufacturers. These areas constitute what we now term inner cities as distinct from city centres. Most of the industries are long since gone, and regeneration of these areas is today heatedly debated.

Beyond this unappealing zone was a large area of mainly terraced dwellings erected as bye-law estates in Victorian times for the workers in the industries mentioned above. These houses are the inner suburbs of today.

Finally, the outer suburbs, the domain of the middle-class families, spread from the inner suburbs further and ever further into the rural areas. The outer suburbs are where Edwardian middle-class housing made its most significant contribution.

The Edwardian period was in many senses a golden era, although seriously blighted by the tragedy of the First World War. In terms of domestic housing the period ties together the conventions of late Victorian Gothic and the speculative housing styles of inter-war suburbia.

Families were, in general, smaller than in Victorian times, domestic help was on a gradual decline (and a perpetual topic of conversation at the popular middle-class 'at-home' gatherings), obsession with health had become fashionable and, last but not least, public transport in the form of electric trams and, in the capital, the London Underground and other railway companies had vastly improved opportunities to commute. Taken together, these changes prompted especially middle-class wage-earners to move further away from the city centres to the less crowded suburbs beyond the estates of bye-law housing.

Tramways and railways had in the latter part of the nineteenth century paved the way for a new way of living for many lower and middle-income families. It had become possible to work at a considerable distance from home by using the new transportation network to commute to and from the work-place. Cheap workmen's fares offered by some companies also allowed the working classes to use trams or trains on a daily basis from the suburbs to the city.

In the early part of the new century railway companies were quick to focus on the more affluent middle classes by promoting the outlying suburbs as being desirable, healthy, affordable and quiet places in which to settle. The Metropolitan Railway in London stressed the rural environments in areas where their lines served north-west

of London, in Middlesex, Hertfordshire and Buckinghamshire. They devised the ingenious name Metro-land for these areas and, from 1915, they published an annual guide, also called Metro-land, see Fig. 5.2, which shows the cover of the 1916 edition. We are left in no doubt about the tranquillity and beauty of the location – which invariably would change when building got under way. The suburban estates created by the Metropolitan Railway and others could not for long match the rural Arcadia so enticingly described by Metro-land promoters. Having said that, it must in fairness be added that to this day many of the Edwardian Metro-land developments have managed to retain something of the countryside spirit that later developments failed to do.

The Metropolitan Railway had cleverly bought up surplus land alongside their lines and they became involved directly in housing development. Their first property venture was in the 1880s and 1890s at Willesden Green Station, only eight minutes by train to Baker Street Station. The houses were unpretentious semi-detached villas for rental by middle-class families. Early in the twentieth century the company developed some more ambitious residences at Pinner and Wembley Park, also offering building plots to private contractors. The description they gave of the area was:

Fig. 5.2. Front cover of the 1916 Metro-land guide (London Transport).

> Beautiful open country. One of the healthiest spots around London. Numerous houses already built and in course of erection. Frequent Metro service. Above sea level, 234 ft [1].

House building was halted by the war, but took off dramatically immediately after.

Other railway companies, not least in the London area, were equally active in advertising the developing railway suburbs. One of the earliest of the north London Underground suburbs was Golders Green, "a place within three miles of Regent's Park where there are roses in the hedgerows and the larks are singing … a place almost unique in rural character" [2]. The relative isolation and remoteness from the city is easily understood, when the main events reported in the local newspaper [2] in the early years of the century were the opening of the Golders Green crematorium, an outbreak of rick fires, one or two burglaries at the big houses and an incident of horse-stealing in the pastures.

The extension of the Charing Cross, Euston & Hampstead Railway to Golders Green was mentioned already in Chapter 1. Following

Fig. 5.3. A 1908 Underground poster for Golders Green. "A place of delightful prospects." Notice the modern electric train in the background. (London Transport).

the opening of the line in the summer of 1907, the growth of estate building was rapid. In the first year, 73 houses were completed and by 1914 the area had 477 houses [3]. The houses were mostly semi-detached, cottagey villas in the Domestic Revival style as illustrated on the Underground poster from 1908 (Fig. 5.3).

Edwardian families and their homes

The nineteenth century had seen an unprecedented population growth, especially in the latter part of the century, see Fig. 5.4. The high Victorian family might easily have boasted five or six children, and one in ten marriages had produced ten or more [4]. Over the Edwardian years the average number of children per family dropped from about 3.5 to 2.8, and middle-class families tended to be smaller than those of manual workers, in many cases having only one or two children. Many middle-class families increasingly had to function without live-in servants. This was mainly due to the better career jobs now offered in offices and shops, especially for women. All in all household sizes had therefore fallen dramatically. These changed circumstances contributed to the size and layout of houses built in the first part of the twentieth century.

Fig. 5.4. Population growth in England and Wales 1801–1911 [5].

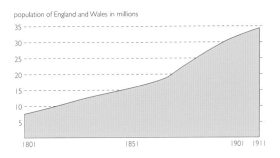

In the period 1851 to 1911 the total population in England and Wales doubled, whereas the urban population grew by three times and house building in and around townships did its best to cope with the demand. However, speculative building was never able to follow closely the fluctuations from country to town in any particular area. There was a peak in house building in England around 1898-1903 with a major down-turn in activity thereafter (see Fig. 5.5). Even building in the outer suburbs declined at that time in spite of the rapid rise of a suburban population. It would seem that the building boom at the turn of the century had created an excess of dwellings, which needed to be occupied before major speculative building was resumed.

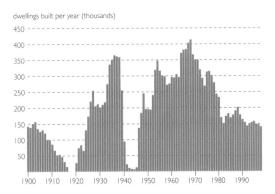

Fig. 5.5. Number of dwellings built in Great Britain 1900-98 [6].

At this time in history, few people in England owned their homes, not even the well-heeled middle-class occupants of suburban villas. As in Victorian times, houses were rented with approximately

5

10 per cent of a middle-class householder's income allocated to rent and taxes. Renting suited the middle classes, who were geographically quite mobile and ready to move into new accommodation adjusted to a changing income and new needs of the family. However, although most new properties were still being built for letting, there was a growing demand, especially in the London area, for houses to purchase. Building societies were becoming more adventurous, and it was no longer so difficult to obtain a mortgage. Nevertheless, at the end of the Edwardian period there were still only about ten per cent owner-occupied dwellings in England, a figure that by the end of the inter-war period had risen to well over 30 per cent [7].

Although Edwardian households were considerably smaller than their Victorian counterparts, many suburban houses were quite substantial, which undoubtedly was a reflection of the extravagance of the times – especially among the upper middle classes. Long (1993) divided the houses of the period into five categories. The houses could be either detached or semi-detached [8]:

Category 1:   Four reception rooms, seven bedrooms, a nursery, a billiard room, dressing rooms and a large conservatory.

Category 2:   Three or four reception rooms, five bedrooms, dressing rooms and a good size conservatory.

Category 3:   Two reception rooms, four bedrooms, a small conservatory.

Category 4:   Two reception rooms, three bedrooms.

Category 5:   Two reception rooms, two bedrooms.

The two top categories were aimed at the upper middle-class households, the third group would represent the middle middle-class, and the two last groups were for the lower middle-classes. The fashion of adding a conservatory had in the last part of the nineteenth century filtered down to suburbia from a vogue started in large country houses. The original use as a place to cultivate exotic plants, not least ferns, had in the process changed to a more social function for use as an extension to the back drawing-room.

The smaller families and the lack of live-in servants did much to change the layout of the rooms. Where Victorian builders had gone to great lengths to comply with the morals of the age by separating servants' quarters from the family and ensuring separate rooms for boys and girls, and for children of different age groups, the

Edwardians set different values on home life. The high-Victorian home with its emphasis on morals and Christianity had given way to a more secular attitude, which dwelled on notions like health, hygiene, comfort, convenience and economy. The rambling corridors and high-ceilinged rooms of the Victorians with each its own function were given over to a more open room layout and lighter rooms, sometimes with folding doors between two rooms, so that they could be opened up to create even more space. In shape the house was usually wider than before, allowing for a substantial entrance hall rather than a claustrophobic Victorian entrance passage. The hall became a focal point of the house as it had been in medieval times. It was furnished with its own fireplace, which easily might be the grandest in the house. Fig. 5.6 shows the ground floor plan of a fairly large Edwardian semi-detached house, where the hall has been given a central position. The additional presence of inglenooks and sometimes window seats encouraged family gatherings. A writing desk was often found in the hall and some halls had a dining area. The larger hall gave the architect the opportunity to create more generous staircases, beginning with a few broad steps, then turning the stairs for effect. The newel post at the foot of the stairs was given especial attention to give it prominence. Turning, routing and wood-carving machines had been developed to produce rich effects imitating the hand-carving of medieval times and the newel post was capped with a fluted urn or some other elaborate design. Fretwork screens were a further embellishment of halls in well-to-do Edwardian homes.

Although the middle classes by this time had much greater confidence in themselves and their social standing than their parents had had, there was still a real need for help in getting the home to be, and look, respectable. Numerous magazines and household guides were at hand to solve any problems of home decoration or social behaviour. One of the most influential and often quoted is Mrs Panton's *From Kitchen to Garrett: Hints for Young Householders* (Panton, 1888). Of the morning-room or breakfast-parlour she advises that it should be decorated in sage-green ("taking care there is no arsenic in it") and the doors painted with pale pink flowers [9]. The appearance of the hall is crucial. There must be no hats or coats to be seen, but an aspidistra in a brass pot was essential.

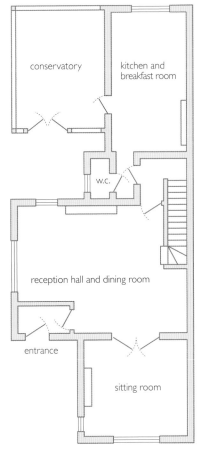

Fig. 5.6. Ground floor plan of a semi-detached Edwardian villa in south London.

5

While the Edwardians were eager to embrace advances in technology such as the telephone[1] and the automobile, they were at heart conservatives when it came to choosing a house for their family. The house should demonstrate the respectability and values of the family and, although the householder liked to be up-to-date, it was best to be safe in one's choice of dwelling. The return to the vernacular styles of the Domestic Revival with its elements of Tudor, Queen Anne Revival and country cottage images was exactly what the average middle-class Edwardian was looking for. The speculative builders changed from Gothic to Domestic Revival for this class of client and the outer suburbs soon became populated with estates of detached and semi-detached houses which today are unmistakably Edwardian.

The Edwardian semi-detached house

The style of the Edwardian suburban house was a product of the Domestic Revival, where the builders sought to create a house which, to the tenant, would speak of country cottages and century-old English traditions. Ingredients from William Morris's Red House at Bexleyheath and from Norman Shaw's houses in Bedford Park were used freely, as were design elements of the Arts and Crafts Movement.

The external characteristics of an Edwardian semi-detached house are best described with reference to a typical example such as shown in Fig. 5.7.

One of the most recognizable features is seen in the window settings. The Edwardians had inherited the bay window from the Victorians, and houses of the first three classes would most likely have a pair of bay windows over two storeys. As the houses were in general wider than in Victorian times, the bays could incorporate more sections, sometimes separated by stone mullions in keeping with Tudor building styles. Casement windows had come into fashion again to supplement the standard Victorian sash window. In their window arrangements the Edwardians found a happy compromise between letting light into the room on the one hand and cosiness on the other. They used a large paned casement (or sash) window for the lower part, and a small paned window for the upper part, often with leaded lights, to impart a feeling of history and rural cottages. The leaded lights were often inlaid with colourful patterns of birds or flowers.

Another medieval window feature that the Edwardians

---

1. They did, however, find the look of the instrument a little too avant-garde and took to concealing it in adapted eighteenth century mahogany knife boxes [10].

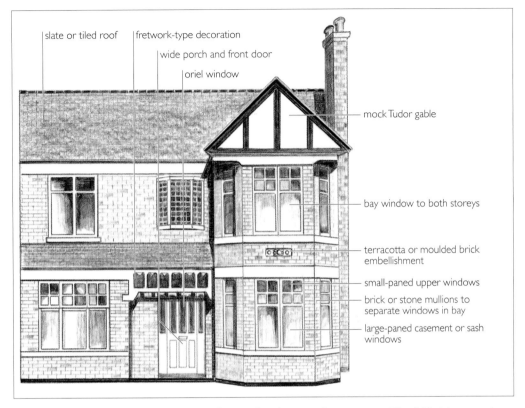

slate or tiled roof | fretwork-type decoration

wide porch and front door

oriel window

mock Tudor gable

bay window to both storeys

terracotta or moulded brick embellishment

small-paned upper windows

brick or stone mullions to separate windows in bay

large-paned casement or sash windows

Fig. 5.7. A large semi-detached Edwardian villa.

introduced in better-class houses was the oriel or bay-oriel window, often seen as the window immediately above the porch (Fig. 5.12). It was used also as the first-floor window style on two-storey bays (Fig. 5.13).

The preferred building material for exterior walling was brick, especially red brick, a legacy of the Domestic Revival and of Bedford Park. Although this was used extensively, there were, of course, regional variations with, for example, stone being widely employed in towns such as York, Harrogate, Bath and Bristol. The illustration from Harrogate in Fig. 5.16 shows a particularly ostentatious specimen of a stone-built Edwardian semi-detached villa.

The Edwardians liked to use regular, machine-made bricks rather than uneven hand-made ones. For decorative purposes moulded bricks and terracotta were very popular and added status to the building. Tile-hanging between the upper and lower bays was much used, as was the inclusion of terracotta panels of flowers or cherubs. Further ornamentation included the use of stucco, which had been shunned by the Gothic Revivalists. Arts and Craft style patterns in stucco were displayed above windows and in the gables to imitate the East Anglian pargetting of the sixteenth and

5

seventeenth centuries. Intricately carved bargeboards and the use of mock Tudor timber patterns in gables had also come into favour, as had elaborate balconies in the style of the Bedford Park development. Brick elevations were often combined with rendering in roughcast or pebble dash. The render could be left in its natural cement (Fig. 5.15) or pebble dash, or it could be painted over in white or cream.

Nearly all progressive architects and architectural commentators lamented the continued insistence of the house-dweller on retaining the parlour or front room, even in the smallest of houses, "for the delectation of the occasional visitor and never used by the family except on Sunday" [11]. Although the term parlour for the front room seemed to be used mostly in lower middle class and working class cottages, such as illustrated in Fig. 5.8 and Fig. 5.9, the room itself remained also in the more urban type houses, but now often called the sitting room. Even the large Edwardian villa, the ground plan of which is shown in Fig. 5.6, boasted a sitting room, albeit with double doors opening onto the larger reception hall and dining area. The more

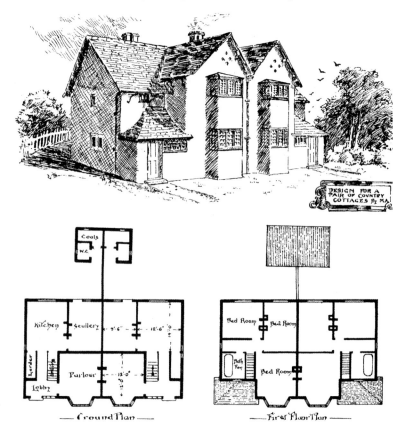

Fig. 5.8. Plan of a small semi-detached country cottage with parlour [12].

moderately sized semi-detached house shown in Fig. 5.10 has a sitting room completely isolated from the living room (which itself is a reception hall and dining area).

The large semi-detached villas of Fig. 5.11 illustrate nearly all the features of the quintessential Edwardian middle-class suburban house. Internally there is a spacious lounge hall – or reception hall – a drawing room and a separate dining room. Externally, the elevation presents brickwork up to string course level[2] and roughcast above, a wide, deeply recessed porch, a balcony with carved wooden railings, mock-Tudor gables, and small-paned casement windows. The treatment of the corner of the building is especially novel. It is a mini-conservatory or bower "in which choice blooms can be raised at little expense" [15].

Figs. 5.12 through 5.16 show examples of Edwardian middle-class villas exhibiting many of the attributes mentioned in the previous paragraphs. Houses such as these came to influence the

---

2. A string course is a continuous horizontal band, usually moulded, on an exterior wall.

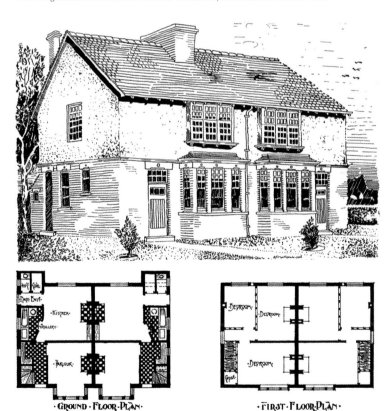

· GROUND · FLOOR · PLAN ·   · FIRST · FLOOR · PLAN ·

Fig. 5.9. Plan of a small semi-detached country cottage with parlour [13].

5

visual scene of the more prosperous of the outer suburbs all over the country. The same building style was used in the terrace estates. Despite the increased popularity of the semi-detached house, the terrace house still retained its dominant position in the first part of the century as a very acceptable, but not necessarily preferred mode of middle-class dwelling. During the Edwardian period the number of terrace houses built outnumbered that of the semi-detached by about three to one.

The two faces of Edwardian domestic building style

We have seen that the speculative builders of the Edwardian period seized upon the Domestic Revival idiom to build houses which appealed to the suburban middle-class families of that age. In this they had been very successful. Many of these estates still stand today and their Edwardian villas, detached or semi-detached, are much sought after.

At the same time as the pattern-book villas in red brick and tile-hanging were being erected in the outer suburbs, a new generation of architects were designing houses – detached, semi-detached and terraces – which visually were totally different. The philosophy of John Ruskin, William Morris and the Arts and Crafts Movement was

Fig. 5.10. Medium-sized pair of semi-detached cottages with the parlour or sitting room unusually set to the rear of the house [14].

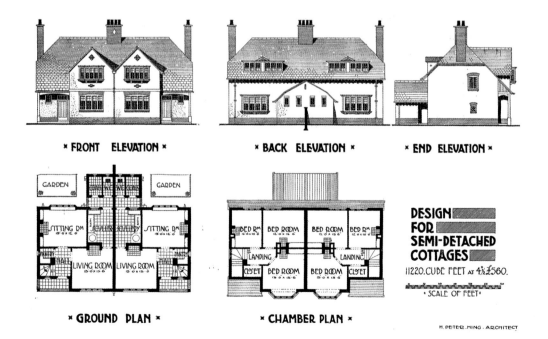

× FRONT ELEVATION ×   × BACK ELEVATION ×   × END ELEVATION ×

× GROUND PLAN ×   × CHAMBER PLAN ×

DESIGN FOR SEMI-DETACHED COTTAGES
11220. CUDE FEET at 4½ £560.
· SCALE OF FEET·

H. PETER .HINC . ARCHITECT

particularly strong within this generation. While the speculative
builders happily pursued the eclecticism of the Domestic Revival,
the avant-garde architects created buildings which in many ways
were simpler and more honest than the ostentatious villas of the new
suburbs. One reason for this was that they often were designing for
a particular client, such as one of the co-partnership societies set up
for the garden cities and the garden suburbs.

Possibly the most influential of the architects, certainly the one
whose 'signature' is seen most often in the architect-designed
vernacular buildings of early Edwardian suburbia, was C.F.A.
Voysey. His houses exhibited decorative buttresses, huge chimneys,
horizontally accentuated windows right under the eaves or raised
to above eaves level, small-paned windows overall, roofs sweeping

Fig. 5.11. Front elevation
and plan of a large
Edwardian semi-detached
villa. Notice the lounge
hall with fireplace and the
special corner bower of this
room designed to impress
visitors [15].

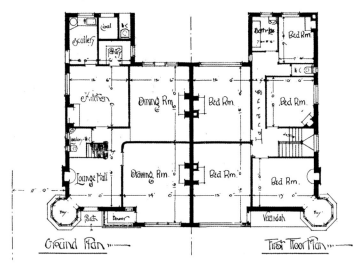

5

Fig. 5.12. Edwardian semi-detached houses in a Manchester suburb. A new enclosed porch has been added to the first building.

Fig. 5.13. Edwardian semi-detached houses in a Manchester suburb.

Fig. 5.14. Edwardian semi-detached houses in a Manchester suburb.

Fig. 5.15. Roughcast Edwardian semi-detached house in a Manchester suburb.

Fig. 5.16. Stone-built Edwardian semi-detached houses in a Harrogate suburb.

to first-floor level and rendering in roughcast. One example of this style of house is seen in the medium-sized semi-detached cottage in Letchworth Garden City, shown as the upper illustration in Fig. 5.17, where it may be compared with the standard Edwardian speculative semi shown in the lower picture of Fig. 5.17 – the two faces of domestic housing styles of this period.

The unpretentious Arts and Crafts style of housing, as in the garden city example of Fig. 5.17, is a far cry from the extravagances that especially the upper middle classes of Edwardian society were looking for. Gone are the elaborate bargeboards (Fig. 5.16), the intricately carved brackets and spindles of the porches, the stylish balconies, the leaded panes, and the copious tile-hanging. Admittedly, many of the houses in the garden city style were designed to house industrial workers and lower middle-class families, so a degree of restraint was only to be expected. However, most of these houses were extremely well balanced, dignified and aesthetically pleasing.

Fig. 5.17. Semi-detached houses in Letchworth.
a: White-painted roughcast, Voyseyesque sweeping roof and horizontally emphasised small paned windows.
b: Standard Edwardian semi in a Manchester suburb. Red brick, tile-hanging, bay oriel windows, mock-Tudor gables.

References

1 *Metro-Land*, 1924, facsimile edition, Southbank Publishing, London 2004, p.89.

2 Alan A.Jackson, *Semi-detached London*, Wild Swan Publications Ltd, Didcot 1991, p.42.

3 *Ibid.*, p.45.

4 John Burnett, *A Social History of Housing 1815-1970*, Methuen, Newton Abbot 1978, p.257.

5 R.R.Lawrence and T.Chris, *The Period House – Style, Detail & Decoration 1774-1914*, Weidenfeld & Nicolson, London 1996.

6 Joe Hicks and Grahame Allen, A Century of Change: Trends in UK statistics since 1900, Research Paper 99/111, House of Commons Library, 21 December 1999, p.12.

7 *Ibid.*

8 Helen Long, *The Edwardian House*, Manchester University Press, Manchester 1993, p.31.

9 John Burnett, *A Social History of Housing 1815-1970*, Methuen, Newton Abbot 1978, p.204.

10 John Gloag, *The Englishman's Castle*, Eyre & Spottiswoode, London 1944, p.158.

11 H.B.Philpott, *Modern Cottages, Villas and Bungalows*, John Dicks, London 1908, p.6.

12 *Ibid.*, p.17.

13 *Ibid.*, p.18.

14 *Ibid.*, p.22.

15 *Ibid.*, p.56.

Garden cities and garden suburbs (1901-20)

" 'Garden City' has a beguilingly soft English attraction about it ..."

Robert Beevers, 2002

The garden city movement

In 1898, the visionary planner Ebenezer Howard (1850-1928) published his book *Tomorrow: A Peaceful Path to Real Reform*, re-issued four years later under the title *Garden Cities of Tomorrow*. Howard was neither an architect nor a town planner (he was a parliamentary stenographer and inventor of typewriters), but his utopian theories were to have a profound impact on town planning throughout the world.

   Howard was influenced by the writings of John Ruskin and William Morris, by the late Victorian currents of social reformism and by the growing enthusiasm for healthy living and the countryside. In his town planning outlines he sought to balance the advantages of the urban city with those of the countryside – avoiding as best he could the disadvantages of both. His idea was to create new towns, based on a circular layout, with a "tightly organized urban centre for 32,000 inhabitants, surrounded by a perpetual green belt of farms and parks" [Howard, cited in 1]. Howard proposed placing such garden cities as satellite towns around a larger, central city with maybe 58,000 people. His concept was illustrated with the diagram shown in Fig. 6.1. Transportation over any longer distance was at the turn of the century dominated by the railways, and for goods also by the canals, which explains the emphasis on these systems in his diagram. Soon, though, the motor car and the electric underground lines in London were to change the pattern of travel and commuting dramatically. Howard could not have foreseen this, but the architects that were engaged to transform his town planning ideas into practice were brilliantly able to lay out the townships so that they function even today, even coping with one or two cars per family.

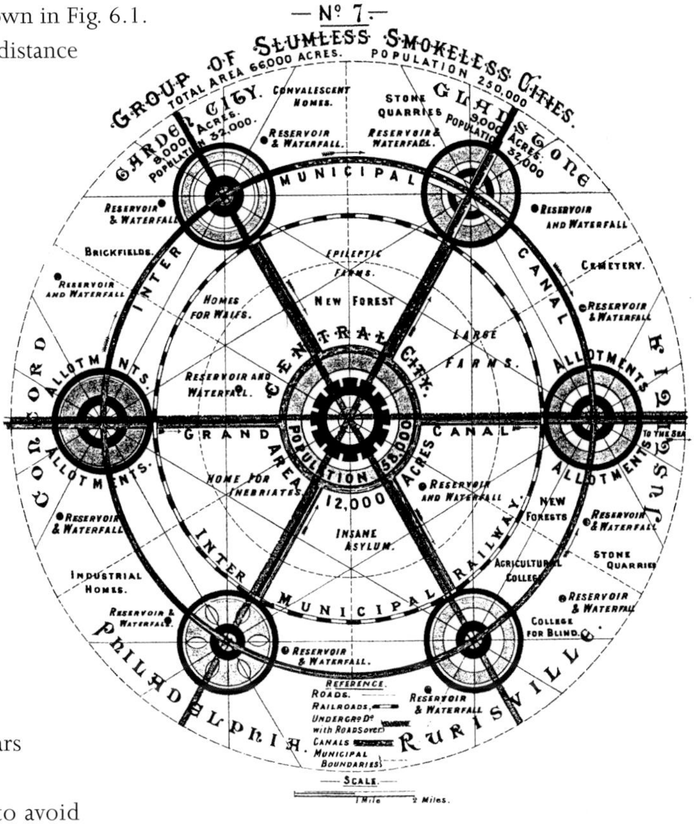

Fig. 6.1. Ebenezer Howard's 1898 diagram of a "group of slumless, smokeless cities" with a total population of around 250,000 inhabitants [1].

Howard wished at all costs to avoid the suburban sprawl, which was beginning to be seen around cities as an unhappy consequence of the bye-law housing and the general lack of town planning principles within the local authorities. The new garden city was to include both agriculture and industry and would have separate zones for housing, factories and municipal buildings.

There has apparently always been some confusion surrounding what constitutes a garden city, a garden suburb, a garden village and a model village. Howard was himself worried about the indiscriminate use of the terms garden city and garden suburb. In a letter to the *Times* from March 26, 1919, he wrote: "The careless use of the two terms meaning quite different things has seriously retarded the growth of the garden city movement, a movement started with the express object of increasing the productive powers of the nation and of solving the twin evils of the over-growth of great cities and the decay of rural districts." An attempt is given below to explain the terms as they are now commonly used, with examples shown for each category.

Garden city	A town of moderate size laid out to include within its boundaries both public buildings, parks, industry and housing. Surrounding the town is an agricultural belt – not merely a green belt, but an integral part of the community – supplying produce to the town.	*Letchworth* *Welwyn*
Garden suburb	A suburb of low-density housing designed with emphasis on trees, grassed areas and hedges to create a rural, village-like presence. The layout should follow the natural contours of the area as well as possible, and the houses themselves arranged in such a way as to give each one an interesting view.	*Bedford Park* *Hampstead* *Wavertree*
Model village	A village created to serve as a housing community mainly for employees of a particular company. Houses would typically have gardens back and front. The village would include a number of community buildings and in general be designed with open spaces and green areas.	*Price's village* *Port Sunlight* *Bournville* *New Earswick*
Garden village	This expression is synonymous with model village.	

In the event, only two garden cities were built in England, one at Letchworth, begun 1903, and the other at Welwyn, begun 1919. They proved difficult and costly to establish, but both were in the long run considered very successful. Howard's philosophy of town planning survived the mass suburban building between the wars, and after the Second World War his ideas were incorporated in the New Towns, which were built as satellite towns to major cities (around London: Hemel Hempstead, Stevenage, Harlow, Basildon and others), see Chapter ten. On a smaller scale, an embodiment of Howard's ideas are found also in the Millennium Communities.

In a historical perspective the model villages of Port Sunlight and Bournville, and the middle-class suburb of Bedford Park, held the ingredients to the housing estates of the garden cities and even more directly to the Edwardian garden suburb movement. Two people in particular became involved in the layout and housing design for the garden cities and garden suburbs – Raymond Unwin and Barry Parker.

RAYMOND UNWIN AND BARRY PARKER

Raymond Unwin (1863-1940) was born in Yorkshire, but the family later moved to Oxford where the young Unwin heard lectures by Ruskin and Morris. He abandoned his first intention of reading theology and moved to Chesterfield where he served an engineering apprenticeship and later worked as an engineer in the planning of mining villages in the Yorkshire and Derbyshire coalfields.

Unwin had quite early become close friends with his cousins Barry (1867-1947) and Ethel Parker (1865-1949), and he eventually obtained consent to marry Ethel. Barry Parker and Unwin set up a partnership in 1896 and were soon commissioned for the design of churches and middle-class houses. Their earliest experiment in semi-detached housing was on Cunnery Road in Church Stretton, Shropshire, where in 1899 they designed a semi-detached pair with a central chimney, a hipped roof, a projecting gable, roughcast walls and decorative buttresses at the sides in the style of Voysey (Fig. 6.2). The pair was possibly intended to house estate servants or act as a lodge to the estate of Major Campell Hyslop, wealthy owner of the Stretton Lunatic Asylum for Gentlemen, for

Fig. 6.2. The earliest semi-detached pair designed by Unwin and Parker at Church Stretton, Shropshire, as they appeared in 2005.

whom Barry Parker had designed a magnificent Arts and Craft mansion in the wooded hills above the village.

In 1901, Unwin, who was the most outgoing of the pair, attended a conference in Bournville, where he met Seebohm Rowntree (1871-1954), second son of the founder of the York cocoa manufacturing company. Shortly after, Unwin and Parker were asked to produce plans for Rowntree's New Earswick model village. This was the first community designed by the two partners. The cottage plans at Church Stretton had been modified by them in 1902 for a development in Starbeck, outside Harrogate, to become generously sized semi-detached pairs with three bedrooms and through living rooms. The cottages served as prototypes for the development of the short terraces and semis at New Earswick, and later for the houses in Letchworth and Hampstead Garden Suburb. They were, however, not popular with the tenants, because Unwin and Parker had made the same mistake as other reformers had done before them by designing houses with enlarged living rooms rather than separate living rooms and parlours. This was not what either working or middle-class families wanted at that time; the parlour or best room was still too close to people's hearts to be excluded.

LETCHWORTH GARDEN CITY

Unwin soon became involved in the first garden city, Letchworth, in Hertfordshire. Ebenezer Howard's writings had attracted the attention of town planners and influential industrialists such as Lever and Cadbury who invested substantially in the Pioneer Company to search for and purchase a suitable site for a garden city. In 1903, the First Garden City Limited was registered as a company. Its remit was to raise capital and to put Howard's theories into practice, in short to develop a garden city. In competition with others, Unwin and Parker submitted plans for the garden city to the company, and early in 1904, their designs were accepted by the board.

Unwin's earliest writings had recommended housing densities of 22 to the acre. However, he soon became a firm believer of much lower densities and suggested an optimal density of 12 units per acre, a figure that, in general, became supported in later housing guidelines. His vision was of wide-fronted semi-detached houses and short terraces in a leafy setting with each house having interesting views. He introduced 'closes' to obtain this ideal. In New Earswick the houses in a close were given access by footpaths, but with the coming of the motor car the closes evolved into *cul-de-sacs* as in Letchworth and Hampstead Garden Suburb.

The Letchworth company ran into financial difficulties very early. The sheer magnitude of building a new town in the middle of the countryside had been seriously under-estimated. There were problems of attracting industries to move to a virgin city, and most of the working capital of the company was used to provide essential services in an attempt to coax both industries and residents to the area. William Lever, who was on the board, was impatient with the lack of progress being made, and he strenuously tried to convince his fellow board members that they should go ahead and start building houses. With housing provided for the city's inhabitants he was convinced that industry was sure to follow. Lever achieved nothing, also due to the fact that the rural district council looked at the scheme with distaste. In protest, he resigned his seat on the board.

Some progress was made when the company's able manager Thomas Adams persuaded the owner of *Country Life* and editor of *The Spectator* to organize a Cheap Cottages Exhibition (the £150 cottage) in Letchworth in 1905. The exhibition was a great success, although many commentators at the time, quite rightly, saw the cottages better suited to middle-class weekenders than to the industrial and agricultural workers they were supposed to serve. For a time, the 121 permanent cottages that were built constituted, as it were, the garden city. The town was started. The control of the estate was, however, soon taken out of the hands of Thomas Adams, who stepped down from the project. Control was handed over to W. H. Gaunt, a northern businessman who cared little for the utopian ideas of Howard, Unwin and Parker. He believed in the money-making as practiced in the harsh ugliness of Lancashire's factories and was offended by any sign of art or taste. He fought hard, but unsuccessfully, to banish 'decadent' red roofing tiles from the town and replace them with grey slates. Not surprisingly, Raymond Unwin was unable to accept the new style of management and he moved from the Letchworth project in 1906, leaving Barry Parker to weather the storms.

Unwin and Parker had even then contributed significantly not only to the overall plan of the garden city, but also to the design of the

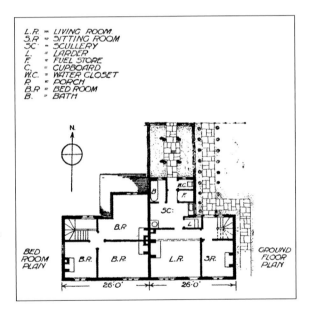

Fig. 6.3. Plan of a typical Unwin and Parker three-bedroomed semi-detached cottage. Care was always taken to give maximum light to the living areas by facing them south (as here) or south-west. All bedrooms had fireplaces [2].

individual dwellings, which they planned as a mixture of terraced, semi-detached and detached houses. In most cases they had to accept that the inhabitants clung uncompromisingly to their best room or parlour, and floor plans for a three-bedroomed semi could typically look like Fig. 6.3.

The houses were mostly in the vernacular style that they had first practiced at Church Stretton. Unwin's street designs used houses in small groupings to relieve the monotony that was so evident in the bye-law streets. The houses themselves were attractive, but Unwin himself was never completely happy with the overall picture. In 1907 he wrote:

> In the streets themselves we have sought to avoid monotonous rows, and perhaps we have erred from an artistic point of view, in allowing too much freedom to the individual, as to the placing of his house. Spaces in the Garden City tend to be too large in proportion to the buildings, and we have much yet to learn as to the best treatment [3].

On the whole, though, the work at Letchworth was praised in the contemporary press, but not all visitors were happy. *The Builder* of December 1908, printed the following critique:

> Hitherto in England we have been in danger of falling between two stools – the practical sanitary considerations on the one hand, and the ultra-sentimental ideas which prompted the Garden City movement (itself largely the outcome of amateur enthusiasms) on the other; while the simple necessity or architectural treatment of the subject has been entirely neglected. The cottages which have been built at Letchworth may have been interesting as a study in cheap materials, but the result has been disastrous architecturally; houses of every conceivable material and design jostling each other in complete confusion, showing that the promoters of the enterprise, though they had a fine enthusiasm and certain excellent ideas about the circulation of air round houses, were yet ignorant of the true basis of town design [4].

It is astonishing today that this highly patronizing article could appear in an otherwise respected publication, and doubly astonishing that it refers to the small handful of people whose visions had a lasting impact on town planning throughout the twentieth century. The jibe at cottages built as a study in cheap materials is probably a reference to the Cheap Cottages Exhibition with which Unwin himself was not too pleased. Two years later, delegates at a housing conference visited Letchworth and they too were not overly impressed. *The Building News* of October 1910, reported that:

Fig. 6.4. Pair of cottages at Letchworth Garden City, 1905. "The Croft", 16 and 18 Baldock Road. Designed by Bennett & Bidwell 1905. From a contemporary postcard.

> … the place is at present wanting in dignity, and looks scattered and unattractive. Many of the shops and houses are extremely ordinary in character, being built in no prearranged style or architectural design, though some of the groups of cottages and villas are more worthy of the opportunity thus furnished for a model scheme of unpretentious and well-built modern residences of artistic merit.

The reporter goes on to say that "the roughcast dwellings discolour badly towards the ground line, and the whitewashed walls of some of the cottages look spotty where soft bricks grin through and stain the limewhite. The city is thirty-five miles from London, and the journey is far from expeditious." He is better pleased with the end of the tour, where "in the evening an exhibition of lantern slides of town plans was shown in the Great Gallery. This informal entertainment proved very popular, as smoking was allowed, and refreshments were provided."

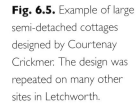

Fig. 6.5. Example of large semi-detached cottages designed by Courtenay Crickmer. The design was repeated on many other sites in Letchworth.

Today, 100 years after the start of building, most of the houses are still standing and, where well maintained, offer extremely attractive residences.

Many architects were employed over the years to design houses for Letchworth Garden City. In the early years nearly all houses,

6

semi-detached or otherwise, followed the basic vernacular and Voyseyesque style employed by Unwin and Parker in their houses at Church Stretton, Starbeck and New Earswick, see the examples of Fig. 6.4 and Fig. 6.5 to the designs of Robert Bennett and Wilson Bidwell, and of Courtenay Crickmer (1879-1971). One of the earliest semi-detached cottages designed by Parker and Unwin is the very basic cottage style in Cromwell Green shown in Fig. 6.6.

One of the most exciting entries to the exhibition was a pair of semi-detached cottages designed by the gifted arts and crafts architect M. H. Baillie Scott (1865-1945). Because of their high price they could not be considered seriously by the exhibition awards committee. Scott was not perturbed. In the exhibition catalogue he wrote:

… the Cottage should be the dream come true, the result of infinite pains, whether it pays five or six per cent is quite a secondary matter. [1]

Fig. 6.6. Early small semi-detached cottage in Cromwell Green photographed in 2005.

Rather than design to a rock-bottom price, he agreed with Unwin that the workers should receive better pay, so that they could afford to live in a dream cottage. Sketches of the Baillie Scott pair are shown in Fig. 6.7. The semi-detached houses had an open plan interior, which was not to everyone's liking; nor was the fact that the scullery section was set some steps lower than the kitchen in order to give

Fig. 6.7. The Baillie Scott entry to the Cheap Cottages Exhibition. At some point, the two cottages were converted into a single dwelling, but the semi-detached form was later re-instated [5].

head room under the cat-slide roof. Later generations have most unfortunately raised the scullery floor level and built flat-roof extensions, see Fig. 6.8, thus taking away the elegance of Baillie Scott's original design.

Some later designs in Letchworth tended to use the neo-Georgian style, which was coming into vogue. It was less cottagey and in many ways much blander. Unwin himself designed in this style, but more so for official buildings in the central areas than for domestic work.

A design competition calling for new high-quality, environmentally friendly, groundbreaking housing in Letchworth was launched in early 2007.

Fig. 6.8. The Baillie Scott semis in 2005. The building of the flat-roof extension eliminated the cat-slide roof and made the house look very ordinary.

WELWYN GARDEN CITY

Critics of the Garden City movement had been quick to voice their opinions, one being that Letchworth would be a one-off experiment, and an unsuccessful one at that. Ebenezer Howard was determined to prove them wrong. Towards the end of the First World War he had his sights set on a plot of land on the Great North Road some 12 miles south of Letchworth. In October of 1918, he boarded a train at King's Cross with two friends and fellow campaigners and set out to Hatfield from where they walked north towards Welwyn, over the grounds of the Earl of Salisbury. Stopping for lunch in Hatfield on their way back, Howard and his friends drew up a rough town plan centred on the village of Welwyn. Howard was convinced that this was where he would establish the second garden city.

Events moved more quickly than could have been anticipated. In May of 1919, Howard saw an advertisement for the sale by auction of a very large plot of land immediately to the north of Salisbury's estate. Within half an hour he got in touch with influential friends to convince them of the urgency in acquiring this land for a second garden city and, having convinced them, he enlisted their help in raising the necessary £5000 deposit for the purchase. Howard was himself not a wealthy man, and he could contribute with only £50 of his own money. When he arrived at the auction a little over a week later he had succeeded in raising all but £200, but nevertheless he emerged as the owner of 1500 acres of shooting estate and in debt to the tune of £50,000.

Howard, now in his seventieth year, was impatient to proceed and was not prepared to wait for uncertain government grants. He was intent on making the garden city a private enterprise, and the same year the Second Garden City Company, later Welwyn Garden City Ltd, was set up with the object of building "an entirely new and self-dependent industrial town, on a site 21 miles from London, as an illustration of the right way to provide for the expansion of industries and population of a great city" [27]. The company succeeded in persuading Lord Salisbury to part with 700 acres of land adjoining the estate purchased at auction. Plans for the town were ready in June 1920, and by 1921 leases had been granted for the building of 200 houses and a new railway station.

The architect chosen to lead the project was Lois de Soissons, who was appointed in April 1920. He was born in Canada and had studied in Paris and Rome. Within two months his overall plan for Welwyn Garden City had been produced, and although some changes were later made, the major layout remained as on the design shown in Fig. 6.9. The railway cuts in a straight line from south to north through the town. The residential areas are placed mainly to the west of the railway and to the south of the industrial area on the east side. This was planned so that the prevailing westerly winds would carry any air-born pollution from the industries away from the housing areas.

The land chosen for the garden city was pleasantly undulating with plenty of old trees, and Soissons and his fellow architect A.W. Kenyon planned the roads to take best advantage of the natural contours and of the existing vegetation. Only the south-west area was more thinly wooded, and each large tree was meticulously marked on the survey

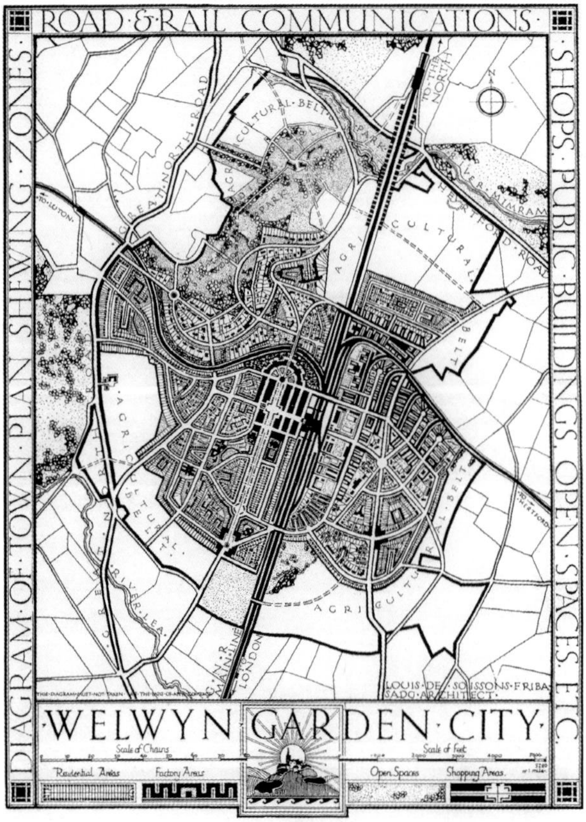

Fig. 6.9. General town plan of Welwyn Garden City [6].

and road plans. All the new roads were planted with trees. The planning was very much in the tradition established by Raymond Unwin in Letchworth and in Hampstead Garden City with *cul-de-sacs* featuring strongly in the layout.

Soissons had chosen to build in the Neo-Georgian style using red bricks made from clay dug locally. Other architects were invited to provide designs for the housing, but all designs had to be approved by Soissons personally, which ensured a pleasing rather than monotonous conformity to the estates. Semi-detached and detached houses figured prominently in the housing schemes. Terraces for workers in the local industries were also provided, and though basically Neo-Georgian they were often rendered in white and embellished with Arts and Crafts style porches.

Fig. 6.10. Plan of Handside Close with a contemporary photograph as well as a recent (2005) photograph of the semi-detached houses [7], [8].

One of the first housing developments to be built was the Dailymail Village, now Meadow Green. *The Daily Mail* newspaper, which had sponsored and organized the Ideal Home Exhibition since 1908, had as a generous gift to the nation – and as a spectacular publicity stunt – offered to build 41 cottages in the new garden city; of these 32 were semi-detached (16 pairs), the rest detached. A model of the Dailymail Village was shown at the 1921 Ideal Home Exhibition, and the village opened in March 1922

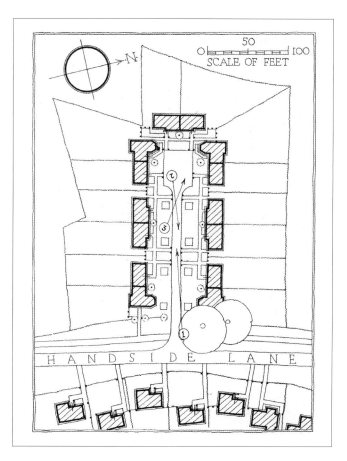

to coincide with the start of that year's exhibition.

The semi-detached properties in Handside Close were built in much the same style as the Daily Mail houses. A plan of this *cul-de-sac* is shown in Fig. 6.10, together with a contemporary photograph and a 2005 photograph of the semi-detached housing scheme. The white-painted rendering seems to be the preferred finish on most buildings today; they were originally left in a soft grey rendering, which much better highlighted the white window frames and door surrounds.

Many of the houses were finished in the red brick of the area, such as shown in Fig. 6.11, which is a no-nonsense semi-detached house

Fig. 6.11. Red-brick semi-detached houses in a *cul-de-sac*, 1920s [9] and 2005.

in one of the numerous *cul-de-sacs* of the town. It is illustrated in its rather bleak surroundings in a contemporary photograph together with a 2005 photograph, which demonstrates the leafy maturity now in place.

In the northern part of the south-west corner of the garden city, a long road named Brockswood Lane curves gracefully on the edge of a wooded area, where once ran the Luton branch of the Great Northern Railway. Large semi-detached houses line the road to the south. The houses are similar to the one in Handslide Close shown above, but by different architects. They are in the unassuming Neo-Georgian style, but there is a hint of modernism in the elongated vertical windows that bring light to the staircases inside. Fig. 6.12 and Fig. 6.13 show the dignified houses.

The residential part of the town was planned with wide grass verges and front gardens without fencing or hedges, following the pattern of suburbs in the United States. Originally, there was an outcry by the residents who valued their privacy, but the landscape architects convinced the inhabitants of some of the larger houses that this was good idea, and they somewhat reluctantly accepted. However, when the landscaping of the front gardens was in place,

Fig. 6.12. Semi-detached houses on Brockswood Lane in the 1920s [10].

Fig. 6.13. Semi-detached houses on Brockswood Lane in 2005.

most admitted that it indeed enhanced the beauty of the estate, and when new developments were laid out the residents asked to have their front gardens like the 'posh ones'. The effect is still very visible in the area, as may be seen on some of the recent photographs shown in this section.

Welwyn Garden City was by and large a success and still is a very desirable place to live. Writing in 1934, the Danish architect and town planner Steen Eiler Rasmussen devoted a chapter in his book on *London: the Unique City* to Letchworth and Welwyn and was impressed and delighted with the two garden cities. He rightly pointed out, though, that the hope nurtured by Ebenezer Howard that the two garden cities by their very existence and success would spawn a generation of new satellite towns, had not been fulfilled [11]. It was only after the Second World War – and with government intervention – that Howard's ideas received renewed interest.

The garden suburb movement

The creation of garden suburbs in the beginning of the twentieth century was, in a way, the practical manifestation of late Victorian and Edwardian philanthropy directed towards improved housing

for the working classes. At the same time there was a growing urge among middle-class house dwellers to live in healthy, pleasant surroundings with a touch of English countryside at their doorstep, and here the garden suburbs fulfilled a role very similar to the speculative housing estates of Metro-land. It was the planned design of a complete suburban community and the non-profit financing of the schemes that set the garden suburbs apart from the speculative estates. The financing was usually handled as a co-partnership scheme, which meant that the houses were owned neither individually nor by a profit-seeking landlord, but by a company, a Trust, in which the tenants of the houses were themselves shareholders. Around 20 garden suburb type schemes were initiated up and down the country before the First World War [12]. The most well known of these is Hampstead Garden Suburb in north London, created by the untiring efforts of the social reformer Henrietta Barnett (1851-1936).

HAMPSTEAD GARDEN SUBURB

"Pretty, witty, and well-to-do," [13] wrote Beatrice Potter of her friend the 19-year-old Henrietta Rowland. Henrietta was born into middle-class comfort. The family fortunes were based on macassar oil, used in hair dressing by generations of Victorians and well into the twentieth century (the Victorian style 'antimacassar' protection for furniture coverings is occasionally still to be found today, although its history and original purpose are mostly forgotten).

Henrietta married Canon Samuel Barnett with whom she worked in the squalor of Whitechapel in London's East End. The extent of the appalling living conditions in London's slums had been charted by Charles Booth (1840-1916) in his 17-volume *Life and Labour of the People in London*, published in the 1890s. In his final volumes, published in 1903, he wrote:

> Put baldly, "lower buildings and wider streets" are
> the things needed, and instead the people are offered
> "depressing streets dark and narrow" or "tall prison like
> dwellings". But their tastes carry them on a good deal
> further ... the demand for "artistic cottages" is noted, and
> gardens are the pride of those who possess them –
> "houses blessed with gardens – a wonderful influence". [1]

---

1. Quoted [13].

Henrietta was determined to channel her energies into providing better living conditions for the poor and Booth's prescription matched her ideas of a garden suburb for all classes.

In 1889, the Barnetts had purchased a ten-bedroomed house on the northern fringes of Hampstead Heath to which they frequently invited parishioners to share their weekends. On learning of Yerkes' plans for the extension of the Charing Cross, Euston and Hampstead Railway to Golders Green and beyond (see Chapter 1) with a station proposed on the Hampstead Heath Extension, which was land viewed from their house, Henrietta Barnett immediately started campaigning to save the land from speculative development.[2] Her ideas of a garden suburb had reached a new urgency. In newspaper articles and pamphlets she outlined her plans for a settlement of houses where, ideally, all classes from the poorest through the artisan classes to all layers of the middle classes would mix in a garden community. Purchase of the Hampstead Heath Extension and more land to the north to accommodate the garden suburb was fraught with difficulties, but eventually the extension was bought in late 1904. Henrietta Barnett was able to raise enough capital in 1906 to launch the Hampstead Garden Suburb Trust, and the following year the Trust was able to purchase a substantial size of open land to the north of Hampstead Heath Extension, the northernmost part of which was to become the Artisans' Quarter of the suburb. While Mrs. Barnett wished to see the classes live side by side, she had firm views as to what housing was appropriate for each class. The lowest earners were allotted the flatter land to the north of the area, whereas the more affluent would be able to enjoy views over the undulating heath land to the south.

Raymond Unwin had become involved in the planning of the garden suburb as early as late 1904. Mrs. Barnett had read one of Unwin's publications and found his way of thinking very similar to her own. In February 1905, Unwin had the first draft plan ready and, although it was quickly superseded, it was a realistic start to the project with a low density of buildings, arranged to take the best possible advantage of the outlying views. On the recommendation

---

2. Before all legalities were finalised building had started on the station, which officially was named North End, but also referred to as Wyldes Station or the Bull and Bush, the name of the local public house about a quarter of a mile away. Shafts for ventilation and lifts were built, as were the underground platforms, which since have been removed. Today you may still see gaps beside the track from the train, where the platforms once stood. Brigid Green, long-time archivist for Hampstead Garden Suburb, reported that the station was said to be the site of one of the shelters for the War Cabinet at the start of the Second World War.

6

of Mrs. Barnett, Unwin was appointed architect to the Hampstead Garden Trust in May 1906. The trustees had studied the model villages of Port Sunlight, Bournville and New Earswick as well as the first garden city, Letchworth, but Henrietta Barnett was not so much concerned with Ebenezer Howard's theories of the "city in a garden" as with creating a spacious and beautiful living environment for the

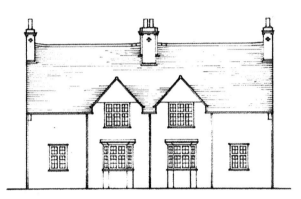

Fig. 6.14. Foundation Cottages, 140-142 Hampstead Way, from an original drawing of the elevations.

Fig. 6.15. Foundation Cottages, 140-42, Hampstead Way, photographed in 2005.

poorest classes, and indeed for all social classes.

Building started in May 1907 when Henrietta Barnett had turned the first sod for the Artisan's Quarter, and six months later more than 1000 men were at work. Unwin and Parker were responsible for the first housing designs. These followed their first cottage designs, which had started with the Church Stretton semi-detached pair and then carried over to Starbeck, New Earswick and Letchworth. The very first house to be completed in the garden suburb was a semi-detached dwelling at 140-42 Hampstead Way, Foundation Cottages, in roughcast with a tiled roof and main entrance doors on either side of the building. The entrances were framed by red brick arches, which also supported the chimneys above. Each semi had four bedrooms and a bath in the scullery. The toilet was outside, accessed from a porch at the back of the house. Fig. 6.14 shows drawings of the side and front

elevations and Fig. 6.15 shows the pair as they appear today (2005).

Unwin was keen to introduce *cul-de-sacs* and roads more narrow than permitted by the council bye-laws (Hendon Urban District Council). The Trust sought independent powers to allow the architects to circumvent the existing bye-laws, and a local Act was passed allowing them to do so. The Act did require an average residential density of eight houses to the acre, somewhat less than the 12 per acre that

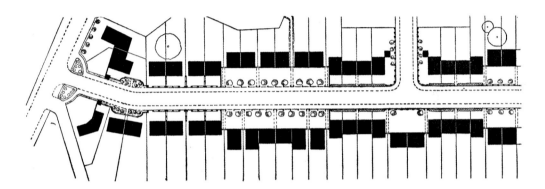

Unwin had planned for, but nevertheless very much acceptable. The Trust had asked Unwin to plan so that "every road may have its own characteristics", a request that Unwin followed conscientiously and the results are indeed a tribute to his versatility and genius as an architect and planner. He was fully aware of the public's preference for a detached or a semi-detached home, although he ascribed the fact mainly to the "very poor quality of the party walls generally built between houses" [14]. His philosophy of planning to create an interesting street picture is perhaps best embodied in the following sentence from *Town Planning in Practice* [15]:

Fig. 6.16. Street layout at Rotherwick Road. Unwin uses groups of detached, semi-detached and short terraces, some retracted from and some set forward to the building line, to create an interesting street architecture [16].

> Even when it is not possible to avoid much repetition of semi-detached or detached houses, they should be so arranged as to give some sense of grouping. The setback of three or four pairs of houses and the arrangement of a continuous green in front of them, with the proper treatment of the houses at each end, which are set forward again to the building line, will of itself produce some grouping.

This approach is exactly illustrated by the layout of Rotherwick Road shown in Fig. 6.16.

6

There was no doubt in the minds of the garden suburb promoters and of its planners that the semi-detached house or cottage should be given a prominent role in the suburb, and the large number of semis built bare witness to this; a very rough estimate taken from published plans of the suburb would indicate that approximately one third of the dwellings are semis. The smallest of the houses were those in the Artisan's Quarters and the houses became larger and more opulent the closer the location was either to the central square (see below) or to the heath itself. The architectural style of the garden suburb was dominated in the early years by the informal Arts and Crafts buildings exemplified by Unwin and Parker's Foundation Cottages and the dark brick houses in the southern part of the suburb. A pair of these semi-detached houses with dark brown brick walls on Rotherwick Road is shown in Fig. 6.17. Other architects followed the vernacular idiom, with the notable exception of Edwin Lutyens discussed below, but many of the larger post-war houses were built in a neo-Georgian style.

Fig. 6.17. Semi-detached pair on Rotherwick Road, set close to the building line.

The Trust did not itself act as building contractor in the development of the suburb. Building activities were administered by the Garden Suburb Development Company set up in 1907, and later with various co-partnership companies such as Hampstead Tenants Ltd. The Trust acted to oversee and advise on the choice of housing design, the commissioning of architects and the quality of the building work carried out. The Garden Suburb Development Company engaged many of the period's leading architects to execute designs for the suburb. Altogether well over 60 architects were involved in the original suburb, though most of them built no more than one or two houses. As architect to the Trust, Unwin guided the designers to make sure that any "building will take its place in the picture already existing. The harmony, the unity which binds the buildings together and welds the whole into a picture, is so much the most important consideration that it should take precedence" [17]. A walk in the suburb today will convince most that in following this maxim he was very successful. Writing in 1951, Nikolaus Pevsner stated that Hampstead Garden Suburb was the "aesthetically most satisfactory and socially most successful of all twentieth century garden suburbs" [18].

The aesthetical ingredient is still there, but the social development did not materialise as Henrietta Barnett had dreamed of. The earliest plans for the suburb showed buildings for working lads and barns for tools and coster barrows. In spite of the low tuppenny return fare to London from Golders Green, neither working lads nor costermongers became conspicuous elements of the social mix. The mixing of classes, never strong to begin with, has now all but disappeared. The population today is made up of the more wealthy part of middle-class society; even the prices of the more modest dwellings in the Artisan's Quarter are now out of reach of the average wage earner.

The suburb was designed with a central square with two churches, the Anglican Church of St. Jude's and the Free Church. Unwin's first plans had included shops along the approaches to the square, but the plan was changed when – probably at the instigation of the chairman of the Trust – Edward Lutyens was brought in as consultant architect. He was perhaps the internationally best known British architect at the time and highly respected for his large country houses. He re-designed the central square to give it a much more formal layout. The churches were also to his designs. The shops were omitted, and the square "became a high-minded enclave of churches and public buildings with a fringe of smart houses" [19]. The lack of shops from the area around the central square meant that it never became the focal point of social activities that Mrs. Barnett and Unwin had hoped for. Unwin and Lutyens got on reasonably well with one another, but relations between Henrietta Barnett and Lutyens were never good and progressed from bad to worse.[3] In the end Mrs Barnett had him dismissed.

Lutyens was also responsible for the design of some of the grander houses on Erskine Hill leading north from the central square. These houses were set in pairs although Lutyens apparently had an aversion

---

3. Lutyens had in a letter to a friend described Mrs. Barnett as "A nice woman but proud of being a philistine – has no idea much beyond a window box full of geraniums, calceolarias and lobelias, over which you can see a goose on a green" [20].

Fig. 6.18. A 'William and Mary'-style Lutyens semi-detached house on Erskine Hill close to the central square in Hamstead. Entrances are on either side of the house to disguise the fact that it is a pair of houses and not a single impressive mansion.

to semi-detached houses. He overcame this by either placing the entrances round to the sides of the building, see Fig. 6.18, or by having one entrance in the centre facing the street and the other entrance at the side.

His choice of style was a far cry from the modest vernacular perpetuated by Unwin and Parker. Lutyens was intent on giving the central square and its surrounding buildings an imposing formality, and he chose the style of the late seventeenth century, a style usually described as 'William and Mary,'[4] whose foremost practitioner was Sir Christopher Wren (1632-1723).[5] Unwin, more adept at collaboration than Henrietta Barnett, worked with Lutyens on the central square and the end result was loyal to Unwin's maxim requiring architectural harmony of the whole picture.

WAVERTREE GARDEN SUBURB (LIVERPOOL) AND THE BUDDICOM PARK ESTATE (CHESTER)

Two smaller garden suburbs, Wavertree at Liverpool and Buddicom in Chester were both planned before the outbreak of the First World War, with building at Wavertree getting under way in 1910 and at

---

4. So called after the joint monarchy of William I and Queen Mary (1689-1702).
5. The use of this building style in the early twentieth century has sometimes been called the Wrenaissance.

Buddicom not until after the war.

The Wavertree estate was originally called the Liverpool Garden Suburb. The financing of the suburb was with a co-partnership scheme in the hands of Liverpool Garden Suburb Tenants Ltd. You may still find manhole covers and rainwater heads all over the estate bearing the initials LGST. The first section of the garden suburb was laid out by Raymond Unwin and the cottage-style housing of the estate bears his imprint, see Fig. 6.19, which shows the first house built,

Fig. 6.19. The first houses from 1910 in Wavertree Garden Suburb. Photographed in 2005.

a semi-detached pair on Wavertree Nook Road. The foundation stone laid on 20 July, 1910 is embedded in the wall under the bay window of No. 13. Unwin again used a layout with *cul-de-sacs* as at Letchworth and Hampstead Garden Suburb. One of the larger semi-detached pairs with a steeply pitched roof and tall chimney stacks reminiscent of Voysey or Lutyens is shown in Fig. 6.20.

In addition to paying rent the early residents of the suburb had to make a down-payment on the property to the co-partnership company. This basically excluded the poorer classes from moving into the area. Among the first tenants were clerks, printing workers, schoolteachers, commercial travellers, managers, a musician, a shipwright and a tram-driver [21].

Building activities ceased in 1915, where only 360 out of the planned 1800 houses had been built. In the 1930s the LGST sold its houses to the owner-occupiers and the undeveloped land was sold off to speculative house builders, thus effectively putting an end to further garden suburb developments. The suburb is now a conservation area and planning

Fig. 6.20. Large semi-detached houses at the head of a *cul-de-sac* in Wavertree Garden Suburb. Photographed in 2005.

permission is required for even moderate changes to a property such as re-pointing brickwork, renewing pebble-dashing or putting up a garden shed. Thanks to the stringent planning restrictions the pleasant atmosphere of the community has by and large been sustained.

In the early twentieth century many working class families in Chester were living in appalling conditions in damp, vermin ridden housing with shared lavatories and often no internal water supply. To alleviate at least some of the housing problems the city

Fig. 6.21. Semi-detached houses from c. 1920 on the Buddicom estate in Chester. Photographed 2005.

council finally decided to provide some respectable housing, as long as it did not become a charge on the rates. They commissioned Patrick Abercrombie (1879-1957) to design a garden suburb at the Chester suburb of Lache. The first plans for what was then called the Buddicom Park Estate (later just the Buddicom Estate) were drawn up in 1914, but building to a revised scheme did not begin until 1919. Abercrombie preferred fairly formal layouts and house designs, unlike the cottage-style images created by Unwin in Letchworth, Hampstead and Wavertree. Using a local architect to execute the detailed designs he produced terraces and semi-detached houses in what could be called an early nineteenth century 'urbancottage' style. The houses were of pink brick patterned with dark diapering as shown in the semi-detached example of Fig. 6.21. By 1922, around 160 houses had been built on the estate.

OTHER GARDEN SUBURBS

As mentioned earlier, around 20 garden suburbs were under way in England before the outbreak of the First World War. Many of these were reviewed by Patrick Abercrombie in the *Town Planning Review* journal in 1910 [22]. It is interesting to note that Abercrombie in his presentation did not emphasise the type of housing being built, ie detached, semi-detached, or terrace, but the plans that he showed in his review demonstrated a preponderance of semi-detached dwellings, a fair number of terraces, and very few detached

Fig. 6.22. Prospect of an avenue in Coventry Garden Suburb by Raymond Unwin [24].

houses. This is not really surprising, as these garden suburb estates were intended to house better-paid workers, artisans and middle-class tenants, but not the very poor or the very wealthy. The upper working class tenants were usually eager to move to the new garden suburbs when at all possible. As Abercrombie explained [23]:

> … it was hoped that the houses vacated by the better class moving out might provide accommodation for the occupants of the condemned houses.

This sentiment was often voiced at the time in connection with slum clearances and re-housing schemes for the poorest.

The ever-present Unwin was involved with the design of several of these garden suburbs, such as the one planned on the outskirts of Coventry, a mere mile-and-a-half from the city centre. A prospect of the planned estate is shown in Fig. 6.22. The

6

Fig. 6.23. The sole surviving semi-detached house in the Grappenhall Estate, Warrington (2005).

Fig. 6.24. An early twentieth century photo of semi-detached houses on Main Avenue in the Burnage Lane Estate.

Fig. 6.25. The same pair of houses in 2005.

housing style is, not surprisingly, in Unwin's vernacular idiom.

Warrington Garden Suburbs was created in north Cheshire as a public company in 1907. Its intention was to ultimately surround Warrington with a ring of garden suburbs. Two sections of land were acquired early on, the Grappenhall Estate and the Great Sankey Estate, to be laid out with 265 and 240 houses respectively. Today the Grappenhall Estate has all but been effaced and built over with new housing, but two terraces have survived, one bearing a tablet with the wording 'The Grappenhall Tenants Ltd, 1911'. A single pair of semi-detached houses overlooking the Manchester Ship Canal are also still standing. One of the pair has been somewhat brutally modernised, but the other still suggests what it must have looked like in early days, see Fig. 6.23. The Great Sankey Estate has faired no better. Most of the area is today covered by inter-war and post World War Two semis. A few roughcast semi-detached houses have survived from the early twentieth century, but their location cannot be recognized on the map shown in Abercrombie's article [25].

In south Manchester the Burnage Lane Estate was planned and built with some 125 houses, 94 of which were fair-sized semi-detached properties. All were in the preferred vernacular style of the age. Many were finished in local greyish bricks in conjunction with roughcast, which according to Abercrombie gave the estate a quiet and restful appearance. An early photograph of one of the semi-detached houses is shown in Fig. 6.24. Much of the estate still stands, set well back from busy Burnage Lane. Even the tennis courts and the bowling green in the centre of the development have survived and are well maintained. Some changes to the original plan were made, as well as to the finish of the buildings. Today most buildings have been rendered in roughcast, often painted white or cream, see for example Fig. 6.25. The greyish brick is hard

Fig. 6.26. Plan of Oldham Garden Suburb in the early twentieth century [26].

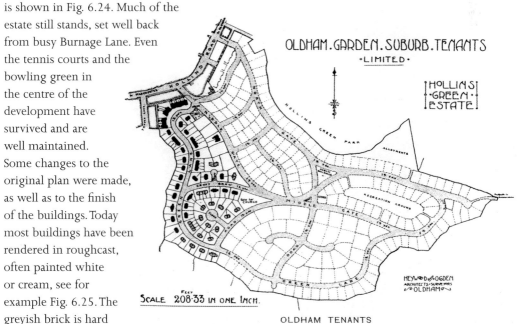

to find today; many houses have red brick elevations at ground level and roughcast above. It is a pleasant enclave.

In Oldham, an eastern suburb of Manchester, a co-partnership scheme had planned to build 600 houses on 60 acres of land in a garden suburb style. The area map is shown in Fig. 6.26. In 1910 only 76 houses had been completed, but the whole area was eventually built upon, although the road layout was altered slightly, and most of the houses seen today are from the inter-war period with many bungalows dominating parts of the estate. The land is on a hillside and from some places there are superb views to the south over open hilly country. A golf club is the suburb's immediate neighbour on the southern border.

Many of the houses shown on the plan are still there. The style is often the same as in the Burnage Lane Estate, but some of the Oldham houses do in fact show the greyish brick, see Fig. 6.27. Many are rendered and painted white, though, and some have pseudo buttresses reminiscent of Voyseyesque houses of the period. On the plan shown above there are twice as many semis as terraced houses.

In an historic perspective it is interesting to realise that semi-detached houses had now

Fig. 6.27. Semi-detached houses in Oldham Garden Suburb in red and grey bricks. None of the windows are original and the pseudo bay window sits uncomfortably on an otherwise unpretentious house, 2005.

come nearly full circle. They started out by being built by wealthy landowners for their farm labourers (see Chapter 2). Only at the turn of eighteenth century did they begin to find acceptance as homes for the middle and upper classes, due in part to John Nash and his Park Villages in London. Throughout the nineteenth century the semi-detached house was essentially the reserve of the middle classes and only with the development of model villages such as Price's Village, Port Sunlight and Bournville were the working classes given the opportunity to move into a semi-detached home; however, in spite of the good intentions of the model village schemes, a majority of the labourers still had to live in terraced accommodation simply because they could not afford the rents in the semi-detached houses. This situation did not change significantly with the garden cities and the garden suburbs, irrespective of the many co-partnership schemes that were set up on a non-profit basis.

Socially, the semi-detached house had nearly, but not quite, come full circle over the past 200 years; they were now at least within reach of the better-paid workers and artisans. However, in Edwardian

England the occupant of a semi-detached house was still most likely to be a middle-class person.

References

1   Mervyn Miller, *Letchworth, the first Garden City*, Phillimore, Chichester 1989, p.15; 57.

2   Raymond Unwin, *Town Planning in Practice,* second edition, T.Fisher Unwin, London 1911, p. 326.

3   Frank Jackson, *Sir Raymond Unwin: Architect, Planner and Visionary*, Zwemmer, London 1985, p.79.

4   'The Systematic Study of Town Planning' (author's name not given), in *The Builder*, 95, December 12 1908.

5   Mervyn Miller, *Letchworth, the First Garden City*, Phillimore, Chichester 1989, p.57.

6   Louis de Soissons and Arthur WM. Kenyon, *Site Planning in Practice at Welwyn Garden City*, Ernest Benn Limited, London 1927, frontispiece.

7   *Ibid.*, p.XLI.

8   *Ibid.*, p.XLII.

9   *Ibid.*, p.XXIV.

10 *Ibid.*, p.XXIX.

11 Steen Eiler Rasmussen, *London*, third edition in Danish, Gyldendalske Boghandel, Nordisk Forlag, Copenhagen1951. I reference the Danish edition, as the abridged English editions that I read do not include Rasmussen's sentiments regarding a generation of new satellite towns. The English title is *London: the Unique City*.

12 Mike Chitty, *Discovering Historic Wavertree*, The Wavertree Society, Liverpool 1999, p.74.

13 Mervyn Miller and A.Stuart Gray, *Hampstead Garden Suburb*, Phillimore, Chichester 1992, p.4; 13.

14 Raymond Unwin, *Town Planning in Practice*, second edition, T.Fisher Unwin, London 1911, p.349.

15 *Ibid.*, p.350.

16 *Ibid.*, p.352.

17 *Ibid.*, p.363.

18 Bridget Cherry and Nikolaus Pevsner, *The Buildings of England*, London 4: North, Penguin Books, London 1998, p.139.

19 *Ibid.*, p.143.

20 Mervyn Miller and A.Stuart Gray, *Hampstead Garden Suburb*, Phillimore, Chichester 1992, p.77.

21 Mike Chitty, *Discovering Historic Wavertree*, The Wavertree Society, Liverpool 1999, p.82.

22 Patrick Abercrombie, 'Modern Town Planning in England', in *The Town Planning Review*, 1, No.2, 1910, pp.111-28.

23 *Ibid.*, p.125.

24 'Progress at Coventry' (author's name not given), in *Garden Cities and Town Planning Magazine*, 11, 1912, p.229.

25 Patrick Abercrombie, 'Modern Town Planning in England', in *The Town Planning Review*, 1, No.2, 1910, plate 34.

26 *Ibid.* plate 47.

27 Beevers R, *The Garden City Utopia,* Olivia Press, Abingdon 1988, p165.

The inter-war years 1: Housing policies, council housing and speculative semis

"We regard it as essential that each house should contain as a minimum three rooms on the ground floor (living-room, parlour and scullery) and three bedrooms above – two of them being capable of containing two beds. A larder and a bathroom are essential."

Recommendation from the Women's Housing Sub-Committee of the Advisory Council to the Ministry of Reconstruction. 1919.

Council housing

The ten years following the First World War were years of political and social unrest, which inevitably came to influence state-initiated as well as private sector house building. The coalition government of Lloyd George (1863-1945) was in 1922 superseded by Conservative rule until 1924, when Labour came into a brief period of power before the Conservatives returned to government even in that same year. The Homes fit for Heroes slogan launched by Lloyd George in the final year of the war was universally accepted by all political parties, but putting the rhetoric into practice would have been difficult under the best of circumstances and became even more so under the short-lived governments of the early twenties.

It is outside the scope of this account to unravel the details of the numerous reports on the housing problems in this post-war period[1], but two documents must be mentioned. One is the Tudor Walters report of 1918, *Report of the Committee on Building Construction in Connection with the Provision of Dwellings for the Working Classes*, the other is the *Housing Manual* of 1919, which translated the recommendations of the Tudor Walters report into actual house plans [2], [3]. These, and a deluge of other reports and Acts of Parliament concerning the housing crisis – a deficit of 600,000 houses in England and Wales had been estimated – were put forward with suggestions for overcoming the lack of decent housing for the returning servicemen and their families. Irrespective of the elements of the various proposals, it is probably true to say that many of the documents strongly influenced the building activities of the twenties and thirties, and that three decisive results surfaced, namely that

1. State-aided housing became an important factor.
2. New residential council and speculative estates were created in the outer suburbs of almost every city and town in England.
3. The semi-detached house was the preferred mode of dwelling.

THE TUDOR WALTERS REPORT

Although local authorities had previously been given powers to build houses for the poor, very little had actively been done as there was no obligation, and state money was not forthcoming. The Government realised even before the war was over that a programme of state-aided house building would be necessary in order to cope, at least partially, with the housing shortage. In 1917, Sir John Tudor Walters MP, was appointed chairman of a select committee that was given the brief of reporting on the design and construction standards of housing for the working classes. Raymond Unwin was a member of the committee, and his influence on the recommendations of the report was crucial. In essence, the report appears as the work of Unwin.

The document was thorough, imaginative and innovative, and it came to influence suburban house building throughout the inter-war years and, arguably, beyond. The report's terms of reference were

---

1. Writers on the history of housing do not always agree on which committee work to emphasize. A useful discussion of the political side of the housing problem facing post-war Britain is given by John Burnett [1].

concerned with working-class housing, and it set out minimum standards for state-aided housing, considering health, comfort and convenience. It was the official design manual for local-authority housing, council housing, but its status was such that it also became a reference for speculative builders catering primarily for the middle classes.

With Unwin at the helm it is not surprising that the garden city and garden suburb ideals were well represented in the report. A housing density of 12 dwellings to the acre in urban areas was recommended (eight in the country), *cul-de-sac* layouts were highlighted for cost effectiveness, and a minimum of 70 feet between houses opposite each other across the street was deemed necessary. The argument for the latter was carefully explained in the report with diagrams showing the height of the sun in mid-winter, and elaborating: "When two-storey houses are concerned … a general width of 70 feet between houses should be regarded as the desirable minimum, otherwise in winter very little sunshine will reach the lower rooms." The argument is not entirely convincing. It presupposed, for example, that there would be sunshine at noon in mid-winter and no trees between the houses to obscure the sunlight. There were other weaknesses and the layout of housing along these lines tends to create an imbalance between the height of the houses and the space in between [4]. Nevertheless the rule became a largely unexplained, but accepted, code of practice throughout Britain.

Bearing in mind the suburban developments on the edges of most towns, the Tudor Walters report stated that the national objective was to provide "spacious suburbs with convenient and attractive houses designed by competent architects, with districts planned so as to provide the amenities of healthy social communities." It was more or less taken for granted that building activities would take place in the outer suburbs. The report's discussion of housing types concentrated on the semi-detached house and on short terraces, usually only four or six in a block, rarely eight. Flat dwelling, or tenement dwelling as it was then called, was dismissed in a short paragraph:

> For large blocks of tenements four or five storeys high, such as have been erected in our great towns and have been commonly adopted in certain Scottish cities, no advocate appeared, though it was admitted that modified types of such buildings might be a necessity in the centre

areas already partly developed with this class of dwelling
or to meet special conditions. Such blocks of tenements
are not dealt with in this report.

The report warned against the narrow-fronted, back extension
houses of bye-law times and recommended a variety of building
types with fairly broad frontages. Ideally, the report said, the
living room should be a "through room" extending from the
back to the front, lighted from windows at both ends. However,
the committee realised that this would not be to everyone's taste,
and admitted that a house with a parlour was "undoubtedly the
type … desired by the majority of the artisan class. It contains
only what is regarded by them as necessary accommodation
for the proper carrying on of family life." Justification for
the parlour was given by explaining the usefulness of having
a quiet room for studies, for the caring of a sick member of
the family, for receiving important visitors and for occasional
formal entertaining.

   The report suggested three basic types of house, or cottages as they
were unchangingly called in the document. The main features of the
basic designs were that

1. The smallest had a living room that also held the
    cooking range. It had a scullery with a bath.
2. The intermediate size had a living room with a grate
    for limited cooking, a scullery with a cooking range,
    and a separate bathroom.
3. The most expensive had a living room with no
    facilities for cooking, a scullery with a cooking range,
    and an upstairs bathroom.

The three basic types could all be augmented with a parlour.

THE HOUSING MANUAL

It fell to the Local Government Board (LGB) to provide designs based
on the Tudor Walters report's recommendations, which they did in
their *Housing Manual* published in 1919 [3]. The following year, an
extended pattern book was published by the newly created Ministry
of Health, which had taken over the responsibility of housing from
the then abolished Local Government Board. Over two-thirds of the
plans shown in the *Housing Manual* and in the pattern book were for
semi-detached houses.

One of the Ministry of Health's plans for a semi-detached house is shown in Fig. 7.1. Designed very much in the vernacular idiom of Unwin, the house is a three-bedroomed parlour type house in the best category. Although the remit of the report was the design of houses for the working classes, the tenants of the council cottage estates that were built in the twenties were largely of a higher income group – artisans, clerks, tradesmen, semi-skilled workers, all with reasonably safe jobs, even during those years of high unemployment.

Most of the designs in both the *Housing Manual* and the Ministry of Health pattern book were uninspiring, but it must be remembered that the cost of building was a major factor in providing new housing for the lower classes, and the Treasury had under the

Fig. 7.1. Plans for a semi-detached pair, adapted from Ministry of Health plan No.164, c.1920, see [5]. This shows a typical three-bedroomed parlour type house in Unwin's earlier vernacular style with brick elevation up to first-floor level and rough cast above the string course. The drawing shows a discrepancy between the width of the main windows on the front elevation and those of the plan. It would be up to the builder to sort this out. Hopefully, the wider windows of the plan drawing would have been chosen to lighten the rooms. Notice also that a space has been allocated to a pram.

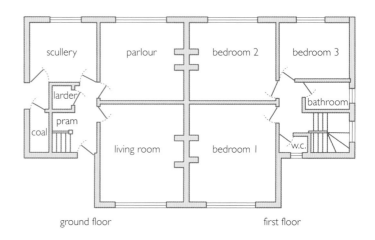

ground floor

first floor

coalition government committed itself to, in principle, underwriting the bill for the local authorities. However, in 1921 the cost of the Addison Scheme[2] as the state-subsidised house building programme was called, spiralled out of control the policy changed and state-funding stopped. By that time 214,000 houses of a high standard had been built.

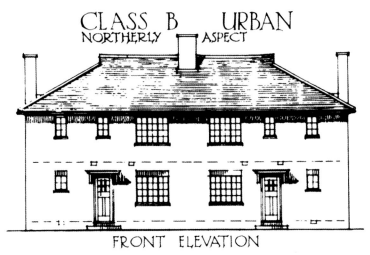

Fig. 7.2. A Neo-Georgian semi-detached design from the Housing Manual, 1919.

The majority of local authority estates were designed in a watered-down version of neo-Georgian, often with some elements of a vernacular Arts and Crafts style added on. The relative uniformity of the council cottages could not, however, aspire to the well-bred elegance of eighteenth century Georgian terraces. One twentieth century critic describes the pattern book designs as "negative, mealy-mouthed pieces of architecture" and continues "now every town and village has its estate of two-storied council houses with hipped roofs, multi-paned casement windows and tiny hoods over the front doors" [6]. Fig. 7.2 illustrates the point.

LATER HOUSING ACTS AND THE COUNCIL HOUSE IMAGE

In 1923, the Conservative Government introduced a Housing Act which completely reversed the policies of the Addison Acts. The new Act encouraged private enterprise by subsidising speculative builders and effectively discouraging the involvement of local authorities by stating that they could only be allowed to build if their building programme would give better results than that of private enterprise. The new Act stimulated private house building and at the same time the cost of building began to fall leading to overall lower house prices. With mortgages now being easier to obtain home ownership expanded, especially among the lower middle classes. All this suited the speculative builder well, because with rent restrictions imposed

---

2. Named after Dr. Christopher Addison (1869-1951), president of the Local Government Board and later the first Minister of Health. He was forced to resign following the uproar surrounding the costs of the state-funded housing.

under the First World War still in place, building to let had become very unattractive.

Both the Conservative Housing Act and that introduced by the Labour Government a year later gave subsidies to private builders. At the same time the Labour Government sought to restore local authorities to their position as house-providers by giving the councils greater subsidies and a promise of a long-term housing programme.

It might seem from what has been said that house building in these difficult years of economic stagnation and mass unemployment was totally dependent on state intervention. This was not the case. Although house construction at the lower end of the housing market was strongly influenced by the subsidies, the majority of the houses built between the wars were built exclusively by private enterprise. Of nearly 4 million houses built between 1919 and 1939, nearly 3 million were speculatively built, a little over 400,000 of them with some state subsidy. Broadly speaking, private, non-subsidised building accounted for more than two-thirds of all houses built in that period.

Fig. 7.3 gives a clear indication of the dominance of private enterprise building in the nineteen twenties and thirties. Although the statistics are for the Greater London area, the trend was the same all over Britain. Only in the first few years following the Addison grants to local authorities did the number of council houses exceed those built privately. From then on the construction of council houses remained fairly constant at around 8000 houses per year (in Greater London), whereas the speculative housing market took off at an unprecedented rate with massive contributions especially in the nineteen thirties. It was the ever-growing population of middle-class families that formed the economic basis for the speculative builder and the vast estates of semi-detached houses that sprang up in the outer suburbs of virtually every city in the country.

The state-aided building of cottage estates was heavily influenced by the Tudor Walters report, the *Housing Manual* and the Ministry of Health pattern book. It has already been mentioned that local authorities showed a preference for using a neo-Georgian style for their buildings, and it was not long before the insipid façades of neo-Georgian semis

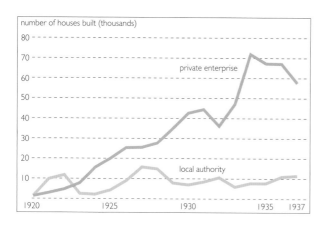

number of houses built (thousands)

Fig. 7.3. Statistics of house building in the inter-war period in Greater London adapted from [7].

and short terraces came to represent the style of council housing during the inter-war period. Following recommendations in the report, many councils also took to providing front gardens with a unifying element of a neatly trimmed privet hedge.

Prospective middle-class home owners were quick to realise that neo-Georgian houses and privet hedges spelt council housing and working class. Consequently, they were at pains to disassociate themselves from this style of dwelling in the choice of their own homes. The speculative builders were equally quick to understand the social implications involved in housing the middle classes, and the Tudorbethan[3] semi (to be discussed in Chapter 8) was a result of this effort to protect one's social status visually.

A bizarre example of the lengths to which middle-class home owners were prepared to go to protect their status and community is the strange story of the Cutteslowe walls. Cutteslowe is a suburb in the northern part of Oxford, where in the early to middle thirties two estates were built adjoining one another, linked by a pair of roads. One estate was entirely middle-class suburbia, the other was a council estate with working class tenants. Residents in the private estate soon complained of the nuisance of the dogs, children and graffiti from the neighbouring community, and they erected seven-feet high walls with iron spikes across the roads on the estate boundary. Though the council did its best to get rid of the walls, the private suburbanites were determined to see them stay, and it was not until 1959 that they were finally removed.

The inter-war speculative semi

The private building boom started in earnest around 1923-24, and over the next ten years or so the semi-detached house developed into the type of house that even today dominates nearly every suburb in this country. We propose to trace its history from pre-First World War times to its unchallenged position as the type, or style, of dwelling that was chosen by the vast majority of lower-middle and middle-middle-class families. It would typically be of two storeys with a hipped roof and have a parlour, dining room and kitchen on the ground floor and three bedrooms and a bathroom on the first floor. We shall call it the universal semi.

---

3. This is an artificial word derived from *Tudor* and *Elizabethan*, strictly speaking the period from 1485 until 1603, when the English monarchs were Tudors. Queen Elizabeth I (1558-1603) was herself a Tudor, but the style predominant in her reign is normally termed *Elizabethan. Jacobethan* is a term often used more or less synonymously with *Tudorbethan*, though it refers to the reign of James I (1603-25).

This was a time when terrace houses were unpopular with the middle classes, largely because they were associated with working class bye-law estates of the late Victorian period. The dream home for a middle-class family would be a spacious detached house in the country, preferably in a romantic cottage style, with a large garden for the children to play in. The semi-detached house proved a tolerable compromise, as it had been for previous generations of middle-class Englishmen.

As always, the speculative builder had his ear to the ground and was able to judge the requirements, aspirations and financial status of his clients, and he built accordingly.

The economic depression of the twenties and increased tax burdens on middle-class incomes resulted in a changed pattern of expenditure. Many families could no longer afford the large houses of the Edwardians and the staff that went with them. Public-school education of the sons of the family, which had been unquestioned for years, now placed a heavier burden on incomes. Over a longer term the average family size decreased, as already mentioned in Chapter 5, and by the nineteen thirties there were on average only 2.2 children per family. Wages for domestic staff had also become a burden, and a solution for many middle-class families had to be a smaller house that could be managed with little or no permanent staff.

In these circumstances the smaller semi-detached house appeared as the most acceptable and indeed desirable solution for the middle classes as well as becoming a mode of dwelling within reach of upper levels of the working classes. The potential clients of the builder were, for example, bank and insurance officials, civil servants, qualified schoolteachers and lower-paid professionals, and for the smallest houses the better-paid skilled workers such as fitters, printers, and engine-drivers. *The Evening News* published a weekly section of up to four pages entitled the 'Homeseekers' Guide'. A 1926 sample of the Guide shows 52 house types offered for sale; of these, seven were detached, eight terraced,

Fig. 7.4. Shrinking plot and house sizes for semi-detached houses 1830-2000. Notice the irregular shaped plots that speculative builders have to cope with in modern estates. The grey areas are either stables (1830) or garages (1935-2000).

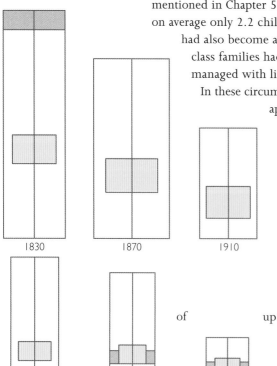

and the remaining 37, or 71 per cent, were semi-detached. Since John Nash in the early nineteenth century made the semi-detached house socially acceptable to the rising middle classes, the size of the houses and the plots of land on which they stood had shrunk noticeably. This is demonstrated by the illustration in Fig. 7.4, which shows the trend from 1830 to the year 2000. The Edwardian and inter-war semis both still had sizeable plots, but the house sizes of the twenties and thirties were significantly smaller than in Edwardian times.

The styles adopted by the speculative builders for the inter-war semis varied from mock-Tudor to International Modern with an endless mixture of pseudo-historical and modernistic styles in between. Chapter 8 will describe the layout and appearance of the universal semi in detail.

The placing of the entrance doors of semi-detached houses created a slight problem for the speculative builders. In most pairs the doors are in the further corners of the building, thus maintaining what might be seen as the greatest possible separation of the dwellings. Many owners and their wives, who were usually at home during the day, were quite content to not have to exchange pleasantries with their next-door neighbours every time they passed through their front door. The other possibility was to place the doors close to the centre of the building. This created the illusion of the pair looking like a single house, and it had definite advantages in terms of minimizing possible noise disturbances, as the main living rooms and bedrooms would be furthest away from the party wall. It also had the very practical and economical advantage for the builder in that most of the plumbing would be grouped around a central location. Many early semis used this arrangement, but in the long run the buyers preferred the alternative setting, and the majority of the houses are therefore found to have their entrance doors in the corners of the front façade. It does underline the feeling of privacy, the very middle-class tendency to keep ourselves to ourselves, "to go home, shut the door and pull up the drawbridge" as Kate Fox points out in *Watching the English* [8].

The front elevation of the universal semi was very often finished in roughcast or pebble-dash, which were first introduced in domestic buildings by the Arts and Crafts architects before the turn of the century and became a favourite with builders until the end of the thirties. Barrett and Phillips in their book *Suburban Style* maintain that it was still very popular in the nineteen twenties, but that its use declined thereafter [9]. This may be true, but nevertheless a very large proportion of nineteen

thirties semis are pebble-dashed and, as quoted in Chapter 1 of this book the semi-detached, pebble-dashed villas are more than the symbol, they are the suburb. The rendering could be painted white, often a later inspiration, or left in its natural cement colour. Brickwork was used on many houses up to the bottom level of the ground floor windows or right up to the string-course.

Inevitably, the huge number of semi-detached houses that were erected in the outer suburbs, with no special attention given by the speculative builders to the layout of the streets, created a picture of monotony. In his 1939 novel *Coming up for Air*, George Orwell places his insurance clerk protagonist and narrator firmly in semi-detached suburbia with the following lines: "Do you know the road I live in – Ellesmere Road, West Bletchley? Even if you don't you know 50 others exactly like it. You know how these streets fester all over the inner-outer suburbs. Always the same. Long, long rows of little semi-detached houses – the numbers in Ellesmere Road run to 212 and ours is 191 – as much alike as council houses and generally uglier. The stucco front, the creosote gate, the privet hedge, the green front door" [10]. Others were equally critical of the stifling repetitiveness of the new estates, where the inhabitants were "happy to walk up a thousand garden paths of the same length and breath and open the same front doors … they could live in the same back room all week and move into the same front room every Sunday" [11].

The builders were aware of the regimented dullness that could be the result of placing long rows of semi-detached houses up and down suburban streets, and they were eager in their advertising to stress the uniqueness of their estates whenever they could, using slogans such as 'no two houses alike' or 'each house individual'.

In his choice of location and house style the middle-class buyer had something of a dilemma. On the one hand he would want to assert his individuality, on the other hand he wanted to be part of a community in which his dwelling did not set him apart from his neighbours. The latter aspiration was fairly easily resolved by the uncompromising sameness of the universal semis, which gave whole streets and estates a feeling of bourgeois solidity. The individuality was helped, sometimes, by the builders who gave houses of the same interior plan a wide range of elevations, thus justifying their advertising slogans. Some houses were given gables over the two-storey bays, some were without. Examples of the several different styles given to the outside view of the universal semis are presented in Chapter 8. The owner himself would personalise his home by his choice of motif in the stained glass front door window, by his choice of paintwork, by his attention to the front garden and by the name he chose to give his home, for example Rose Cottage, Dunroamin, The Laurels, Belle Vue, or, more bizarrely, Insanity.

By the nineteen thirties the increasing popularity of the motor car forced municipal authorities to modernise the roads leading to and from the cities and to create by-pass roads in an attempt to take the pressure off the city high streets. The speculative builders were quick to seize upon the vacant land bordering the new roads, and rows of semis were built which in the ironic comment of Osbert Lancaster "enriched the landscape on either side of our great arterial roads." These ranks of houses lining the main roads came to be known as ribbon development – "as like as a string of sausages" wrote one commentator at the time. A Restriction of Ribbon Development Act was passed in 1935, but it was not until after the Second World

Fig. 7.5. Nineteen thirties ribbon development in Chester. The car park adjacent to a shopping centre is a recent addition. Jefferson Air Photography, 2002.

War that anything constructive came to be done. The inter-war ribbon development estates are still conspicuous elements of most major roads close to a city. Fig. 7.5 is an aerial photograph of such a development – in the words of a report published by The Council for the Preservation of Rural England in 1939 "Ribbon development is bad for the road and bad for the houses … it cuts off the view of the country and its amenities … it is monotonous, unsightly, unhealthy, expensive and dangerous" [12].

Houses of the period were not only criticized because of their blatant eclecticism, but for being poorly built. The disparaging term jerry-building was often applied.[4] This criticism is not really acceptable, as most houses were built to high standards, especially those that were erected by the major builders of the period.

The universal semi-detached house was indisputably the most popular house style built in the inter-war period. However, another housing type did receive some popularity in this period; this was the bungalow, which became especially prominent in areas where land was cheap, for example, in semi-rural areas and in coastal towns. The bungalow was essentially a detached type of dwelling, although semi-detached versions did appear, as shown in Appendix 2.

In complete contrast in appearance to the universal semi, very few houses were built in the International Modern or Modernist style. They never became popular with the English home owner, though modified Modernist derivatives were tried out successfully by some of the larger building firms. At the time these derivatives were popularly called 'sunspan' or 'suntrap' houses. The term Art Deco is sometimes now used to describe these styles. Modernist and Art Deco houses will be discussed in chapter nine.

---

4. Jerry-building is a term used to describe shoddy, inadequate or downright bad work. It derives from the nautical term "jury-rig", meaning temporary repairs to masts and rigging. It is thought to originate in the word ajurie, an Old French word for aid. Jerry-building usually meant skimping on materials or labour. In this connection the expression was first used in the nineteenth century.

References

1 John Burnett, *A Social History of Housing 1815-1970*, Methuen, Newton Abbot 1978, Chapter 8.

2 Tudor Walters report, *Housing Manual on the Preparation of State-aided Housing Schemes*, Report of the Committee on Building Construction and Dwellings for the Working Classes, HMSO, London 1919.

3 Local Government Board, *Housing Manual*, HMSO, London 1919.

4 Arthur Edwards, *The Design of Suburbia*, Pembridge Press, London 1981, p.106.

5 John Burnett, *A Social History of Housing 1815-1970*, Methuen, Newton Abbot 1978, p.224.

6 Arthur Edwards, *The Design of Suburbia*, Pembridge Press, London 1981, p.103.

7 Alan A.Jackson, *Semi-detached London*, Wild Swan Publications Ltd, Didcot 1991, p.64.

8 Kate Fox, *Watching the English*, Hodder, London 2005, p.213.

9 Helen Barrett and John Phillips, *Suburban Style*, Guild Publishing, London 1987, p.129.

10 George Orwell, *Coming up for Air*, Secker & Warburg, London 1954, p.13.

11 E. Reid, in a letter to the *Illustrated Carpenter and Builder*, 21 February 1936.

12 CPRE, *Building in Cheshire*, Council for the Preservation of Rural England, 1939, p.12.

8

The inter-war years 2: The universal semi, layout and style

"… the need to remain an individual within a crowd."
Ian Davis in "Dunroamin", 1981

Layout

The room layout of the universal semi was very simple and was applied to nearly all semi-detached houses throughout the period. It is quite possible that the speculative builders had studied the *Housing Manual* of 1919 and found that the suggestions included there were appropriate to their middle-class clients [1]. The ground floor and first floor plan of a small, three-bedroomed semi-detached house is shown in Fig. 8.1 and may be compared to the layout taken from the *Housing Manual* in Fig. 7.1. Variations in this layout were rare, the differences between the houses being primarily in the size of the rooms and the placing of the staircase. Larger houses might have an integral garage and space for a fourth bedroom. Many designs incorporated French doors leading from the back reception room, which was typically the dining room or family room, into the rear garden.

It is interesting to find that irrespective of the best efforts of architects and reformers over the preceding 50 years, the front parlour or best room has been maintained. It might not always be called the parlour on the drawings, but its function is little different from Victorian times. The builders might call the front room the drawing room, sitting room, lounge or reception room – terms that

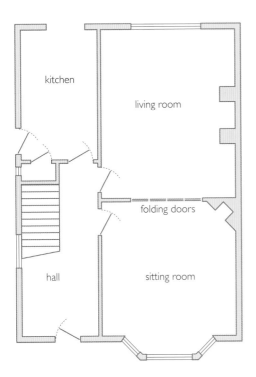
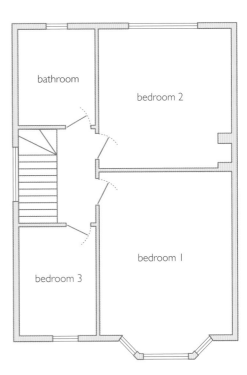

gave the room a slight snob-appeal and elevated it from the word parlour, which many middle-class home owners considered to be working-class.

Style

To many people, semis of the inter-war suburbs are associated with just one style of housing, the mock-Tudor or Tudorbethan style. This is not surprising, as it is probably the most predominant of the many eclectic styles that evolved over this period. There were many others, however, as can be witnessed by walking through any inter-war suburb today.

It was mainly through the imaginative efforts of the speculative builders, who needed to advertise their estates as having 'no two houses alike' that a diversity of housing types came about – when viewed from the outside. There were a few basic rules, however, that were followed religiously by the inter-war builders. These rules applied to both Tudorbethan and non-Tudorbethan styles. Nearly all houses had a hipped main roof rather than a simple pitched one. The houses were given two storeys and most had two-storey bays, whose windows served the front reception room and front bedroom. Only at the lower end of the housing scale did the builders omit the bay

Fig. 8.1. Plan of the universal semi. This plan was repeated ad infinitum, with only small variations, in tens of thousands of semi-detached homes during the building boom of the nineteen twenties and thirties. It was the outside view that defined the style of the house.

windows. A much-used design was to combine the first floor front elevations under an M-shaped gabled roof. This allowed the builder to sweep the outer sides of the gables low down to porch level in the style of Voysey. A pair of inter-war semis in this style was shown in Fig. 4.9 and further examples will be provided later in this chapter. The Arts and Crafts architect Courtenay Crickmer, who had designed houses for the First Garden City at Letchworth, used the M-shaped roof so often that it came to be seen as his trademark design.

We will suggest a grouping or classification of the inter-war styles as shown in the table below. Within the two major groups we have called Tudorbethan and non-Tudorbethan it is possible to identify four styles commonly used for the universal semi, classes 1 through 4. The neo-Georgian style houses, the suntrap houses and the bungalows complement the list.

Inter-war styles of semi-detached housing
The shaded areas are the non-universal type semis

Class	Tudorbethan	Non-Tudorbethan
1. Two-storey bays crowned with a pitched (saddleback) gable roof	X	X
2. Two-storey bays crowned with a hipped gable roof	X[1]	X
3. Two-storey bays without gables		X
4. M-shaped gable, with or without bays	X	X
5. Neo-Georgian, no bays		X
6. Suntrap		X
7. Bungalows	X	X

1) Rare

All the housing styles presented in the above table will be mentioned in the following sections with appropriate illustrations. As a supplement to the table a sketch of the seven basic styles of the non-Tudorbethan houses is shown later as Fig. 8.12. We begin by looking at the Tudorbethan or neo-Tudor style semis and discuss possible reasons for their extreme popularity in the inter-war years.

THE TUDORBETHAN IMAGE
In a historical perspective it would have seemed natural for the inter-war middle classes to have preferred one of the highly successful building styles practiced in Letchworth or Hampstead Garden

Suburb. This was not to be. It was the mock-Tudor or Tudorbethan house style that emerged as the single most lasting symbol of suburban living in this period.

Many timber-framed Tudor dwellings in England have survived, not least in Chester and in Shrewsbury, and their characteristic black and white façades were to become a defining feature of the mock-Tudor housing of the inter-war period, although in a much watered-down form. An original

Fig. 8.2. Late sixteenth century timber-framed Tudor town house in Chester.

Tudor town house is shown in Fig. 8.2. This particular building was in fact built as two houses, which were later united to serve as an inn, Ye Olde Edgar, but they are now again separate dwellings. It may possibly be a very early example of a semi-detached house.

The neo-Tudor style was also to become the most derided of the several house styles that were used by speculative builders in the twenties and thirties. The label Tudorbethan was maybe the kindest, whereas popular wit and the scathing comments of architectural critics used expressions such as 'floor-board Tudor', 'brewer's Tudor' or 'stockbroker Tudor' to ridicule the imitation half-timbering adorning the gables and frontages of these popular suburban dwellings, see Fig. 8.3. The question is why did this building style became so universally loved by the new middle-class home owners? How did Tudorbethan become the popular style of the universal semi?

Fig. 8.3. A cartoon drawing from 1937 making fun of the fake adornments of Tudorbethan houses of the inter-war period [3].

There are several reasons. One is the conservative, and sometimes confused, romanticism of the middle classes. The Tudorbethan house was an embodiment of their dreams of being lord of the manor – within their limited budget. But I think the most perceptive explanation was given by the critic Anthony Bertram, who, following a series of radio broadcasts on design in the 1930s, wrote:

> Probably the popular love for the Tudor, whether genuine or bogus, is based on fear and a wish to escape. When I was broadcasting I had many letters

that said quite frankly: "The suggestion of those quiet old days gives us the restful atmosphere we seek in our homes." This is self-deception, because the old days were far from quiet, but it is not surprising. These are insecure and frightening times and I believe that economic depression and the fear of war are the chief promoters of the Tudoresque [2].

We need to remember that it was after a horrific world war that the survivors from all social classes emerged to start a family and find a living and a home in peace-time Britain. For many, a mythological Elizabethan age and the Tudor past represented an age of stability and secure living. The home owner, living in a period where recent history had destroyed so many hopes and ambitions, and faced with a future where rumblings of a new conflict could be heard, needed to protect himself and his family in a house that at least gave an outward impression of unshakable stability. The timber-framed buildings of the Tudors did just that, and it mattered not so much that it had to be a make-believe construction.

The use of Tudor style timbering and Tudor style leaded panes in casement windows had been used already by Lord Leverhulme at his model village, Port Sunlight (see Chapter 4), and in Barry Parker's late eighteen nineties design for the mansion in Stretton, Shropshire, mentioned in Chapter 5. Mock-Tudor gables are a common sight in the Edwardian suburbs, as are leaded windows, oriel windows and herringbone pattern brickwork on the more expensive houses, see the illustrations in Chapter 5. Baillie Scott had used structural timber framing in his terraces in Hampstead Garden Suburb, at the 'Baillie Scott Corner', a visually pleasing design executed in his preferred Arts and Crafts style. Unwin had been most satisfied with the result, although he admitted that they might not appeal to people who like houses of the suburban villa type. In this, later history proved him wrong.

The neo-Tudor style was thus not an invention of the twenties and thirties, but it was in this period that it filtered down to the middle and lower middle-class housing of the semi-detached estates run up by speculative builders. The Tudorbethan house became the dream house of a troubled generation.

Since the first Daily Mail Ideal Home Exhibition had opened in London in 1908, the Tudorbethan style had figured prominently among the show houses on display. In 1910, one of the main attractions of the exhibition was a Tudor village with half-timbered cottages grouped around a village green. It was a fantasy, but one that (especially after the Great War) spoke to the patriotic feelings of a large number of prospective home owners. The Empire was declining, and the Tudorbethan image evoked a glorious and very English past. It was perhaps an unvoiced protest against the foreign classicism of Roman and Greek architecture and the ecclesiastical styles of Pugin's Gothic Revival.

Fig. 8.4. Tudorbethan semis (class 1) in a north London suburb. Built about 1905.

The architectural styles chosen by the speculative builder just before and just after the war were typically examples of suburban mock-Tudor, see for example Fig. 8.4 showing a row of semi-detached houses built about 1905 in a north London suburb, and Fig. 8.5 which shows a 1924 advert for a Tudorbethan semi, also in north London. Both designs have timber decorated gables under a small pitched roof. The earlier house is rendered in white-painted roughcast or pebble-dash, but quite likely it started out in its natural cement coloured rendering. The later house is rendered in untreated roughcast. The porch on this house is created by the jettied first floor supported on white painted brackets, which, however, would not be part of the load bearing construction. The windows still have an Edwardian feel to them, and the garden gate and chain fence are also typical of the period. Notice in the advertisement that the builder gives travel times by rail to London Baker Street and Marylebone; many home owners living in the London suburbs had jobs in the city, and easy access to rail services into London was an important selling point.

The inter-war suburbs display a very high percentage of Tudorbethan semis, but the Tudoresque contribution is many times found only in the sham timbering on the gables above the two-storey bays, such as shown in Figs. 8.4, 8.5 and 8.6. This is a fairly modest acknowledgement of a historical past, but on the other hand the Tudor message is displayed on the most noticeable part of the building. For some reason the builders only rarely used mock-timbering on the elevations above the front doors, although

GLEBE ESTATE. ROXBOROUGH ESTATE. HOOKING GREEN ESTATE.

SEMI-DETACHED Brick-Built Villas on this Estate, ideally situated within 3 minutes of North Harrow, 5 minutes West Harrow Stations. Train journey about 16 minutes Baker Street or Marylebone.

3 Bedroom Semi-Det. Houses from £750 to £875.
4   „   „   „   „   £950 „ £1050.
REPAYMENTS AS RENT.
Over 12 Years 19s. 11d. ⎱ per Month for each
„ 15   „   17s. 2d. ⎰   £100 advanced.
Ordinary Mortgages arranged.   Repayment £12 10s. per quarter, plus interest.   £200 down, balance as rent.
Electric Light, Large Gardens, Pinner Parish, Decorations to suit Purchasers. Rates 8s. in the £ per year.

A. CUTLER, *Builder,*
Estate Office, Pinner Road, North Harrow.
Phone—Harrow 139.

SAY YOU SAW IT IN "METRO-LAND."

Fig. 8.5. Early nineteen-twenties Tudorbethan semi-detached house in north-west London as advertised in Metro-land, 1924, [5], (class 1).

8

exceptions are shown later in Fig. 8.8 and Fig. 8.9. On the front elevations, as well as on the bays between the two floors, they often chose to apply tile-hanging as in Figs. 8.4 and 8.5, a fashion adopted by the Domestic Revival of the late nineteenth century. Apart from the gables, the front façade could be finished in roughcast or pebble-dash as in Figs. 8.6 and 8.7. An unusually strong application of neo-Tudor decoration was given to the houses shown in an advertisement by the builders F & C Costin in their 1928 brochure, see [4]. Of the eight semi-detached houses in the advertisement seven were Tudorbethan and only one was non-Tudorbethan. Most of Costin's houses had mock-timbering not only on the gables, but also on the first-floor bays. One of the houses was the rare class 2 type Tudorbethan house, where the hipped bay-roof itself cannot accommodate timber decoration, but mock-timbering had been applied to the bays. Other builders had different mixes of styles, and in the nineteen thirties there was a tendency to build many more non-Tudorbethan style houses. This was partly because of the increased competition, and builders sought to save on their expenses where they could; this meant that even sham timbering disappeared, and the non-gable style bay came into use more and more (see the overview of building styles in Table 8.1 and in Fig. 8.11).

Fig. 8.6. Inter-war class 1 semi in Chester with mock-Tudor gables above the two-storey bays. The Tudoresque contribution was very often restricted to the gables, but it is nevertheless eye-catching and imparted to the buyer the coveted hint of Englishness and a glorious past.

Fig. 8.7. A nineteen thirties semi-detached class 1 pair with a unifying mock-timbered pediment proclaiming its Tudor legacy.

Many semi-detached houses of the period were given a unifying pediment to make them appear as a single, detached dwelling; this discreet deception had been used freely in late Georgian and early Victorian semi-detached estates, such as in the Lloyd Baker estate and the Park Villages in London (Chapter 2). It gave the builder

Fig. 8.8. Semi-detached houses in Bexley, south London, with a very strong Tudor motif.

more space to promote the Tudor image as illustrated in Fig. 8.7.

Occasionally, the half timbering effect would be used on the entire first-floor elevation to the street, see Fig. 8.8 which shows a semi-detached house in Bexley, south London. Notice, though, the absence of two-storey bays, but there is the M-shaped roof sweeping down to become part of the entrance porch (class 4).

Only very rarely did the Tudorbethan form step outside its class 1 pattern (two-storey bays each crowned with their own gable roof or sharing a wide pediment, itself crowned with a gable roof) or its class 4 pattern (M-shaped) with prominent mock-timbering. However, a variation was sometimes to be found in a combination of a hipped and pitched gable above the bays, a small triangular

Fig. 8.9. An exceptional early inter-war semi near Chester. Such an extravagance of mock-Tudor is difficult to classify neatly in the classes proposed in Table 8.1.

8

shape called a 'gablet' being left just below the saddleback ridge. This space could on occasion just manage to show some vertical mock-timbering, barely enough, though, to qualify as Tudorbethan.

An example of a quite unusual use of mock-timber on the front elevation of a semi-detached pair in a Chester suburb is illustrated in Fig. 8.9. The building is probably early post-First World War and displays a rarely seen exuberance of black and white decoration on a private house. The builder might well have found inspiration in the many larger mock-Tudor buildings that were erected in the city of Chester in the latter part of the nineteenth century.

THE NON-TUDORBETHAN SEMI

Throughout the twenties and especially in the building boom of the mid-nineteen thirties the builders started erecting estates of semi-detached houses for the lower end of the middle classes, where the houses were devoid of mock-Tudor embellishments. Houses with two-storey bays topped by a gable and a saddleback roof were built in large numbers, but often without the mock-timbering of the Tudorbethan style as the builders turned to capture the lower end of the market and cut back on building expenses. Increasingly, the speculative builders experimented with the façade variations shown in Fig. 8.11 and found that they sold well, not least because of the individualism given to the outside view. Streets were run up where houses of several different classes stood side-by-side, such as illustrated in Fig. 8.10

Fig. 8.10. Advertisement by Wates builders in the late thirties captioned "Each house individual".

The following sections will demonstrate mainly by drawings and photographs the wide variety of inter-war, non-Tudorbethan semis, which together with the Tudorbethan styles still describe the outer suburbs of most English cities. A pictorial overview of the seven

Fig. 8.11. The seven classes of non-Tudorbethan semis described in Table.8.1. The first four classes are the universal semis. Classes 1, 2, and 4 become Tudorbethan by the addition of mock-timbering. Bungalows can also be Tudorbethan.

1. Two-storey bay crowned with a gable roof.

2. Two-storey bay crowned with a hipped roof.

3. Two-storey bay with no separate roof.

4. M-shaped gable.

5. Neo-Georgian.

6. Suntrap.

7. Bungalow (entrances on either side).

non-Tudorbethan buildings styles listed in the table at the beginning of the chapter is given in Fig. 8.11.

Class 1

Two-storey bays crowned with a pitched (saddleback) gable roof

As with the Tudorbethan style the non-Tudorbethan variations were seen well before the First World War. A pattern book of 1908 shows several examples that look like archetypal nineteen twenties semis, such as the pair of semi-detached houses (or cottages, as they were called at the time) shown in Fig. 8.12. This design was described as a superior type of cottage – it had at the time the book was published been erected at Tamworth in Staffordshire – and the pattern book took pains to describe the materials in some detail: "All walls up to the first floor level, also the front boundary wall, were carried out in the best sand-faced Staffordshire bricks with neatly rubbed joints; all

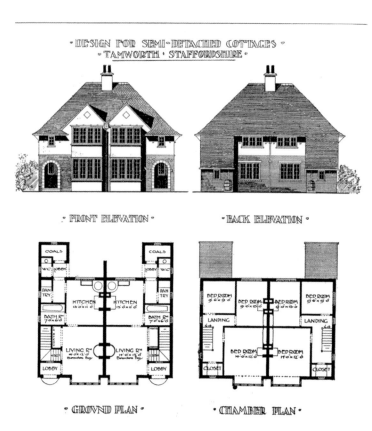

· DESIGN FOR SEMI-DETACHED COTTAGES ·
· TAMWORTH · STAFFORDSHIRE ·

· FRONT ELEVATION ·   **· BACK ELEVATION ·**

· GROUND PLAN ·   **· CHAMBER PLAN ·**

Fig. 8.12. Design for a pair of semi-detached houses at Tamworth, Staffordshire [6].

walls above, and also the chimney stack, were finished in roughcast painted white. The roofs were covered with the best Broseley tiles of a rich strawberry colour. All outside woodwork – also eaves, gutters and downpipes –were finished white. The inside wall, partitions &c., were finished in plaster, and all woodwork was finished green …".

Fig. 8.13 shows a row of typical non-Tudorbethan semis (mainly class 1) in Ewell, South London photographed about 1930, distinguishable

Fig. 8.13. Class 1 semis in Ruxley Lane, Ewell, Surrey, around 1930.

from the Tudorbethan semis only by the lack of mock-timbering (compare with Fig. 8.4). The same general picture is found in Edgware, North London, see the recent photograph of Fig. 8.14. The porches look a bit out-of-place but may easily be original. Fig. 8.15 shows a similar row in West Derby, a suburb of Liverpool. Here the houses have tile-hanging to the gables and bays. All the windows seen in the picture are newer (double-glazing). Those on the second-to-last pair have at least made an attempt to emulate the original smaller-paned windows, whereas the others have fitted incompatible large paned windows, which just don't agree with the nineteen thirties buildings. The side extension with garage on the house on the right with the projected porch also looks out of place.

Fig. 8.14. Row of nineteen thirties class 1 non-Tudorbethan semis in Edgware, north London (photo 2003).

Class 2
Two-storey bays crowned with a hipped roof

This style, illustrated in Fig. 8.11 (2), was extremely popular and may be found inter-mixed with class 1 and 3 semis in nearly all inter-war estates, especially those built in the thirties. A mid-thirties development in Ewell, Surrey, is shown on a contemporary photograph in Fig. 8.16. The hipped roof occasionally extended over both bays to create the illusion of a single dwelling, while individual hipped roofs to the separate bays maintained an illusion of individuality. This just emphasizes the challenge set by the middle-class homeowners to the speculative builders – to fulfil a dream of living in a detached house, while reality dictates that they share a party wall with their neighbours. The situation is basically unchanged

Fig. 8.15. Row of nineteen thirties class 1 non-Tudorbethan semis in West Derby near Liverpool. Notice tile-hanging to the gables and bays (photo 2003).

8

today, but the estate builders have shown new inventiveness in creating this illusion, although sometimes only by adapting designs from Victorian pattern books as shown later in this book.

Two advertisements shown in Fig. 8.17 show class 2 semis for sale in North London. The Reid advertisement proclaims (in a continuation of the part shown): "With a Reid house there is no such thing as monotony for they are so varied as to preserve the individuality of each and all." The builders were fully aware of the

Fig. 8.16. Mixed classes of semis in Ewell with class 2 dominating this picture taken around 1937.

criticisms that they laid themselves open to in the building of their estates, and they did what they could to allay the possible concerns of their customers. In North Harrow, Cutlers were mindful also of the homeowners' desires to escape to rural England and they promised "Ideal homes in North Harrow … for pedestrians who delight in rambles, the region might be called an enchanted ground." The enchantment was soon to become less easy to find

Fig. 8.17. Two nineteen thirties advertisements for class 2 semi-detached houses.

due to the building activity in this area all through the thirties, promoted also by the Metropolitan Railway that had extended its network far and wide into the suburbs of North-west London. Cutlers quoted train times to Baker Street and the City in their advertisement and they promised special financial terms to civil servants, bank officials, railway and insurance officials and the L.C.C (London County Council) Staff Association – a typical cross section of middle-class home buyers of this decade.

Fig. 8.18. Two class 2 semi-detached houses in Brook Avenue, Edgware, North London (photo 2003). Both houses in the top picture have each a quite elaborate stained glass window giving light to the staircase and hall, but these windows are quite out of balance with the rest of the elevation. In the same picture the added outer porch and the blue painted brickwork with white-painted pointing on the house to the right defies comment. The house in the other picture has its original door with amber-coloured panes and stained glass side windows; it looks much as it did when built in the mid-thirties.

The recent photographs of Fig. 8.18 show hipped bay semis on the same street of the North London suburb of Edgware, the archetypal suburb of the inter-war period, mentioned already in Chapter 1. Much has changed on the estate since the houses were built, and many of the alterations have been done with little sensitivity such as in the example at the top. Other houses have been left by and large as they were and carefully maintained. The photo at the bottom shows an example of this. In nearly all cases where changes have been introduced the original symmetry of the pair has been destroyed, and the intended placid (if boring) picture presented to owners and visitors alike is no longer in evidence.

Class 3

Two-storey bays with no gables

The two-storeyed bay had become such a prominent feature of middle-class housing in the inter-war period that very few builders ventured to cut costs by either providing houses with bays only at ground-floor level or by eliminating them completely and adapting a neo-Georgian style. However, especially in the late nineteen

8

Fig. 8.19. A proud housewife poses in front of her brand new semi in 1936 [7].

Fig. 8.20. An example of class 3 type semi with flat-topped bays. The picture is from a 1933 advert [11].

thirties the builders had to look very closely at their building costs to stay in business. The gradual cutting back on mock-Tudor embellishments has already been mentioned. By eliminating the gables with the costly extra roofing required, either the saddle roof or the hipped roof, further cost reductions could be found. The cheapest solution was to keep the bays with just a protective flat roof at eaves level. Thousands and thousands more were built in this way for the cheaper end of the market.

An example of this type of class 3 house is illustrated in Fig. 8.19. Other examples are shown in Fig. 8.20 and 8.21. While the style is not really displeasing, the bays do appear incomplete. Some of the quality builders of the period recognized this and improved the appearance immensely by letting the hipped main roof extend fully

Fig. 8.21. Another example of a class 3 type semi with flat-topped bays. In this recent photograph, the house with cream and green window frames is an unusually well maintained nineteen thirties semi right down to the original front door, the sunburst garden gate and the neatly trimmed box hedge. Unfortunately, the neighbours have not displayed the same degree of sensitivity (photo 2003).

over the depth of the bays. This resulted in the eaves becoming very deep, which, however, only added to the feeling of solidity and gave the houses a near cottage-like image, see Fig. 8.22.

The technique of incorporating the bays totally under the eaves was used extensively by builders of the suntrap houses to be discussed in Chapter 9.

Class 4

M-shaped gable with or without bays

This is probably the housing style that is the rarest among the four classes of universal semis that we have defined. Nevertheless, it can be seen on most inter-war housing estates around the country, either in its Tudorbethan form as was illustrated in Fig. 8.8, or in

Fig. 8.22. Class 3 semis with the roof extended over the bays to give the houses a more finished look as well as giving them a certain cottagey appeal. Both pictures are from the suburbs of Liverpool. The black and white photo is from *The Illustrated History of Liverpool Suburbs* [8].

Fig. 8.23. Nineteen thirties advertisement for class 4 houses by Costin.

its non-Tudorbethan structure as shown in Fig. 8.22, Fig. 8.23 and 8.24. The design was aesthetically quite successful, either with or without bays, and the roof sloping down to near ground level created a natural porch.

Variations

The speculative builders had to put in a lot of effort to break the monotony that was an unfortunate by-product of building standardised semi-detached estates; the buyers needed to be convinced that they were purchasing something individual in a sea of look-alike boxes, and the builders combined freely the four basic classes discussed above to create variety in the street elevations. New distinctive features were added whenever they were deemed appropriate and when they were not

Fig. 8.24. Contemporary photograph of a late nineteen thirties estate showing a mix of class 4, M-type houses with no bays, and class 3 houses. Heston Avenue, Hounslow, London. There were no garages to these houses, nor was there space between the houses for building one. Evidently, the estate was built to attract lower middle-class and upper working-class buyers. The solitary parked vehicle, which evidently pre-dates the houses, might even have belonged to the photographer or estate developer.

Fig. 8.25. One of many variations used to make the houses on an estate seem individual [10]. This pair of semis has elements of three of the classes defined in the table on page 160 and Fig. 8.11.

too expensive. An example of such a hybrid is shown in Fig. 8.25. The front door entrances in this pair have been moved to either side of the building. On the front elevation a porthole type window at first-floor level gives light to the inside staircase and an oriel type bay window has been added at ground level. The two-storey bays are capped with a small, pitched roof finished off with a gablet. The roof is a basic M-shape. The pair thus contains elements of class 1 (the gablet), class 2 (the pitched roof above the bays) and class 4 (the M-shape of the main roof).

The relative weighting of the four different classes of the universal semi

No studies have been found that have tried to assess the relative number of inter-war semi-detached houses of different styles; indeed, no studies have surfaced that have proposed a classification such as the one suggested in this chapter. The following comments must therefore be seen only as the personal experience of the author based on the suburbs of London, Chester and Liverpool.

First of all it is useful to remember that the nearly three million homes erected in the inter-war period were built by more than 76,000 builders, according to Oliver et al. in their book *Dunroamin* (1981, dedication note). Many builders put up maybe only a few houses at a time, while larger building contractors like Wates, Costin, Reid, Cutlers and Laing developed massive estates using large workforces. Some of the contractors employed their own architects, but, in general, there was in this period a feeling of animosity between architects and the speculative builder. The architects were

unwilling to accept that the speculative builder was able to satisfy popular tastes without any input from the architectural profession.

Houses erected by the larger estate builders sometimes displayed a distinct style and preference for one or other of the various classes described in this chapter. The houses chosen by the builder Laing, for example, are more than likely to belong to class 3 with the hipped roof extending over the bays. Laing houses could be quite austere with barely any decoration, but they set themselves apart from those of other builders by adopting a modified International Modern style and promoting the suntrap houses to be shown in Chapter 9.

As has been suggested earlier in this chapter, there was a discernible change in building styles in the nineteen thirties as the builders sought to cut back on expenses, and the simpler styles became more and more predominant. The Tudorbethan gave way to the non-Tudorbethan, and the simpler style of class 3 semis was seen more and more.

Regional variations seem also to play a role in determining which type of semi dominates in any particular suburb, but this can easily be connected to which builder or builders were most active in that area.

We thus have the following factors, all of which influence the style of houses being built:

1   Builder
2   Purchaser
3   Area
4   Year of build
5   Cost

There are most likely others to consider also. While the Tudorbethan style has been mentioned several times as dominating the semi-detached estates of the period between the wars, there seem to be significant differences between areas. Tudorbethan houses appear most numerous in estates from the nineteen twenties and early nineteen thirties in neighbourhoods that are clearly affluent middle class. The simpler class 3 non-Tudorbethan semis seem to prevail in areas which are less prosperous, in lower middle-class and working-class districts. These generalisations reflect only a personal experience, and hopefully a statistically designed exercise will be undertaken at some point to sort out the real situation.

References

1   Local Government Board, *Housing Manual*, HMSO, London 1919.

2   Anthony Bertram, *Design*, Penguin Books, Harmondsworth 1938, p.58.

3   H. Myles Wright, *Small Houses £500-£2,500*, The Architectural Press, second edition, London 1946, p.12.

4   Alan A.Jackson, *Semi-detached London*, Wild Swan Publications Ltd, Didcot 1991, p.109.

5   *Metro-Land*, 1924, facsimile edition, Southbank Publishing, London 2004, p.112.

6   H.B.Philpott, *Modern Cottages, Villas and Bungalows*, John Dicks, London 1908.

7   Greg Stevenson, *The 1930s Home*, Shire Publications, Princes Risborough 2000, frontispiece.

8   David Lewis, *The Illustrated History of Liverpool Suburbs*, Breedon Books, Derby 2003, p.100.

9   Alan A.Jackson, *Semi-detached London*, Wild Swan Publications Ltd, Didcot 1991, p.84.

10 Finn Jensen, 'Mine's a half', in *Period House*, November 2003, p.59; 175.

11 Frank Green, *Manchester and District*, Souvenir Magazines Ltd, London 1933, p.137.

The inter-war years 3: Modernism and Art Deco

"Whether it is possible to 'Go Modern' and still 'Be British' is a question vexing quite a few people today"
Paul Nash, 1932

Of the approximately four million houses built between the wars only a very small number were of the type that could be termed Modernist or Art Deco. The white-walled, flat-roofed houses were not popular with the English home buying public at the time; they were made fun of by cartoonists such as Osbert Lancaster in *A Cartoon History of Architecture* (1975) [1] and they have until recently been derided by the public, the architects and the media alike. Nevertheless, many if not most have survived. Houses in a watered-down version of the style were given hipped roofs and two-storey bay windows and became known as Suntrap or Sunspan houses (see Fig. 8.11). They were built speculatively as semi-detached homes in relatively large numbers and were well received by the middle-class clientele.

In this chapter, we will first look at the background of the Modernist style and go on to present a selection of semi-detached houses in England built to this idiom. Many of them were not uncompromisingly Modernist, but included ornamental elements of the Art Deco style. Art Deco is a term that is generally applied to the decorative and applied arts, the jazz-style that followed in the footsteps of the Paris exhibition in 1925 (see below).

Some speculative builders were cautiously modern and used a building style that was essentially Modernist, but without any decorative features and with a plain brick elevation rather than the crisp white rendering of the Modernist and Art Deco houses – this building style will be referred to as Restrained Modernism.

Modernism

It is probably true to say that the greatest single influence on modern European architecture in the inter-war years came from the German school of Bauhaus founded in 1919. One of Germany's leading architects Walter Gropius (1883-1969) had been asked to set up a new school of arts in Weimar. Gropius firmly believed that art, design and construction should be united. This had been the philosophy also of the Arts and Craft movement, but now Gropius was able to put his ideas into practice at the Bauhaus school, which attracted artists and architects from all over Europe. Gropius left the school in the late twenties and in 1930 Mies van der Rohe (1886-1969) took over as director. However, the increasing political attack on the school by Nazi Germany led to its closure in 1933, and many of its faculty members eventually fled Germany. Gropius and van der Rohe relocated to the United States to head architecture and design schools. They were to influence American architecture with their Bauhaus background and ideas of modern design.

The Bauhaus promoted the philosophy of form follows function which had been expressed first by the American architect Louis Sullivan in the late nineteenth century, although earlier Pugin and slightly later William Morris had designed in accordance with the same doctrine (see Chapter 3). Bauhaus architecture was very different from the prevailing building styles of the early twentieth century. Gropius, who worked in England for three years in the mid-thirties, introduced re-inforced concrete, glass and steel in his buildings in a manner not seen before. The designs demonstrated a predilection for asymmetrical compositions, cubic shapes, flat roofs and white rendered walls. Bauhaus buildings were unadorned and austere, but the horizontal windows, the liberal use of glass and the white façades did much to make the structures appear exciting – and modern. The structural and design elements of the Bauhaus group embodied the key features of the style now termed Modernism.

The white cubist houses of Modernism never endeared themselves to the house-hungry English middle classes of the inter-war years. Promoting the flat roofs of the houses as areas for sun-bathing, a sun loggia, was something of a travesty in the English climate. The flat roofs soon gained a poor reputation because of problems with rainwater penetrating to the upstairs rooms. The concrete houses were in general not adequately insulated. The beautiful, white-painted outside walls did not stand up to the vagaries of the climate and became streaked from the rain. This end result was unfortunately

exacerbated by the frequent lack of copings at the head of the walls, copings having been eliminated by the architects as being fussy and archaic. The reluctance of the house buying public and of the speculative builders to take on a largely unknown building technology with a poor track record was understandable. Things did improve over the years, when the houses became brick-built and rendered in favour of the concrete construction. With the addition of a hipped roof the modern style became palatable to the public, but a thorn in the eye of the purists.

Even before Gropius and van der Rohe moved to the United States the modern movement had by and large been accepted there. The programme of skyscraper buildings in major cities and the American's love of new technology were contributing factors. In 1932, the Museum of Modern Art in New York held an exhibition entitled The International Style, and the term International Style or International Modern became synonymous with Modernism. The expression Moderne was also used, especially in America, to denote either a pure Modernist or an Art Deco style. Jazz Moderne ands Streamlined Moderne became popular terms in America for the Art Deco style.

Art Deco

Applying the term Art Deco to the *avant-garde* architecture of the inter-war period is not strictly correct, but the dividing lines between Art Deco and Modernism have become somewhat blurred in recent times.[1] The name Art Deco was first used by Bevis Hillier in 1968 to identify explicitly a decorative style, the word being coined from the prestigious and definitive Paris Exhibition of 1925, Exposition Internationale des Art Decoratifs et Industrielle Moderne [2]. The exhibition programme required that exhibits should be 'modern', achieving the maximum of novelty and showing a minimum of traditional influence. The exhibition successfully brought together the artistic and the industrial, with exhibits ranging from architecture and interior design and furniture to textiles, jewellery, fashion and household goods. Distinguishing features of the styles exhibited were geometric forms such as zigzags, sunbursts and chevrons, and abstract patterns in bold colours.

Art Deco designs in the nineteen twenties were opulent and

---

1. Several important books on the subject lend support to the non-purist view, e.g. Patricia Bayer's *Art Deco Architecture* (1992), Ingrid Cranfield's *Art Deco House Style* (2001), Colin Hines's *Art Deco London* (2003), and most recently Alan Powers' *Modern: The Modern Movement in Britain* (2005) [3], [4], [5] and [6].

expensive. They were all about escapism – as were the Tudorbethan semis of England's suburbs – and for many they represented an unobtainable world of sophistication and moneyed living. Make-believe was an important factor in the hardships that followed in the footsteps of the First World War and of the Great Depression, and gradually the mass production techniques and new materials, such as Bakelite, brought everyday objects in a modern design within reach of standard households.

The exuberance of Art Deco designs was far removed from the new Modernist building style, which used plain white walls and large expanses of glass brought together in a strict, mainly cubist geometry. The Swiss architect Le Corbusier had designed a pavilion in the new style for the Paris exhibition. The organizers were shocked and displeased, however, and they tried to hide the pavilion among the trees at the back of the Grand Palais. Mies van der Rohe hardly faired better – his minimalist pavilion caused such dismay among the organizers that they wanted to build a 12ft high wall around it.

Modernist company estates

The introduction of Modernist housing in England is interesting. In many ways it followed the housing pattern set out by wealthy landowners of the seventeenth and eighteenth centuries, who had built small villages or estates of semi-detached houses for their farm labourers, as described in chapter 2. Later, in the nineteenth century, Victorian factory owners had established model villages for their workers such as Price's Village, Port Sunlight and Bournville. Now, in the twentieth century, it was the turn of the wealthy industrialists to provide housing for their factory workers.

The first substantial estate of semi-detached Modernist houses in England, and maybe the most aesthetically successful, was built at Silver End, near Braintree in Essex. The construction of this estate was commissioned in 1926 by F. H. Crittall, whose company had pioneered the manufacture of metal-framed windows. Detached houses in the new style were built for the managers of the company, while workers could rent semi-detached homes, also in the clean, white-walled and flat-roofed style designed by the outstanding architect Thomas Smith Tait (1882-1954), see Figs. 9.1 and 9.2.

The houses in Fig. 9.1 are very unassuming, but the semi-detached pair in Fig. 9.2 are more exciting with their V-shaped windows on the front elevation. The inspiration for these windows

9

is believed to stem from what was probably the very first Art Deco house built in England, New Ways in Northampton, see Fig. 9.3. New Ways was built for Bassett-Lowke, the engineer manufacturer of accurate model railway locomotives coveted by both young and old enthusiasts alike. In *Modern: The Modern Movement in Britain* Alan Powers records that the idea ultimately derived from designs by Frank Lloyd Wright (1867-1959), whom Tait had met on a visit to the United States in the early years of the First World War [7]. The

same window style was used on the detached houses, where the V-shaped structure was painted a striking green as were all the metal-framed windows. Thanks to planning protection the Crittall estate has been well preserved, although some of the houses are looking a little tired (2003). Many of the inhabitants do not seem to be keen gardeners and the front gardens are less tended than you would expect to find in an English

Fig. 9.1. Semi-detached houses on the Crittall Estate at Silver End near Braintree (photo 2003).

Fig. 9.2. An interesting pair of semi-detached houses on the Crittall Estate at Silver End (photo 2003).

2. The houses are still regarded as weird by local inhabitants. One gentleman at the bar of the village pub noisily proclaimed to the author that they should all have been flattened years ago (2003).

suburb; this is probably a by-product of the houses not being owned by the residents.[2]

The other company estate to be mentioned briefly in this section lies in East Tilbury, in a bleak Dickensian landscape on the Thames Estuary. The housing estate was built for its workers by the British Bata Company, a shoe manufacturer with headquarters in central Czechoslovakia. Building started in 1933 and continued right until 1950. Fig. 9.4 shows a picture of the estate of very Spartan houses. However, the houses did have front and back gardens, and the company was able to attract workers to the area from the more traditional shoe manufacturing centres in the Midlands.

Fig. 9.3. New Ways, the modernist house built for Bassett-Lowke in Northampton 1925-26. The V-shaped window is the prototype for similar windows on the Crittall Estate at Silver End. It is reputedly derived from designs by the American architect Frank Lloyd Wright.

Speculative modernist semis

Although the public in the inter-war period was eager to embrace ideas and technologies that were modern and that in one way or the other could create a sphere of well-being in an unstable world, there were limits to how far people were prepared to go, not least when it came to choosing house and home. The pure Modernist movement in housing was a case in point, even though especially the 1934

Fig. 9.4. Semi-detached concrete houses on the Bata Estate in East Tilbury, London.

Ideal Home Exhibition did its best to promote the white-walled, flat-roofed concrete structures of the new age. The Modernist house being a foreign import did not help its image in middle-class circles. Convincing the English house buying public that it was time to take on the brave new world of Modernism was an uphill struggle, predestined to fail. "The modern movement does not yet speak English" wrote John Gloag in 1944 [8]. Corbusier's edict that "the house is a machine for living in" never became truly accepted in this country. As John Gloag stated in his criticism of Modernism and Corbusier in particular, the Englishman's house

> is something more human and civilised and comfortable – it is a home. Despite a hundred years of confusion and vulgarity in taste and lack of education and judgment in design, the English home still shows the Englishman's mastery of the art of living a private life [9].

In the event only a handful of Modernist semis were built in the ten years before the Second World War. In no way did they make an impact on the speculative suburbs, dominated as these were by the universal semis.

THE ARCHITECT AND THE SPECULATIVE BUILDER

Apart from the poor public image of these houses there was also a very real problem for the speculative builder that Modernist houses used a technology of steel and concrete with which the smaller builder was not familiar. Architects had learned about the use of these materials in housing construction and most Modernist houses were designed by architects. Unfortunately, this was a period where the speculative builder and the architect were not on the best of terms. In 1920, members of the Royal Institute of British Architects, RIBA, were obliged to follow a code of practice, which effectively barred them from being involved in speculative development [10]. Suburban estates in the boom years were run up by the speculative builders with no input from architects, except maybe indirectly from trade journals and pattern books. However, the economic realities for architects worsened in the nineteen thirties and RIBA changed its tune. The minimum architects' fees adhered to previously were reduced considerably and efforts were made to demonstrate the positive contributions which architects could make to the design and building of speculative houses. In the introduction to his 1937 book on small houses, the architect Myles Wright was at pains to stress the advantages of employing an architect in the building process of smaller houses in the price range £500 to £2,500 [11].

As the speculative builders were eager to cut their building costs and saw the Modernist houses as potentially cheaper to build than the universal semis, a certain improvement in the relations between the builders and the architects did come about. Several Modernist semi-detached houses were built speculatively in the nineteen thirties, mainly – although not exclusively – in the London area, but the number was small. Several of these houses are shown below.

THE ARCHITECT AND THE AUTHORITIES

The avant-garde architects, who embraced the new technologies of steel and concrete and the minimalist design of Modernism, had also the authorities to contend with when seeking planning permission. In *The Modern House in England*, Yorke gave some convincing examples of the inertia typical in planning departments populated by architects of the old school [12]. Yorke illustrates by means of several examples the ease with which cottagey and Tudorbethan building plans in the nineteen thirties would be accepted "on the nod", whereas plans for a modern house in the best sense of the word were more than likely to be rejected, or modifications and new designs asked for. On a first submission the house shown in Fig. 9.5 was turned down on grounds of it being "injurious to the amenities of the neighbourhood" [13]. It seems unbelievable that a design of such beauty should have invoked the displeasure of the authorities.

Fig. 9.5. Detached Modernist house that was turned down by the planning authorities at an early stage. Thankfully, permission was finally given after a considerable amount of discussion and delay.

EXAMPLES OF MODERNIST SEMI-DETACHED HOUSES FROM THE NINETEEN THIRTIES

From the discussions above it must be clear that finding examples that show pure Modernist semi-detached houses is far from easy. Only very few suburban estates were attempted. One was built around 1934 at West Molesey, Surrey, with the advertising extolling the advantages of the flat-roofed houses: "This flat roof offers you a whole floor of extra space … your children can play in safety and in unrestricted sunshine … enjoy the peace of moonlight and sleep al fresco if you wish" [14]. Potential buyers were not enticed by the advertiser's efforts, and a year after their construction many of the houses had had a pitched roof added. Whereas Modernism had become an accepted style for the new factories that lined the main roads leading into London, many people did not wish to come home to a house that looked like a miniature copy of their workplace, and rural cottage or mock-Tudor remained the preferred style for home-owners.

Since the early part of the century the middle classes had become obsessed with healthy, open air living. The seaside and the sun figure prominently in the repertoire of posters such as those used by the main railway companies. Because of the supposed prevalence of sunshine in coastal areas some housing developers ventured to build Modernist estates on the Essex coast in Old Felixstowe and further south in Frinton-on-Sea [15]. The architect Oliver Hill, best known for his Art Deco style Midland Hotel in Morecambe Bay, designed the Frinton Park Estate, which was heralded as the first Modernist resort in Britain. Although the project never reached its intended goals, it did at one point form the largest collection of Modernist houses in England.

A small speculative estate was established on the Altrincham Road at near Manchester with quite attractive semi-detached houses in the Modernist style, see Fig. 9.6. Only few of the original flat-roofed versions remain today, most having been furnished with hipped roofs over the years.

Fig. 9.6. A Modernist pair of semis on the Altrincham Road at Wythenshawe, Manchester. The symmetry of the original pair has been destroyed and the modern glazing, different on the two houses, adds to the imbalance. The zig-zag decoration on the front wall is an Art Deco feature. Modernists did not really condone adornments like this (photo 2004).

Fig. 9.7. A small group of brick Modernist houses by Lubetkin and Tecton, 1936. Only the centre house is a semi-detached pair [16].

These latter day modifications are in fact quite pleasing to look at, and the climate problems of the flat roof have been eliminated.

A handful of Modernist houses formed the centre piece of an estate at Haywards Heath in Sussex, 1936. They were, unusually, finished in brick, but their minimalist cubist design was unmistakably Modernist, see Fig. 9.7.

Fig. 9.8 shows a photo, plan and description of a white-walled semi-detached pair in an uncompromising Modernist style. Also shown is a plan of the houses. The plan shows an interior layout, which is in essence exactly the same floor plan that was shown for the universal semi in chapter 8, Fig. 8.1. The architects and builders had not in this instance followed the teachings of Bauhaus and Corbusier by including an open plan layout of the downstairs rooms. The living room is just the new term for the old fashioned parlour.

In Fig. 9.9 is shown the front elevations of a pair built for Hampstead Garden Suburb. The houses are more spacious than the ones shown in Fig. 9.8 and the interior layout is quite

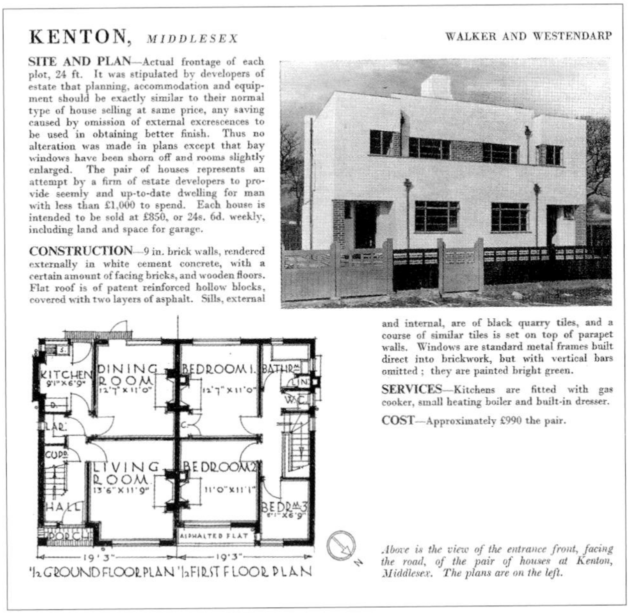

Fig. 9.8. A small semi-detached pair at Kenton in Middlesex with very clean lines [17].

KENTON, *MIDDLESEX*   WALKER AND WESTENDARP

SITE AND PLAN—Actual frontage of each plot, 24 ft. It was stipulated by developers of estate that planning, accommodation and equipment should be exactly similar to their normal type of house selling at same price, any saving caused by omission of external excrescences to be used in obtaining better finish. Thus no alteration was made in plans except that bay windows have been shorn off and rooms slightly enlarged. The pair of houses represents an attempt by a firm of estate developers to provide seemly and up-to-date dwelling for man with less than £1,000 to spend. Each house is intended to be sold at £850, or 24s. 6d. weekly, including land and space for garage.

CONSTRUCTION—9 in. brick walls, rendered externally in white cement concrete, with a certain amount of facing bricks, and wooden floors. Flat roof is of patent reinforced hollow blocks, covered with two layers of asphalt. Sills, external

and internal, are of black quarry tiles, and a course of similar tiles is set on top of parapet walls. Windows are standard metal frames built direct into brickwork, but with vertical bars omitted ; they are painted bright green.

SERVICES—Kitchens are fitted with gas cooker, small heating boiler and built-in dresser.

COST—Approximately £990 the pair.

Above is the view of the entrance front, facing the road, of the pair of houses at Kenton, Middlesex. The plans are on the left.

½ GROUND FLOOR PLAN ½ FIRST FLOOR PLAN

Fig. 9.9. Modernist semis in Vivian Way, Hampstead Garden Suburb, c. 1935 [18].

different, with a larger kitchen and French doors between the dining room and lounge or living room. At some time all three houses shown in the picture have been given hipped roofs of slightly varying design, but their original Modernist image is still visible. The centre house now appears as in Fig. 9.10.

In Gidea Park, near Romford east of London, a competition was held by the directors of Gidea Park Ltd to provide various types of well planned small houses at low cost. The houses were exhibited at the Modern Homes Exhibition at Gidea Park in 1934. Fig. 9.11 shows a winning pair of unpretentious, three-bedroomed semi-detached houses in class B of the competition. The internal plan was very standard except that the living room on the ground floor had become one single, large open-plan room extending the width of the house.

In a sea of universal semis in Upton near Chester a solitary white-walled cubist pair may still be found, see Fig. 9.12. Both houses have had double-glazing installed, thereby losing the streamlined,

Fig. 9.10. One of the Vivian Way semi-detached pairs as it appears now with an added-on hipped roof and other less substantial modifications (photo 2005).

Fig. 9.11. A winning pair of small semi-detached houses in the Gidea Park competition of 1934 [19].

horizontal effect given to the pair by the original windows, which most likely would have been by Crittall. The pair share a sloping roof hiding behind the ziggurat top of the façade – a discreet attempt at decoration in the Art Deco manner.

Fig. 9.12. Semi-detached cubist pair in Upton near Chester. The stepped, shared gable is a modest Art Deco embellishment (photo 2006).

What must be one of the most exciting and stunning designs for a semi-detached house in the Modernist style can be found in Lytton Close, a small *cul-de-sac* in Hampstead Garden Suburb, see Fig. 9.13. The houses were designed in 1935 by the architect G.G. Winbourne.

Fig. 9.13. Cubist Modernism, but with Art Deco leanings in the curved windows and in the balconies. Lytton Close, Hampstead Garden Suburb. One of the finest examples of a Modernist semi-detached house in England (photo 2005).

There are no external adornments, but the curved corner windows and the prominent balconies at first floor and roof level are Art Deco style features. The glass staircase tower seen leading to the flat roof is no less than spectacular.

ART DECO AND RESTRAINED MODERNISM

While exhibiting a refreshing departure from the Tudorbethan image of most houses built in the inter-war period, the Modernist houses did tend to display a starkness that was alien to the traditional middle-class house buyer. The individually designed detached Modernist houses built for wealthy clients could be truly impressive (see for example Fig. 9.5), but in general it was difficult to transfer the same feeling of lightness and subdued grandeur to the modest-sized boxes of suburban semis. The unique semi-detached houses at Lytton Close described above are, it must be said, an exception.

It was not that the English public was opposed to being modern, far from it. The charleston, fox-trot, jazz music, cocktails and fast, streamlined cars were in vogue. The Art Deco style invaded the household in the form of abstract patterned carpets and fabrics as well as in the vibrantly decorated pottery by Clarisse Cliff (1899-1972), or the more restrained designs by Susie Cooper (1902-95). It was not uncommon to find stunning Art Deco interiors hiding in a Tudorbethan shell semi. Somehow the architects and speculative builders had to transfer some of this joie-de-vivre to the outside of the house, balancing the frugality of Modernism with the exuberance of Art Deco. Of course, compromises had to be made in the process, but what emerged was a style of suburban semi-detached or detached houses which are recognizably Art Deco.

These Art Deco houses started appearing in England about the same time as the Modernist speculative houses, that is to say in the early thirties. The principle of creating an Art Deco house was in reality not very complicated. Each semi in the Modernist semi-detached pair was complemented with a two-storey bay with curved corner windows, as manufactured by Crittall. The bays nearly always appeared as a central section uniting the two halves of the building. Very often a hipped roof with deep eaves covering the bays was set on the flat roof. Windows with curved glass had been developed by Crittall to catch as much sunlight as possible; they became known as Suntrap windows and the houses themselves as Suntrap houses. Modernism remained intact in the white rendered walls and the horizontal emphasis of the metal-framed windows, but the bays and the hipped roof took away some of the "bizarre or Continental look" [20], to quote one builder's characterization of a Modernist house.

An example of a flat-roofed Art Deco house built in the mid-thirties in Hampstead Garden Suburb is shown in Fig. 9.15.

The narrow horizontal glazing bars of the Crittall windows and the horizontal, streamlined emphasis given to the houses by using bands or string courses of coloured stucco were defining features

Fig. 9.15. Semi-detached pair in the Art Deco style using a central double bay with Suntrap windows and a horizontal emphasis in the string course at parapet level and in the concrete finish over the windows and porches. Vivian Way, Hampstead Garden Suburb. The houses are well maintained and in nearly their original finish. The owners have thankfully agreed on the colour scheme for their houses, which adds to the stature of the pair (photo 2005).

of the Art Deco house style. Other characteristics seen on Art Deco houses were motifs such as chevrons (often used on the opening top centre window pane of the bay windows), sunbursts (on garden gates, on windows of entrance doors and garage doors), zigzags (on façades), ziggurats (above porches, on the roofline or on the garden wall), stepped porches (often in brick to set them off from the white walls), plain horizontal or curved porch canopies in white concrete, and also tall, narrow windows contrasting the overall horizontal aspect of the front elevation. Front door leaded panes with geometric motifs were popular. Houses with hipped roofs could be covered with standard reddish-brown roof tiles or could more exotically use glazed green or blue tiles. Many of the above attributes will be pointed out on the illustrations in the rest of this chapter.

In 1931-32, the building firm of Haymills erected a small estate of white-walled, flat-roofed houses in Ashley Lane, Hendon, North London. They were designed by Herbert Welch acting as

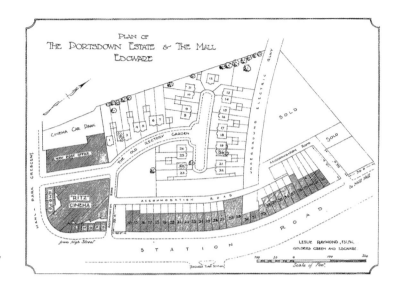

Fig. 9.16. Layout of the Portsdown Estate or Old Rectory Gardens, Edgware, North London, 1932 [20].

consultant architect to the firm, one of the early instances where a speculative builder employed outside professional help. The houses were not a success, however. In 1932, Roger Malcolm, a builder in North London, decided nevertheless to use Welch to design a new style of house for his Old Rectory Garden Estate in Edgware, see the estate plan in Fig. 9.16. The houses were to embody the principles of Modernism, but had to be sure of public appeal. The Art Deco house style with a prominent hipped roof was the result.

Fig. 9.17. Semi-detached Art Deco houses on the Portsdown Estate in Edgware. These houses, from c.1932, are among the earliest Art Deco style houses built in England. Many have retained their original Suntrap windows, but quite a few have, unfortunately, inserted modern sheet glass windows, which look totally incompatible with the stylish horizontal effect given to the houses by the original windows (photo 2005).

Roger Malcolm was at care to point out that his houses, though considered moderne,[3] were "not contrived with the frigid austerity of geometrical modernism" [21]. These houses were probably the earliest Art Deco style houses with hipped roofs to appear in England, see Fig. 9.17. Welch also designed houses for Hampstead Garden Suburb and there are several small estates in the Suburb that are populated with houses nearly identical to the ones in Edgware. The houses were moderately successful and other speculative builders soon began to copy the style.

Fig. 9.18. Another semi-detached house designed by Welch and his associates, 1938 [22]. The original colour theme would most likely have been white walls with window frames painted green.

Another design by Welch is shown in Fig. 9.18. The pair would probably have been finished in white rendering with window frames picked out in green. The roof is covered in green glazed pantiles in a fairly subdued colour compared with some of the roofs that were erected in this period. The house is a little unusual in that the bays do not continue to full height. The building demonstrates the sleek, horizontal proportions of Art Deco housing; the horizontal bands between the ground floor windows and the grooved rendering around the doors accentuate the horizontal theme.

A pleasantly proportioned semi-detached bungalow from 1938 is illustrated in Fig.9.19. The corner windows and the narrow horizontal glazing bars are both typical of the Art Deco style, which is even more strongly underlined by the sunburst pattern of the entrance doors. Abstract, geometrical patterns were a large part of the decorations adopted by the Art Deco generation. The opening of Tut-ank-Ahmun's tomb in 1922 had created a veritable Egyptomania in Europe; this, and renewed interest in the

Fig. 9.19. Semi-detached bungalow in the Art Deco style, 1938 [22]. Notice especially the sunburst motif on the entrance doors.

---

3. The expression 'moderne' was in England commonly applied to Art Deco and Suntrap houses and is still used in this way.

Aztec cultures of Central America formed the inspiration for new patterns of decoration. The flowing lines of Art Nouveau at the turn of the century were replaced with straight lines in rigid geometric elements of chevrons, ziggurats and sunrays. The late twenties catalogue of leaded lights shown in Fig. 9.20 gives an example of typical decorative panes used in windows and front doors of Art Deco buildings of the thirties.

An Art Deco semi-detached house that exhibits several of the features mentioned above is shown in Fig. 9.21: white rendered walls, Suntrap windows, chevron symbol on the opening panes in the bay windows, a horizontal band on the façade with a decorative wavy line, the sunburst garden gate and the ziggurat style garden walls.

The white-walled elevations taken over from the Modernist movement were the most common finish to Art Deco buildings, but some builders preferred to have their houses standing in plain brick. In the competitive years of the nineteen thirties many small builders had to close business or join forces with other companies. Major companies became household names such as Costain, Wates, Taylor-Woodrow, New Ideal Homestead, Wimpey and Laing. Of these, especially Laing became well known for his fairly austere houses with brick elevations.

In 1904, John William Laing took over the running of the building firm started by his father and, after the War, he obtained several contracts for building municipal housing. His housing designs complied with the Government's Housing Manual of 1919 and the firm came personally recommended by Raymond Unwin. The company moved its headquarters from Carlisle to Mill Hill in north London in 1926 where it was well placed to deal with the building boom of semi-detached houses in London's new outer suburbs.

John Laing's own architect, David Adam, was responsible for many of the estate designs in the thirties, but Laing involved himself in most details. Early on, he introduced cavity walls, effective damp courses and deep concrete foundations and insisted untiringly on the best-quality materials and workmanship. Laing

Fig. 9.20. Window designs in common use in Art Deco houses of the nineteen thirties.

had some very personal ideas concerning how his houses should appear. He did not accept roughcast, because it disguised the quality of the bricks. He wanted windowsills in the downstairs rooms to be low, so that anyone sitting inside could look out. On the first floor the sills should be higher up to keep small children safe. He considered curving staircases to be dangerous. As far as possible every house should have a sunny aspect: David Adam had at one point to totally redesign his layout for an estate at Canons

Fig. 9.21. Art Deco house from the late thirties showing several typical features: Suntrap windows, chevrons on small ventilation panes, decorative brickwork on porch, decorative horizontal band above ground floor windows, sunburst garden gate and ziggurat motif on garden wall [24].

Park because Laing did not think that enough houses had a sunny and attractive outlook.

Laing believed in value for money and simple designs with no gimmickry. This could have led to estates of Modernist houses, but Laing was a very practical builder, tuned to the tastes of the house-buying public, and he chose a different approach. He did not wish to compete with the Tudorbethan builders in their own field, nor did he wish to follow the Art Deco penchant for decorative effects that to his mind served no practical purpose. His favourite house designs might reasonably be called Restrained Modernist. It was a building style that vacillated between the sparseness of Modernism

and the softer, decorative Art Deco with its curved bay windows. A hipped roof was an essential part of Laing's designs, as were the brick elevations such as seen on the cautiously modern semi-detached house from 1936 in Fig. 9.22.

Over the past centuries we have seen just about every possible revival of building styles, starting with neo-Classicism and later continuing with Gothic Revival, Queen Anne, vernacular and Georgian revivals bringing us into the twentieth century. Mock-Tudor, more a romantic declaration than a revival, captured our hearts in the inter-war period and never totally left us. Now, 70 years after the zenith of Modernist housing in England it is not unreasonable to ask if we ever will see a Modernist Revival in domestic housing. It may never happen, but it is a question that will be considered in Chapter 11.

Fig. 9.22. John Laing semi-detached pair from 1936 with wide eaves and Suntrap bay windows. An essay in Restrained Modernism. The string course above the ground floor windows continues over the porches to define the simple, but elegant canopies [25].

References

1   Osbert Lancaster, *A Cartoon History of Architecture*, John Murray, London 1975.

2   Bevis Hillier, *Art Deco of the 20s and 30s*, Studio Vista, London and New York, 1968.

3   Patricia Bayer, *Art Deco Architecture*, Thames & Hudson, London 1992.

4   Ingrid Cranfield, *Art Deco House Style*, David & Charles, Newton Abbot, 2001.

5   Colin Hines, *Art Deco London*, Park House Press, Twickenham, 2003.

6   Alan Powers, *Modern: The Modern Movement in Britain*, Merrell, London 2005.

7   *Ibid.*, p.61.

8   John Gloag, *The Englishman's Castle*, Eyre & Spottiswoode, London 1944, p.163.

9   *Ibid.*

10 Arthur Edwards, *The Design of Suburbia*, Pembridge Press, London 1981, pp.132-4.

11 H. Myles Wright, *Small Houses £500-£2,500*, The Architectural Press, second edition, London 1946, pp.7-20.

12 F.R.S. Yorke, *The Modern House in England*, The Architectural Press, third edition, London 1948, pp.9-18.

13 *Ibid.*, pp.15-17.

14 Greg Stevenson, *The 1930s Home*, Shire Publications, Princes Risborough 2000, p.14.

15 Jean Gardner, *Houses of the Art Deco Years*, Braiswick, Felixstowe 2004, p.74.

16 F.R.S. Yorke, *The Modern House in England*, The Architectural Press, third edition, London 1948, p.47.

17 H. Myles Wright, *Small Houses £500-£2,500*, The Architectural Press, second edition, London 1946, p.84.

18 *Ibid.*, p.50.

19 *Ibid.*, p.108.

20 MoDA, *Little Palaces, house and home in the inter-war suburbs*, Middlesex University Press, Barnet 2003, p.28.

21 Alan A. Jackson, *Semi-detached London*, Wild Swan Publications Ltd, Didcot 1991, p.211.

22 John Prizeman, *Houses of Britain: The Outside View*, Quiller Press, London 2003, p.39.

23 *Ibid.*, p.94.

24 Paul Oliver et.al., *Dunroamin, the Suburban Semi and its Enemies*, Barrie & Jenkins, London 1981, p.185.

25 Berry Ritchie, *The Good Builder*, the John Laing Story, James & James, London 1997, p.72.

10 Post Second World War developments (1945-90)

"Since the Second World War housing has been through a rollercoaster change unprecedented in the previous 150 years"
Rudlin and Falk, 1999

There was a drastic shortage of housing after the Second World War, when enemy bombing had destroyed some 500,000 homes and severely damaged a further 250,000 in or near major cities [1].[1] Building had all but stopped during the war, but as in the First World War the government had established several committees to plan for the housing situation when peace came. In 1945, the coalition government pledged a separate house for every family that wished to have one.

Notably three reports were to influence house building in post-war Britain. For the capital, the Greater London Plan of 1944 was prepared by Patrick Abercrombie, while The Dudley Report from the same year and the Parker-Morris Report from 1961 addressed the issues of town planning and housing on a broader basis. Although the impact of these reports was felt most strongly on public or municipal housing, in essence council housing, their findings did to a degree influence also speculative building in the second half of the twentieth century.

We will briefly consider the three reports in the context of semi-detached housing and the role of the reports in shaping the post-war suburbs of this country.

---

1. Some authors give considerably higher figures – up to two million homes destroyed [2].

The Abercrombie plan

To prepare for the resurrection of London after the war, Abercrombie had been given the task of finding ways to redistribute the existing population to reduce the pre-war congestion in the built-up areas of Greater London. He defined four rings around Central London as shown in Fig. 10.1: the urban ring, the suburban ring, the green belt ring and the outer country ring [3]. In Chapter 5 of this book we defined four slightly different rings or zones. Referring to Fig. 5.1, the city centre, the inner city and the inner suburbs correspond to the inner urban ring defined by Abercrombie; the zone of outer suburbs in Fig. 5.1 is the suburban ring of Fig. 10.1. Abercrombie's third ring from the centre is the green belt ring. This ring was intended to act as a barrier against the sprawl of the existing London suburbs that were poised to expand even further into the countryside.

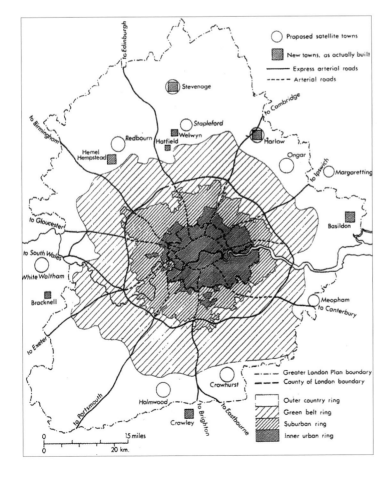

Fig. 10.1. New Towns or satellite towns around London. From the Abercrombie *Greater London Plan*, 1944 [35].

Abercrombie's solution was one of new urban communities, new towns, outside the green belt. The towns could either be planned afresh in rural or semi-rural areas, or they could be placed around existing towns. These new towns or satellite towns were planned to accommodate a mixture of social classes and a range of industries that would provide employment for the inhabitants. It was a return to the philosophy of Ebenezer Howard and the garden city movement.

In 1945, the new Labour Government appointed Lewis Silkin MP, as Minister of Town and Country Planning, and within weeks proposals for new towns were ready. In spite of opposition, the New Towns Act was given royal assent in August 1946 and the Government now had the power to name possible sites for new towns. Stevenage was England's first new town, designated as such in November of the same year. Between 1946 and 1970, 21 new towns were planned in England, eight of which were the localities shown in Fig. 10.1. The other new towns were geographically located north of London and close to industrially important cities such as Birmingham, Manchester, Liverpool and Newcastle. Milton Keynes, the last major New Town, was started in 1970 and expected to grow to 250,000 inhabitants. In 2005, the number was close to 220,000. Most new towns were planned much smaller, between 50,000 and 80,000 inhabitants.

The creation of new towns and their housing estates was important to the Labour Government and a high priority was given to public housing. It was decided at an early stage that the new towns were to be created by Government-sponsored corporations financed by the Exchequer.

In the early years speculative building was actively discouraged by restricting licences for private building to only one in five licences issued. These controls were finally abandoned in 1954 under the Conservative Government, who encouraged private building enterprise. There followed a surge in speculative building, which peaked in the late sixties, see Fig. 10.2.[2] In the seventies, the public and private sector contributed nearly equally to the housing output, but from the early eighties public sector housing decreased as private housing increased, until private enterprise in 2005 accounted for nearly 86 per cent of the houses being built.

---

2. Please note that the statistics shown illustrate the trend in house building and are taken from different sources. The absolute figures should, if necessary, be confirmed by consulting official Government statistics.

The statistics of Fig. 10.2 do not include the contribution made by housing associations. These associations have existed since the mid-nineteenth century, but their house-building role was limited until council housing was reduced so radically in the nineteen-eighties. Before the Housing Act of 1988, associations could receive large grants for building, but they were under strict rent control and limited in the type of housing they were allowed to build. The Housing Act changed this. Development risks were transferred to the associations, and building was financed through a combination of private investment and substantially reduced government grants. By 1990, housing associations were contributing nearly as many completions as the public sector, and by the mid-nineties they had practically taken over the role previously performed by the local authorities.

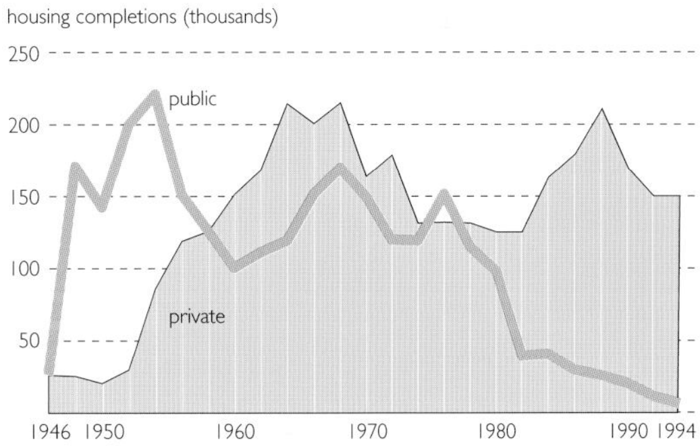

Buildings in the new towns were mostly to a high standard. In terms of numbers their contribution to the housing market was, however, negligible. In *A Social History of Housing* [5] Burnett reported that only 216,000 houses had been built by 1972. Many of the new towns were considered successful as social experiments, but the provision of shops, schools and other amenities did not always keep up with the housing. Burnett, *op.cit.*, summarised his review by stating: "No brave new world had emerged from the new towns, no radical shift in the established pattern of cities and suburbs."

For some reason promoters of the new town concept were loath even to mention the word suburb when discussing the residential areas of the town. Theirs was an urban perspective, and suburbs in post-war England had for many years been derided by the architects and critics. This was especially true of the massive, inter-war speculative estates of predominantly semi-detached houses. Also the new towns received their share of criticism, even as they were being built. In an article titled 'Failure of the New Towns' in *The Architectural Review* J.M. Richards dismissed the new towns as the building of suburbs dignified by the name of towns [6]. Edwards took a similarly critical view when stating that the new towns are "less like towns than vast overgrown villages" [7]. Later, a critical appraisal of newly built speculative estates in Milton Keynes concluded: "The most modern town in Britain has a housing stock which reads like a trip down memory lane" [8]. Some of the semi-detached houses had

Fig. 10.2. Public and private sector housing completions 1946-80. Adapted from [1] and [4]. Private enterprise housing did not take off until the Conservative Government in 1954 abolished the restrictive building licenses imposed by the previous Labour Government shortly after the war.

housing completions (thousands)

porches with pseudo-classical columns; some houses had thatched roofs.

In spite of all the efforts spent in dissociating new towns from traditional suburbs they do appear, certainly to an outsider, to comply with the criteria for suburbs – they are mostly residential areas built outside the nucleus of a town. It is just unfortunate that suburban living in the twentieth century became the object of ridicule and scorn from urbanites and social and architectural critics alike. Somehow suburban life must suit the English. Surveys show that most people aspire to suburban living even with the renewed encouragement now being given to city centre living [9].

As the new towns were publicly funded it is not surprising that their communities had a definite council estate atmosphere. The use of *cul-de-sacs* in the style of Unwin and a street layout that followed the contours of the land should have created a pleasant and civilised finished product. The architects of the new towns had stressed the social mixture and the natural presence of a neighbourhood spirit. In the event few, if any, of the developments could live up to the ambitions of the planners, either in terms of their architecture, street layout or social qualities. The word that springs to mind when walking the streets of some our post-war new towns is joyless. This is not because of a lack of architectural merit as far as the individual buildings are concerned, but the areas carry the unmistakable stamp of oppressive officialdom. The building plots are too small, the spaces back and front do not give garden lovers any opportunity for inspired creativity. The grass verges, the trees and the open spaces appear contrived and not a natural part of the housing landscape. Even the pubs, if they can be found, sit uncomfortably in the townscape. A town centre is often hard to find, and shopping has by and large been moved out of the main dwelling area to mammoth shopping malls.

The new towns were founded on Ebenezer Howard's ideas, but the communities that evolved did not measure up to the first garden cities of Letchworth and Welwyn. Even the speculators' semi-detached suburbs of the inter-war period appear today to be more sociable and desirable places to live in.

The buildings in new towns were often semi-detached, but with a fair proportion of terraces and occasionally some low-rise flats. Examples of quite different architectural styles from Runcorn New Town are given in Fig. 10.3. On the left are nineteen-thirties style semis with hipped roofs, on the right an example of a non-traditional semi-detached pair.

Runcorn New Town was the setting for an avant-garde prize-winning experimental estate in the nineteen-seventies. Designed by James Stirling in the Southgate area of Runcorn, it attracted enormous attention with its multi-coloured cladding and round windows. The buildings were of concrete, exposed at its roughest, and the architectural terms Brutalism or New Brutalism were aptly applied to Stirling's structures. Three-storey town houses and several blocks of flats were built, but living conditions were poor, and it was not long before the residents were campaigning for their demolition. The authorities eventually agreed to this and in consultation with the community a new estate was planned. This was, not surprisingly, a much more traditional suburban layout with rather non-descript semi-detached houses as shown in Fig. 10.4. The houses seem quite spacious with typically three or four bedrooms, but garden sizes are small.

Fig. 10.3. Left: Traditional hipped roof semis in Runcorn New Town. Right: A more adventurous semi-detached pair, also in Runcorn New Town (photo 2005).

Fig. 10.4. Traditional semi-detached houses in the Hallwood Park Estate of Runcorn New Town. These houses took the place of the avant-garde dwellings on the Southgate Estate that were demolished following vigorous campaigning from the residents (photo 2006).

The Dudley Report

As in 1918, the Government had in the last year of World War Two prepared a housing report which was to set the standards for public housing in the early part of the post-war era. The Dudley Report [10], published for the Ministry of Health in 1944, took much the same approach as the Tudor-Walters Report of 1918. Two main issues discussed were the question of internal space standards and the importance of street layout and its social implications. The report recommended increasing the house sizes from an average of 750-850sq ft for a three-bedroomed house to a minimum of 900sq ft. The report suggested 'social units' or 'neighbourhoods' with a population of between 5,000 and 10,000 organised around a well-defined centre. Due consideration was to be given to car parking and a system of safe pedestrian walkways. In retrospect, it appears sometimes that the architects and planners of Britain's new towns had surged ahead without consulting The Dudley Report. Indeed, a careful study of Raymond Unwin's seminal *Town Planning in Practice* (1911) could have averted many of the unfortunate townscapes of post-war Britain [11].

With reference to semi-detached housing the report maintained that the advantages attributed to the semi-detached configuration, for example that the sound insulation was better than in terraced houses, were largely illusory. The only concession given to the semi-detached house by The Dudley Report was the ease with which an approach to the back door can be provided. For all its social considerations and logical arguments the report failed to take into account that the semi-detached house for many people represented the ultimately desirable dwelling, not only for the middle classes but increasingly also for the upper levels of the working classes.

Hopes for decent and spacious public housing ran high in the wake of The Dudley Report and the accompanying *Housing Manual* [12]. However, the economic realities of post-war Britain soon forced public investments to back down from the recommendations of the report; space, for example, was often reduced from the report's minimum of 900sq ft right down to 750sq ft. The tighter budgets encouraged a move away from semi-detached houses to terraces and to flats, which never became popular with the English public. Architects and town planners had promoted flat dwelling, although The Dudley Report had noted their lack of popularity with the public in stating that "while flats are open to many objections for families with children, they are less objectionable for other persons" [13]. Many councils saw the high-rise buildings as an ideal solution to the re-housing of occupants evicted from slum clearance schemes. Over a ten-year period beginning in the mid-fifties high-rise buildings dominated municipal housing projects in many cities. A sharp decline followed, partly due to reduced government subsidies, but mainly precipitated by the Ronan Point disaster of 1968: In the early hours of the morning a gas explosion caused the entire corner of a new, 22-storey building in London's dockland to collapse. A public inquiry concluded that the catastrophe was due to substantial defects in the design and construction of the building [14]. The flats were rebuilt after the incident, but the building was knocked down in 1986 and replaced with low-level terraced houses.

The 1944 *Housing Manual* was revised and re-issued in 1949. The new version was considered a vast improvement and contained information and house plans that even today could be used to good effect. In the introduction to the house plans, the *Manual* states:

> Elevations are shown in line diagrams to indicate
> suggestions for linking houses in pairs and to show the
> varied treatment that is possible in the design of terrace
> houses. [15]

It goes on to stress

> ... the need for considering the street scene as the unit
> of architectural design. All elevational treatments should
> be considered in relation to the site and landscape where
> the houses are situated and should accord with regional
> characteristics; for this reason it is emphasised that the
> particular designs shown would not lend themselves to
> exact or uniform reproduction.

There are strong echoes of Raymond Unwin in these paragraphs.

The houses shown in the 1949 *Housing Manual* are still generous in size and exceed the space requirements set out in The Dudley Report. For semi-detached houses, the *Manual* presents plans for rural and urban locations and distinguishes between The Kitchen-Living Room House and The Working Kitchen House. Figs. 10.5 and 10.6 show plans taken from the Manual.

The *Housing Manual* showed approximately equal numbers of designs for semi-detached and terraced houses. Also shown were bungalows, or old people's dwellings as they were termed, and

ELEVATION TO THE ROAD

FIRST FLOOR PLAN

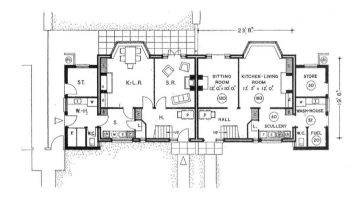

Fig. 10.5. Plan and elevation of a rural semi-detached house of the Kitchen-Living Room type [16].

a few layouts for flats and maisonettes.[3] On the other hand, the *Manual* included suggestions for townscapes which emphasised terraces and flats. The terraces shown in these townscapes, which were illustrated with photos of scale models, were extremely long; even as models they appeared somewhat out of character with the text of the *Manual*, which had taken pains to underline the aesthetics of street layouts.

Public authority housing in post-war Britain had benefited from the guidelines of The Dudley Report. The building programmes initiated by the Labour Government created an unprecedented public injection to the housing market, which lasted until the mid-fifties.

3. A maisonette is nowadays also called a duplex apartment. It is a self-contained dwelling of two floors with internal stairs, in an apartment house [18].

ELEVATION TO THE ROAD

Fig. 10.6. Plan and elevation of an urban semi-detached house of the Working-Kitchen type [17].

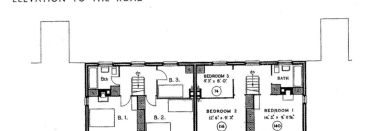

FIRST FLOOR PLAN

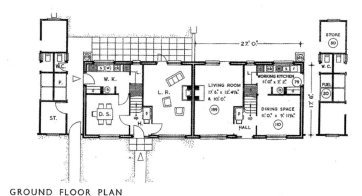

GROUND FLOOR PLAN

Public housing peaked around 1954 (see Fig. 10.2) and it was only the restrictive economic climate, and a change in government, that slowed down the development of public housing.

The Parker-Morris Report

The poor state of Britain's economy was a significant factor in the decline of public house building programmes, not only in the number of dwellings completed annually, but also in the quality of the housing offered. As mentioned in the previous section, house sizes had by the fifties become smaller than the minimum called for in The Dudley Report. Not only that, but building standards had fallen, and many of the new estates deserved the uncomplimentary term jerry-building, more so than most inter-war speculative semis. The fall in standards had not passed unnoticed. In 1959, the

Conservative Government set up a committee under Sir Parker Morris to advise on house building requirements. The terms of reference were "to consider the standards of design and equipment applicable to family dwellings and other forms of residential accommodation, whether provided by local authorities or by private enterprise, and to make recommendations" [19]. The committee reported in 1961 with the document *Homes for Today and Tomorrow* [19].

The Parker-Morris Report included a thorough investigation of how people lived. It set out space standards based on occupancy and the need for storage space. The internal design and layout of the house was given new consideration. Also improved room heating, to include central heating, was carefully evaluated. The trend for all social classes to take some meals in the kitchen was duly considered, supporting the Working Kitchen configuration introduced in the *Housing Manual* of 1949. In larger homes the Edwardian concept of a dining-hall was re-introduced (see for example, Fig. 5.6). A parlour or best room was not included in the recommendations.

Additionally, the report addressed the question of garden sizes and warned against the post-war trend to build on smaller and smaller plots, but in this respect it had little impact. Plot sizes for semi-detached houses fell from around 9,900sq ft in the inter-war period to only 5,100sq ft in the nineteen eighties [20]. A space for a garage or car was discussed, as the report had estimated that by 1980 an average of one car per household was expected in Britain.

The findings and recommendations of the report may not have been revolutionary, but they were sound. Even at the turn of the new millennium discussions of housing developments still referred to the benchmarks of the Parker-Morris Report. A contemporary set of housing standards has long been considered overdue.

In specific terms the report recommended a minimum of 910sq ft floor-space for a five-person family, plus an extra 50sq ft of storage space. This was a real increase from the average 900sq ft, which included storage space. The space recommendations and other improvements suggested by the report added an extra 8-15 per cent to the price of a five-person house, even without central heating. Under these circumstances local authorities were slow to take up the findings of the report and in 1969 the Labour Government therefore declared that the Parker-Morris recommendations would be mandatory for all public sector housing. This requirement was overturned by Margaret Thatcher's Government in 1980. The private sector – the speculative builders – had never adopted the standards.

Unlike its predecessors, the Tudor-Walters Report and The Dudley Report, the Parker-Morris report was not followed by a Housing Manual, although examples of house plans were shown in publications issued by the Ministry of Housing and Local Government over the next few years [21].

Architectural styles for the suburban semi 1945–65: public housing

In spite of the somewhat negative comments on semi-detached housing embedded in The Dudley Report, and its undisguised preference for terraces, local authorities were not blind to the fact that their tenants would prefer to live in a semi-detached house if given the choice. A survey carried out in 1968 on behalf of the National Housebuilders Registration Council indicated that 85 per cent of those interviewed would choose a detached or semi-detached house rather than a larger house in a terrace [22]. There is no reason to believe that a similar response would not have been found in the forties and fifties.

The inclusion of the many designs for semi-detached houses in the 1949 *Housing Manual* underlines the continued popularity of this housing type in early post-war Britain. In fact, the semi-detached house remained the type of dwelling built in largest numbers until well into the sixties.

With its introduction of restrictive building licenses, the Labour Government had effectively throttled private speculative housing for nearly a decade after the war finished (see Fig. 10.2). The builders were contracted to build public housing estates to the designs and financial constraints imposed by the local authorities.

Building materials were in short supply after the war and there was a positive famine of bricks. Pr methods had been pioneered in the inter-war period and refined during the war and they were now put into good use. Precast concrete blocks and larger panels were used extensively, with heavy machinery handling and placing the individual slabs, see Fig.10.7. There was also a lack of skilled labour, which encouraged the trend for prefabricated units.

The dominant position of public housing and the general lack of traditional building materials go a long way to explain the

10 architectural styles that prevailed in post-war Britain. There were some significant and immediately visible changes to the semi-detached house style, when compared with pre-war designs:

1. The hipped roof had been replaced with a gable, or saddleback, roof.
2. Bay windows had all but disappeared.
3. Mock-Tudor was no longer seen.
4. Prefabricated concrete structures dominated the elevations.

Fig. 10.7. Erection of an early post-war prefab [23].

Fig. 10.8. A 1947 semi-detached house from Wates using walls of insulated concrete [24].

The houses were much plainer than their most recent ancestors of the inter-war period, but many of them were architect designed and aesthetically appealing. Concrete itself can be of many shades from nearly pure white to murky, brownish grey; however, it can be coloured by the addition of iron oxides. Black, red and yellow concrete may be created in this manner. If the walls were left untreated, the general attraction of the house depended much on the colour of the concrete and the smoothness of the finish.

Even well before the 1949 *Housing Manual* was published, major builders of the day such as Wates and Laing had started building houses in the new idiom. A Wates semi from 1947 is shown in Fig. 10.8.

Soon after the First World War, John Laing & Son Ltd developed

a technique, Easiform, for building in concrete. Its basis was a steel shuttering which formed a hollow mould into which unskilled labour could pour a concrete mix to make instant walls. In 1945, Laing was, therefore, more than ready to build housing for local authorities, and around 10,000 homes were being built using this technique in 1947. An example of Laing's semi-detached houses from one of their advertisements is illustrated in Fig. 10.9. The gabled houses are nearly identical in appearance to the ones built by Wates shown above. A little variation is offered by finishing some pairs with a hipped roof as may be seen in the photograph. The text to the advertisement reads: "These photographs show some of our present day contracts of national importance at home and abroad, and we look forward to the time when houses for sale will be added to these activities" [25].

Fig. 10.9. A Laing development of semi-detached houses using its patented Easiform technique for a local authority.

It is interesting to note that the houses outwardly bear a strong resemblance to the Parker and Unwin semi-detached houses in Cromwell Green, Letchworth, from 1905, see Fig. 6.6, although those were slightly smaller.

Very much in the same style, but of a slightly different construction, is the semi-detached pair shown in Fig. 10.10 [26]. This is a 1946 building having steel frames, a first floor clad in profiled steel sheets, and a non-load-bearing brick ground floor. This system was promoted by the British Iron and Steel Federation (BISF) and proved very successful, although popular wit referred to these estates disparagingly as tin towns. About 30,000 houses were built between 1946 and 1951 [27]. Several of these houses have survived, but often repairs and refurbishment by the council became necessary in the nineteen-nineties. With a new lease of life they again appear quite appealing, although the tenants sometimes display a lack of interest in

Fig. 10.10. A 1946 semi-detached pair with a steel cladded first floor.

Fig. 10.11. Part of a nineteen-fifties estate of prefabricated semi-detached houses with steel cladding to the first floors, Ellesmere Port, Cheshire (photo 2006).

keeping the gardens and surrounding areas attractive. A recent photograph of a row of these semi-detached houses is shown in Fig. 10.11.

Another council estate of semis to a slightly different design, but following the same idiom, was built in the nineteen fifties on a development pleasantly centred around a green in the Chester suburb of Blacon, see Fig. 10.12.

While the prefabs illustrated above display a certain poise and dignity, some of the other building systems using untreated concrete blocks or slabs produced houses that were no less than grim. Many of the prefabs still survive on the outskirts of villages and townships all over the country, although they were built for a lifespan of just ten years.

Fig. 10.13 illustrates an unusual house from the early post-war period in a flat-roofed modernist design using a reinforced concrete frame

Fig. 10.12. An unpretentious estate of council houses was erected in a suburb of Chester in the nineteen fifties (photo 2006).

212

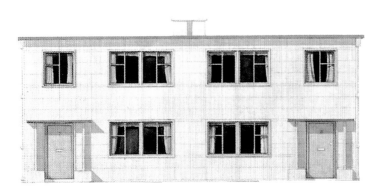

Fig. 10.13. An early post-war semi-detached pair built of concrete in the modernist style.

and walls of concrete blocks [28]. Apart from the flat roof, the main difference between this house and the others shown above is that the ground floor windows are set higher. Post-war domestic architecture tended in general to favour tall ground floor windows set quite low, which not only makes the rooms lighter, but "makes life more agreeable for the toddler" as one commentator put it at the time [29].

A pleasant estate of modernist houses with gable roofs is pictured

Fig. 10.14. An estate of modernist houses in Norfolk. Constructed of brick with colour-washed walls. Roofs are covered with red Norfolk pantiles.

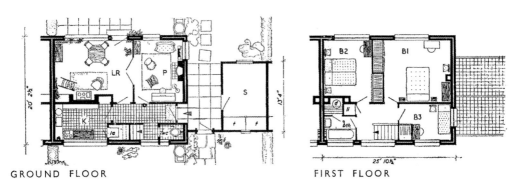

GROUND FLOOR

FIRST FLOOR

Fig. 10.15. The ground floor and first-floor plan of one of the Norfolk semi-detached houses. Notice that the parlour (P) has been retained in this design [31]. There are small discrepancies between the plan shown and the sizes and placement of the ground floor windows as they appear on the houses when actually built.

213

in Fig. 10.14 and the layout of one house of a pair in Fig. 10.15 [30]. Surprisingly, the parlour (P) has been preserved in this design, as has the presence of a fuel cooking range in the living room (LR).

Mid-century modern

As may be seen from the illustrations provided in this section there was a great deal of commonality between the semi-detached house styles built in the late forties. Although the houses were constructed under extremely difficult conditions and for cost reasons were totally unadorned, they conferred an architectural virtue of their own by being truly un-eclectic. With the exception of the pure modernist buildings of the twenties and thirties, this is probably the first time in the history of domestic housing that homes in England were being provided without elements copied from either classicism, Tudor, Queen Anne, Gothic, vernacular styles or Egyptology.

In the houses of this period some historians have detected Georgian influences in the tall ground-floor windows and in the placement of the windows on the façade, and others have focused on the porches, which could have been inspired by the Arts and Crafts Movement or by modernist architecture. Some terraces from the fifties were built with concealed roofs behind a parapet, a clear reference to the Georgian roof style. All this is true, but it seems more fair to acknowledge the intrinsic honesty of the first ten years of mainly public domestic housing in post-war Britain. Mid-century Modern might be an appropriate term for the architectural style of 1945-55, before buildings again began to adopt features borrowed from earlier periods and from other countries.

Fig. 10.16. Linked semi-detached houses planned for the Live Architecture exhibition at the Festival of Britain, 1951. The linked sections provided bathrooms at first floor level and storage at ground floor level.

A review of Britain's role in design and architecture was presented to the public at the Festival of Britain in 1951. The festival was set up to commemorate the Great Exhibition of 1851. It was designed to be the autobiography of a nation, as the official programme described it. New ideas in architecture were given space at a Live Architecture exhibition in the Limehouse area in London's East End. It included a development programme of housing, as well as of schools and shops. The estates were planned by the London County Council (LCC), with flats, terraces, maisonettes and individual houses, mostly designed by private architects. An example of the linked semi-detached houses planned for the area is shown in Fig. 10.16 [32]. The design is basically a conventional three-bedroomed house with a through living room on the ground floor. The unusual link between the houses provides a bathroom on the first floor and fuel and bicycle storage at ground level. The architects chose to build with a hipped roof, rather than the gable roof that was most commonly used in public housing at the time. Instead of bay windows, the houses now had ground floor windows set low down in deep, concrete-lined recesses typical of the period. The porches are faintly modernist.

The Live Architecture exhibition of the Festival also showed an unsympathetic parody of a mock-Tudor inter-war home, Gremlin Grange. The purposely crooked building was generally felt to be somewhat in bad taste and insulting to the millions of families who lived in and were happy with their Tudorbethan homes of the twenties and thirties.

By the early fifties the supply of building materials was becoming more plentiful, although brick production was still slow in recovering. Nevertheless, a number of estates erected by local authorities in this period were brick built, such as the Dallum Estate at Warrington, Cheshire.

Fig. 10.17. An early nineteen fifties semi in a suburb of Warrington, Cheshire. Brick built with a hipped roof, it is a continuation of the class 3 building style of the inter-war period, see Fig. 8.11 (photo 2006).

This estate comprises a mixture of short terraces, semi-detached houses and bungalows all built in a traditional style and with hipped roofs, see, for example, Fig. 10.17 showing a class 3 universal semi. In a nearby estate the authorities some years later built a very large number of houses, again using brick, this time in a modernist style with flat-roofed terraces and semis.

In the fifties, architects of public housing were tiring of the simplicity or even crudeness of prefabricated building elements and, as in the estates mentioned above, they had begun to use brick more freely as the production became sustainable once more. They

Fig. 10.18. An example of modest semi-detached houses in the Scandinavian style (photo 2006).

also attempted to give some variation to the elevations by applying tile-hanging or weatherboarding, but the overall impression of uniformity changed very little with the adoption of what came to be known as the Scandinavian style: a low-pitched gable roof and an unpretentious, even plain, façade. An example is shown in Fig. 10.18.[4] The style became exceedingly popular and survived with little variation until the nineties.

Architectural styles for the suburban semi 1945–65: private housing

With private building on the rise from the mid-fifties, the perennial problem of making sure that council housing and privately built housing could be distinguished from one another posed a challenge to the speculative builders. More often than not the speculative builders resorted to the universal semis of the inter-war period,

Fig. 10.19. A typical row of speculatively built semi-detached houses from the nineteen fifties in Hoole near Chester. These are class 3 type universal semis, see Fig. 8.11 (photo 2006).

4. It should be noted, however, that most private houses built in Scandinavia over this period, most notably in Denmark, were single-storey, bungalow-type houses. The term Scandinavian style is slightly misplaced, but will nevertheless be used in this text.

and many of the semi-detached estates from the mid-fifties are virtually indistinguishable from their nineteen-thirties counterparts. Fig. 10.19, for example, shows a small suburban development in Hoole near Chester of class 3 universal semis (see Fig. 8.11), which would have been the cheapest to build. Even more frugal were some of the working-class estates where the bay windows were omitted.

With bricks being available again after the immediate post-war shortage many speculative houses were once more brick-built. An interesting class 4 universal semi from c.1955 is illustrated in Fig. 10.20. The house is part of a small estate of mainly semi-detached houses and both owners have retained their distinctive Critall windows. Unfortunately, many of the other similar houses on the street have had PVC double-glazed windows put in; sometimes just the one owner has made this improvement, while the other half of the semi has kept its original windows. The result is architecturally disastrous.

After the Second World War, the neo-Georgian style which had followed in the wake of the Tudor-Walters report in 1918 had gone out of fashion with the public authorities. The speculative builders turned tentatively to building in this style or to the closely relate neo-Queen Anne style, as illustrated in a 1965 advertisement for a semi-detached house in Fig. 10.21. For a while it seemed as though private housing vacillated between pre-war universal semis, neo-Georgian and Scandinavian. With municipal housing displaying front elevations with semi-Georgian window settings on the one hand, and adopting the low-pitched gable roofs and unobtrusive frontages of the Scandinavian style on the other, the private and public dwellings converged in appearance to the frustration of the speculative builder and his clients. The major building companies of the age had the benefit of using architects for their housing designs, but even so it was becoming increasingly difficult to differentiate between owner-occupied new builds and tenanted local authority housing. As the size and structure of the two types of housing came closer together, it became even more important for the owner-occupier to set his house apart from those of the municipal estates. Perhaps the most significant difference on the outside view was the inclusion of garages for the private middle-class housing estates, often using linked garages to

Fig. 10.20. A class 4 universal semi from c.1955 with its original windows intact, Upton near Chester (photo 2006).

Fig. 10.21. Speculative builders' advertisement from 1965.

10

fill the gaps between the semi-detached pairs as in Fig. 10.22.[5] Of course, the much emphasized easy access from the front to the back of a semi-detached house was lost with the intrusion of this space. The motorcar had appeared in middle-class estates in the nineteen-thirties, but it was only after the war, and after petrol rationing had been removed in the early fifties, that car ownership among the middle classes became common. Ownership in Britain trebled between 1949 and 1961. With the status of house ownership and house style having been watered down, the motorcar took over the function of proclaiming the semi-detached homeowner's standing in the estate. A Morris Minor was, of course, acceptable and even trendy, but real status came with having a Rover, Humber or Wolseley parked in the driveway.

Fig. 10.22. Semi-detached houses with linked garages, believed to be 1960s, Ellesmere Port, Cheshire (photo 2006).

Another visible accentuation of an owner's status and tastes lay with the front garden, which in a sense took on the role that the front parlour or best room had played in previous generations. A well-kept lawn, a neatly trimmed hedge and an abundance of flowering plants, especially rose bushes, spoke of real middle-class values. The situation is not very different today.

One might wonder why the speculative builders did not re-introduce the highly successful Tudorbethan style they had used before the war. The simple explanation to this is twofold. Firstly, speculative building was, as we have seen, severely curtailed by government restrictions until the mid fifties; secondly, there was a severe shortage of timber, and unnecessary adornments had to be kept to a minimum. When timber again became more readily available, public taste had changed to prefer timber cladding in a more Scandinavian style. Class 1 universal semis with a mock-Tudor gable had gone out of fashion for a while, but the style had not been forgotten by either the public or the builders, it was just lying dormant. A visit to any newly built middle-class estate today will confirm that

5. This design had been used also before the Second World War in some of the more affluent estates [33].

mock-Tudor has been resurrected, as will be demonstrated
in Chapter 11.

Public and private housing: 1965-90

By the early sixties and for the next 20 years or so, the number
of houses completed in the public and private sectors was by
and large the same. Only when the Conservatives came to power
in 1979 did a dramatic change take place with publicly funded
housing decreasing abruptly, soon to become insignificant;
correspondingly, private housing rose to take over the major share
of the housing market.

Fig. 10.23. Scandinavian
style semi-detached houses
built in the early seventies
Chester (photo 2006).

If we look at the styles
of semi-detached houses
built over this period, two
conclusions arise:

1. There was very little
   difference between
   public and private
   semi-detached
   estate houses.
2. There was very
   little innovation in
   housing style.

By this time the Scandinavian style had become the most used, and
both small and very large estates of these houses may be found
all over England. Fig. 10.23 shows part of a typical early seventies
estate in a suburb of Chester. The style was adopted also for some
of the later new towns, such as in Warrington, Cheshire. Fig. 10.24
illustrates some typical examples.

Fig. 10.24. Semi-detached
houses on two estates in
Warrington New Town. The
pair in the left-hand picture
is from c.1974; the one in
the right-hand picture
c. 1985 (photos 2006).

Fig. 10.25. A nineteen eighties dormer style semi-detached pair in Bramley, Surrey (photo 2006).

Fig. 10.26. A different style of semis designed for Crawley New Town in 1969. They are constructed using honey-coloured concrete blocks [34].

The dormer-style became popular for semi-detached houses in most of the country in the nineteen eighties and nineties. An example of a three-bedroomed house in the south of England is shown in Fig. 10.25. Although they may appear a little cramped from the outside, they can be quite spacious. In the house shown in the illustration the three bedrooms are of a reasonable size, and there are also two bathrooms on the first floor. Downstairs, there is a small study as well as two living rooms and a kitchen.

A refreshing departure from the bland, self-effacing styles shown in Figs. 10.23 and 10.24 is the pair built in honey-coloured concrete blocks for a 1969 estate in Crawley New Town, see Fig. 10.26.

Under the Conservative Government in the nineteen eighties, the speculative builders found a new freedom and became more adventurous until new regulations under Labour rule placed obstacles in their path. The preferred housing type was now the detached house, but all major building contractors were still providing semi-detached houses on most of their estates.

References

1   John Short, *Housing in Britain*, Methuen & Co Ltd, London 1982, p.42.

2   David Christopher, *British Culture*, Routledge, London and New York 1999, p.182.

3   Patrick Abercrombie, *Greater London Plan 1944*, His Majesty's Stationery Office, London 1944.

4   David Rudlin and Nicholas Falk, *Building the 21st Century Home*, Architectural Press, Oxford 1999, p.69.

5   John Burnett, *A Social History of Housing*, David & Charles Ltd, Newton Abbot 1978, p.280.

6   J.M. Richards, 'Failure of the New Towns', in *Architectural Review*, 114, 1953, p.29.

7   Arthur Edwards, *The Design of Suburbia*, Pembridge Press Ltd, London 1981, p.165.

8   Julienne Hanson, 'Selling the dream', in *Architects Journal*, 15 April 1992, pp. 36-37.

9   In Suburbia Partnership, *In Suburbia, Delivering Sustainable Communities*, Hampshire County Council 2002.

10 Central Housing Advisory Committee, *The Design of Dwellings*, His Majesty's Stationery Office, London 1944. The Dudley Report.

11 Raymond Unwin, *Town Planning in Practice*, Second edition, Fisher Unwin, London 1911.

12 Ministry of Health, *Housing Manual*, His Majesty's Stationery Office, London 1944.

13 Arthur Edwards, *The design of suburbia*, Pembridge Press Ltd, London 1981, p.152.

14 F. Berry, *Housing: The Great British Failure*, 1974, p.86.

15 Ministry of Health, *Housing Manual*, His Majesty's Stationery Office, London 1949, p.50.

16 *Ibid.*, p.52

17 *Ibid.*, p.56

18 Penguin Reference, *Dictionary of Architecture & Landscape Architecture*, Fifth edition, Penguin, London 1999.

19 Central Housing Advisory Committee, *Homes for Today and Tomorrow*, His Majesty's Stationery Office, London 1949. The Parker-Morris Report.

20 John Halsey and Josephine Webb, *Twentieth-Century British Social Trends*, MacMillan Press, London 2000, p.48.

21 John Burnett, *A Social History of Housing*, David & Charles Ltd, Newton Abbot 1978, p.291.

22 Arthur Edwards, *The design of suburbia*, Pembridge Press Ltd, London 1981, p.243.

23 *Concrete Quarterly*, September 1950, p.11.

24 *Daily Mail Ideal Home Book*, The Daily Mail Home Exhibition Department of Associated Newspapers Ltd, London 1947-48, p.7.

25 *Ibid.*, p.12.

26 John Prizeman, *Houses of Britain: The Outside View*, Quiller Press, London 2003, p.105.

27 Colin Davies, *The Prefabricated Home*, Reaktion Books Ltd, London 2005, p.64.

28 John Prizeman, *Houses of Britain: The Outside View*, Quiller Press, London 2003, p.104.

29 Eric Bird, *Daily Mail Ideal Home Book*, 1947-48, The Daily Mail Home Exhibition Department of Associated Newspapers Ltd, London p.8.

30 F.R.S. Yorke, *The Modern House in England*, The Architectural Press, London 1948, p.38.

31 *Ibid.*, p.39

32 *Daily Mail Ideal Home Book*, 1950-51, The Daily Mail Home Exhibition Department of Associated Newspapers Ltd, London p.31.

33 Council for the Preservation of Rural England – Cheshire Branch, *Building in Cheshire*, 1939, p.65.

34 John Prizeman, *Houses of Britain: The Outside View*, Quiller Press, London 2003, p.105.

35 Richard Rogers and Anne Power, *Cities for a Small Country*, Faber and Faber, London 2000, p.68.

Into the new millennium

"New estates are designed to be inoffensive. They are equivalent to the national preference for magnolia wall paint"
Vesna Goldsworthy, March 2005

The final decades of the twentieth century were years of confusion and frustration for the house-building industry. Council housing had all but ceased and the output from housing associations declined in quality to a level where the associations were seen as "mass providers of poor homes for poor people" [1]. The private sector had a boom period in the mid-eighties, but this was followed by a slump as house prices fell by 30 per cent between 1989 and 1992.

Throughout the nineties and into the new millennium, the building industry faced an uncertain future and struggled to cope with new legislation and guidelines brought in by the Labour Government, not least the Planning Policy Guidance, PPG3 Housing, released in the year 2000 [2]. This document detailed the Government's housing objectives and effectively limited the scope of the speculative builder. The Government's proposal was introduced in the House of Commons stating – with maybe unwarranted confidence: "The old 'predict and provide' approach to housing which under the Tories gave us urban sprawl, out-of-town shopping and pepper-pot development is dead."

The document was well-intentioned, but sometimes unduly restrictive. It recognized, for example, that the average density of housing in recent estates was about 25 dwellings per hectare, or 10 dwellings per acre, but it would like to see this figure doubled.

It reviewed car parking standards and requested developers to "not provide off-street parking when there is no need or where there is a demand for car-free housing." This policy has unfortunately, and predictably, led to estates being built where parked cars now clutter narrow roads and reduce the safety of pedestrians, especially children, by obscuring their view along the street.

It is a little early to assess the full impact of the new planning procedures on the pattern of speculatively built estates,[1] but it is fairly certain that the requirement for higher density housing has encouraged some developers to include more semi-detached houses in their estate portfolios, although the detached house is still the preferred choice. The rising cost of land has also played a part in a move to building more semis, as has a tighter economy for many middle-class families who have had to compromise on their aspirations.

Semi-detached status and styles

The number of semi-detached houses completed annually in the second half of the twentieth century never came to match that of the boom years of the inter-war period. Nevertheless, the semi-detached house has been extremely resilient and is still, in the first years of the twenty-first century, the most common type of dwelling in this country, as shown by the statistics presented in Chapter 1. According to David Christopher, Britain had in 1996 the oldest housing stock in Europe [4]. This is not necessarily a bad thing, as it could reflect the high quality of the houses built over the past few hundred years. However, modern houses are without a shadow of doubt better insulated and heated, they are easier to maintain and they are compatible with today's safety standards. These facts notwithstanding, estate agents can confirm that most house-buyers seem to prefer older houses to new ones: "We can't seem to find enough two- or three-bed Victorian homes" was a lament from one agent in February 2006.

It is somewhat disconcerting to admit that so little innovation in domestic architecture took place in the final decades of the twentieth century. One observer has remarked that the architectural profession rewards the iconic buildings of our age, but that "no prizes are

1. The RIBA (Royal Institute of British Architects) Practice Bulletin of 21 July 2005 reported that "House builders are celebrating what they see as a U-turn on planning policy by the planning minister Yvette Cooper, confirmed in this week's consultation on a successor to PPG3, now expected in the autumn. 'Responding to market demand' is the new mantra being handed down to planners." [3].

given to the architect who makes an ordinary suburb liveable" [5]. Where architects have ventured into designing homes for the middle classes or the working classes, their attempts have been rejected. This happened to houses of the Modern Movement and, later, to the rough dwellings of New Brutalism.

It seems to be the innate conservatism of the average English house-buying public that has dictated the style of newly built estate homes, whether detached, semi-detached or terraced. The favoured styles were for many years the Scandinavian and the neo-Georgian (sometimes now called mock-Georgian). These were still popular with the builders around the turn of the century, but the major estate builders turned increasingly to more and more historic, vernacular styles.

Speculative builders, estate agents and mortgage lenders are cautious people and they know where to invest safely. In the nineteen thirties, for example, it was very difficult to borrow money to purchase a Modernist home; today, architect-designed homes are valued typically 10 per cent less than standard estate homes [6]. A safe investment is in a traditional style, semi-detached house with little to recommend it other than its ordinariness. Middle-class buyers do not want to be adventurous; a spokesman for one estate builder asserted that they did not want "some massive glass gherkin that looked as if it had been beamed down from Mars" [7].

Critics of typical speculative estate houses have dubbed them toy town architecture or noddy housing (after Enid Blyton's stories for small children), but this may

Fig. 11.1. Estate layout by Bryant Homes 2002. Predominantly detached homes, five are semi-detached pairs.

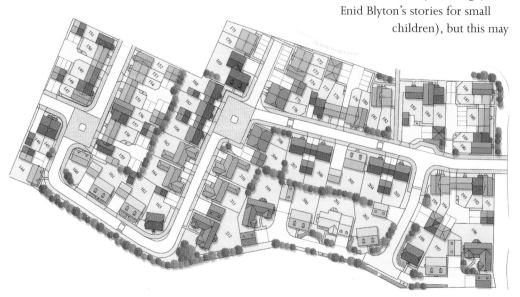

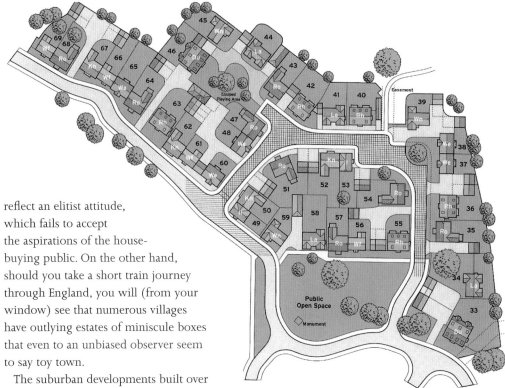

reflect an elitist attitude, which fails to accept the aspirations of the house-buying public. On the other hand, should you take a short train journey through England, you will (from your window) see that numerous villages have outlying estates of miniscule boxes that even to an unbiased observer seem to say toy town.

The suburban developments built over the past few years have been tuned mostly to the requirements and economies of middle middle-class families. They are often located in semi-rural areas and are typically quite small estates, ranging from maybe five to 100 dwellings. For estates of any reasonable size there will be a mixture of detached and semi-detached houses, short terraces and occasionally some low-rise apartment buildings. Typical layouts of some modern developments are shown in Fig. 11.1 and Fig. 11.2.

The gardens in the estates are small, but most are large enough for owners to enjoy old-fashioned gardening rather than just making do with a patio and container planting. Some newer and quite prestigious estates have gardens which are no more than minute, token areas separating the plots from each other or from the road.

Fig. 11.2. Estate layout by Willson Connolly 2002. Predominantly detached homes, four are semi-detached pairs, some are terraces.

ECLECTICISM UNLIMITED

The architecture adopted for many estate houses in the beginning of the twenty-first century was either unashamed replicas of Victorian house styles or one of many eclectic styles believed to represent traditional, middle-class values.

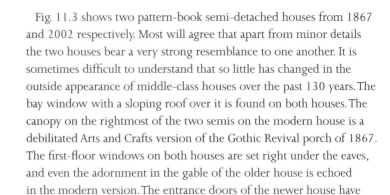

Fig. 11.3 shows two pattern-book semi-detached houses from 1867 and 2002 respectively. Most will agree that apart from minor details the two houses bear a very strong resemblance to one another. It is sometimes difficult to understand that so little has changed in the outside appearance of middle-class houses over the past 130 years. The bay window with a sloping roof over it is found on both houses. The canopy on the rightmost of the two semis on the modern house is a debilitated Arts and Crafts version of the Gothic Revival porch of 1867. The first-floor windows on both houses are set right under the eaves, and even the adornment in the gable of the older house is echoed in the modern version. The entrance doors of the newer house have simple leaded glass patterns of the kind popular in the late Victorian period. Both houses have prominent quoins on the front elevation. Variations on the modern house can be seen on estates all over the country.

Estate builders have succeeded in creating modern houses with the traditional, conservative look favoured by middle-England purchasers. In doing so they have borrowed freely from

Fig. 11.3. Pattern book semis from 1867 and 2002. The entrance to one semi of the 1867 pair is on the left-hand side of the building [8], [9].

Fig. 11.4. Mock-Tudor semi built 2005 (photo 2006).

Fig. 11.5. Modern 2005 semi near Liverpool. It has Georgian/Victorian ancestry in the placement of the windows, a near-Edwardian style porch and the sensible simplicity of the Scandinavian style (photo 2006).

all periods of English domestic architecture, from Tudor through Georgian, Victorian and Edwardian to post-war Scandinavian. The mock-Tudor so beloved by the inter-war speculative builders has had its renaissance after lying dormant for many years. 'Inspired by the past. Designed for the future' is an advertising slogan that perfectly describes the majority of estate developments today and mirrors the aspirations of potential buyers. The eclecticism of early twenty-first century semi-detached houses is demonstrated in the selection of buildings shown in Fig. 11.4 to Fig. 11.8.

Fig. 11.6. A 2004 semi with a watered down Tudor pediment over the entrance doors. Porches are prominent in houses built around the turn of the new century. With a third-floor living space added to the traditional two-storey semi these houses are often advertised as town-houses [10].

Fig. 11.7. Another town-house-style semi built in 2005 by a different estate developer. The style is eclectic but pleasantly subdued. The Arts and Crafts style entrance doors, the modest canopy, the sand-coloured lintels on a brownish brick background and the slate roof give the building an old-fashioned dignity (photo 2006).

Fig. 11.8. Part of a late-twentieth century estate with two pairs of semi-detached houses. They are mirror images of one another except for the choice of finish to the elevations and the roofs (photo 2005).

Although a significant number of buyers still wanted a "best room", according to a 1999 survey [11], a browse through estate builders' brochures today indicates that the best room or parlour has finally disappeared from most semi-detached houses on offer. A typical layout of the ground floor of a modern semi can look like the plan shown in Fig.11.9.

There is very little variation in the layouts provided by different estate builders, but there is hardly any agreement on what the downstairs living area should be called. On the illustration here it has been called just that: living area. However, you will just as easily find the terms drawing room, living room, living space, living/dining room, sitting room, family room, lounge or even the rather pretentious reception room.

Fig. 11.9. Typical ground-floor plan of an early twenty-first century semi-detached pair.

Living area	Living area
C	C
WC	WC
Kitchen	Hall	Hall	Kitchen

SEMIS WITH A DIFFERENCE

In spite of the speculator's preference for conservative style houses that are considered a safe investment, a number of innovative housing projects have been developed in recent years, albeit in small numbers. Some of those that include semi-detached houses are presented in this section.

It has been said that many groundbreaking and award-winning home designs never survive the process from the architect's drawing board to construction on site, at least not without being watered down because of the speculative builders' fear that all buyers are traditionalists at heart. One turn-of-the-century design for a semi-detached pair that did make it through to completion can be seen in Stevenage. A photograph of the pair as seen from the rear is shown in Fig. 11.10, and a plan of the houses is reproduced in Fig. 11.11 [12].

The smooth brown and grey tiled cladding on the gables matches the colours of the roofs and makes the houses stand out from the traditional brick houses all around them. Much of the building used prefabricated elements with a timber panel system to form the structure. The double pitch to the roofs underlines the dual occupancy of the building. The plots, and hence the gardens, are quite small in keeping with the high-density requirements for dwellings on most suburban estates.

In the Dulwich Village Conservation Area, several quite spectacular semi-detached houses were erected in 2003 [13]. Designed by architect Peter Huf, these so-called Huf houses use a post and beam system, which allows a very large degree of flexibility in the

Fig. 11.10. View of an unusual pair of semi-detached houses in Stevenage built at the turn of the century (Sergison Bates, 2006).

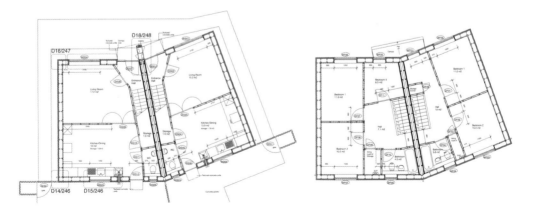

Fig. 11.11. Room layouts for the semi-detached pair shown in Fig. 11.10. The house on the left-hand side is three-bedroomed, the other two-bedroomed. Both houses have quite spacious landings, large enough to give them a "room-like" feel (Sergison Bates, 2006). [12]

internal room arrangements by using demountable, non-load bearing walls. The elements are precision-manufactured abroad and assembled on site in this country.

Fig. 11.12. Non-traditional semi-detached housing in Dulwich Village (Huf Haus, 2006).

Typically, the semi-detached houses are two stories high with a basement such as the houses shown in Fig. 11.12. This type of house might have four bedrooms and an open plan ground floor, with the drawing room, dining room and kitchen flowing effortlessly into one another, see Fig. 11.13.

The pair of semis shown in Fig. 11.14 were built on the site of an earlier semi that had been wrecked in a gas explosion (the remaining semi of that pair is the now a detached house just visible in the picture). The pair is a pilot project designed to have very low

Fig. 11.13. Plans for a four-bedroomed Huf semi-detached house. Notice the huge amount of extra space offered by the basement with its two bonus rooms (Huf Haus, 2006).

running costs for heating, lighting, water and general maintenance [14]. A substantial amount of pre-fabrication was involved using timber frame cassettes for the walls and floors. The cassettes are filled with cellulose fibre insulation manufactured from recycled newsprint. Some of the internal walls are removable, which opens up the possibility of providing an extra bedroom or study. The houses have more floor space than is normally provided in semi-detached houses. This has been accomplished by using the roof space as living space, a feature appreciated by the families living there.

Fig. 11.14. Semi-detached pair in Cherhill, Wiltshire (Bree Day Partnership, 2005).

An urban village of more than 400 new homes including apartments, terraces and semis was developed at Didsbury near Manchester on the brownfield[2] site of the former Withington Hospital.

The architects have given the estate some novel housing designs in a definite contemporary style [15]. One of the larger houses is a four-bedroomed semi-detached house. The front elevation of this house type is illustrated in Fig. 11.15 and the internal layout, spread over three floors, is shown in Fig. 11.16.

As in some of the other more recent semis shown in this chapter, the Didsbury semi demonstrates a seemingly consistent trend to build houses with three rather than two storeys. This sometimes means incorporating a basement level as in the Huf houses mentioned above, or using the space under the roof as a living space. Quite often this latter plan results in adding dormer windows to the roofs of the building as shown in Figs. 11.6 and 11.7, but the Didsbury development has cleverly avoided this and on the larger houses created a balanced and appealing façade towards the street. Some might criticize the houses as being overly eclectic and although there are traces of Arts and Crafts (the front entrance doors), Scandinavian (the wood cladding)

Fig. 11.15. Large semi-detached houses in a development at Didsbury near Manchester, 2005.

---

2. A brownfield site is land that has previously been developed. It can e.g. be a disused airfield, a closed colliery site or gasworks, or the grounds of a derelict factory.

Fig. 11.16. The floor plans of one of the semi-detached houses in the Didsbury development. This is a large house, and, by using the space under the roof, the architects have added an attractive second-floor living area. The kitchen and dining room are surprisingly far from one another, but most informal meals are probably served in the family room adjacent to the kitchen.

Ground Floor

Family / Kitchen	5.627m x 6.589m	18'6" x 21'8"
Dining	3.902m x 2.777m	12'10" x 9'1"
Garage / Car Port	11.062m x 2.830m	36'4" x 9'4"

First Floor

Master Bedroom	3.460m x 4.611m	11'4" x 15'2"
Bedroom 2	3.486m x 3.039m	11'5" x 10'00"
Bedroom 3	3.689m x 3.036m	12'1" x 9'11"
Bedroom 4 / Study	2.802m x 2.777m	9'2" x 9'1"

Second Floor

Living	5.255m x 6.601m	17'3" x 21'8"

and Modernism (the spectacular stair-well) the final result is a unique turn-of-the-millennium design.

A totally different approach to the design of a semi-detached house is the pair commissioned by two brothers and their families on an exclusive sight overlooking Hampstead Heath, see Fig. 11.17. Designed by the architect Jonathan Woolf, the large, flat-roofed houses with a decidedly Modernist flavour are each roughly similar but not identical. The entrance front of the houses is quite austere with just one window in the whole façade, but the houses open up towards the heath with large amounts of glazing facing the gardens and giving views to Kenwood House and beyond.

Fig. 11.17. A night-view of the unique semi-detached pair of houses in Hampstead (Jonathan Woolf, 2006).

A MODERNIST REVIVAL

In the conclusion at the end of Chapter 9, we asked if the time was ripe for a Modernist Revival. This is not very likely, given the history of domestic

housing which reflects a high degree of conservatism and
cautiousness. It is nevertheless interesting
to reflect on the situation today and
review the factors that may influence
a revival of the stylish Modernist
houses of the nineteen thirties.

The factors stacked against their
acceptance in the nineteen thirties were
indubitable:

1. They were considered
   non-English.
2. Promoting the flat roofs as a place
   for sun-bathing or al fresco
   dining was, in this country,
   a travesty.
3. The flat roofs created
   problems with rain water
   penetrating to the rooms
   below.

4. The concrete shell provided
   inadequate insulation.
5. The white outer walls were
   difficult to maintain in pristine
   condition.
6. The metal window frames were prone to rust.

Fig. 11.18. Ground-floor
and first-floor plans of the
semi-detached pair shown
in Fig. 11.17 (Jonathan
Woolf, 2006).

The first point is debatable today, where television and travel have
conditioned the average person to more readily accept influences
from abroad. The second point hardly merits discussion, but the very
idea of a flat roof was contrary to middle-class conceptions of what
a proper house should look like. This is in itself interesting, because
the prestigious Georgian terraces would appear from street level to
be flat-roofed, the low-pitched roof being hidden behind a parapet.
Indeed, one recent visitor from abroad being shown Georgian terraces
in Islington remarked on all the houses having flat roofs.

The final four points above are all technical problems that have
nothing to do with house style, and modern building technology
has effectively solved these early problems.

Apart from the extreme conservatism of the housing market,
the overriding problems in building Modernist houses today lie
in the stringent planning policies imposed by the Government.

Restrictions are placed on housing densities and the land space allowed for a family home is not generous. Modernist houses were at their best when they were able to appear streamlined and were dominated by horizontal lines. This was attainable most easily for custom-designed individual houses such as shown in Fig. 9.5. It was more difficult to design suburban semis to look just as striking, although some of the Modernist semis shown in Chapter 9 were, in fact, extremely successful.

There are three observations that could point towards a possible renaissance of Modernist housing in the twenty-first century. One is that a growing number of contemporary architect-designed homes are built in a Modernist style [16]. Another positive factor is that modern methods of construction, often based on off-site pre-fabricated elements, can keep the costs down, as well as circumventing the disadvantages mentioned above for the Modernist inter-war houses. Thirdly, at least some local planning departments have shaken off a reputation of mediocrity and are prepared to give planning permission to unusual designs. One planning inspector was recently cited as having said of such a Modernist design: "I consider that the scheme is an exciting example of modern architecture, with the potential to enhance the conservation area by contributing to the continuing evolution of its architectural heritage" [17].

Of the semi-detached houses shown in this chapter, the speculatively built Didsbury houses shown in Fig. 11.15 demonstrate elements of Modernism, while the privately commissioned pair on Hampstead Heath seen in Fig. 11.17 is nearly pure Modernism.

The millennium communities

In 1997, the Labour Government launched the Millennium Communities Programme with the aim of setting a benchmark for future regeneration projects. Developments are primarily on brownfield sites. The programme encourages the use of modern methods of construction, and in constructing homes the developers are required to reduce the energy spent by 50 per cent. The amount of metered energy consumption in the finished buildings must be reduced by 20 per cent, as must the amount of water used.

When finished, the communities will include different types and sizes of homes to attract a broad range of residents. Green spaces, wildlife areas and recreational facilities have been highlighted in the planning process, as has the inclusion of sensible transport links, shopping facilities, schools, etc.

At this time seven Millennium Communities have been designated and are in various stages of development and construction. They are:

- Greenwich Millennium Village, London
- Allerton Bywater Millennium Community, Leeds
- New Islington Millennium Community, Manchester
- South Lynn Millennium Community, King's Lynn
- Telford Millennium Community
- Oakgrove Millennium Community, Milton Keynes
- Hastings Millennium Community

The plan is to create 6000 homes by 2010 and 9000 homes in total. Greenwich Millennium Village was the first community to be identified; it is situated on a brownfield site of what was previously the largest gas works in Europe. The first residents moved into their new homes in 2000. It is worth observing that the residential areas of this community were designed to have only apartments and terrace houses.

Smaller in scale, but interesting in the context of the semi-detached house are, for example, the developments at Allerton Bywater near Leeds and at East Ketley, near Telford.

ALLERTON BYWATER

Allerton Bywater was the home of the last colliery in Leeds. It closed in 1992 and the 24 ha (59 acres) former colliery ground is now the site of the second Millennium Community. Phase 1 is under construction and the first homes were ready in late 2006. The development has a mixture of apartments, terraces and semi-detached houses as well as some detached homes. Fig. 11.19 shows the layout of Phase 1 [18].

Fig. 11.19. Plan of the first phase of the Allerton Bywater Millennium Community.

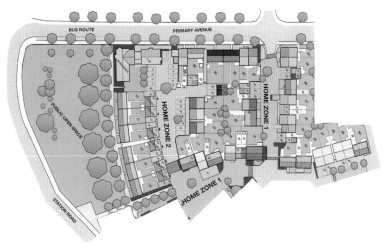

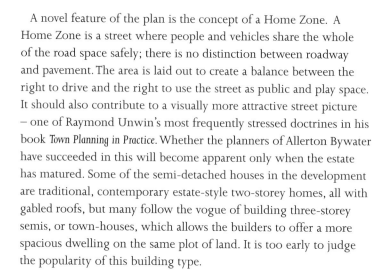

A novel feature of the plan is the concept of a Home Zone. A Home Zone is a street where people and vehicles share the whole of the road space safely; there is no distinction between roadway and pavement. The area is laid out to create a balance between the right to drive and the right to use the street as public and play space. It should also contribute to a visually more attractive street picture – one of Raymond Unwin's most frequently stressed doctrines in his book *Town Planning in Practice*. Whether the planners of Allerton Bywater have succeeded in this will become apparent only when the estate has matured. Some of the semi-detached houses in the development are traditional, contemporary estate-style two-storey homes, all with gabled roofs, but many follow the vogue of building three-storey semis, or town-houses, which allows the builders to offer a more spacious dwelling on the same plot of land. It is too early to judge the popularity of this building type.

EAST KETLEY

A 40 ha (100 acres) brownfield site on the north-western outskirts of Telford was chosen in 1992 to become the Telford

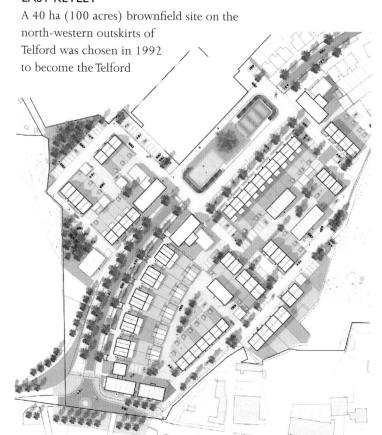

Fig. 11.20. A 2005 plan of the first phase of the East Ketley village. The gardens to the semi-detached houses are not large, but bigger than in some contemporary developments. The planners have guaranteed a garden depth of at least 10 m.

Millennium Community. The location at East Ketley includes former colliery workings, a disused golf driving range and playing fields. The site had been left fallow for many years and had become an important habitat for wildlife, including the protected Great Crested Newt.

The first plan for the new village was presented in early 2004, and following consultations with local residents and other parties involved, a revised plan was drawn up as a basis for a planning application. Around 750 new homes are planned for the site. The revised plans would seem to include more semi-detached houses than the first plan had shown. A plan of the first phase of the development to include around 100 dwellings is shown in Fig. 11.20 [19]. There are some apartment buildings, but most of the units are houses, either terraced or semi-detached. One of the concerns voiced in the consultations was that the density of housing as originally planned would be too high. There was also a reminder to the developers that houses should be of a pleasing design: "We don't want ugly buildings" was the simple statement made by one commentator [19]. An artist's impression of the rear elevation of one of the semi-detached pairs is shown in Fig. 11.21; the houses are of three storeys in a restrained design [20].

Building has yet to start. In February 2006, the area was being readied for the infrastructure work – and for the relocation of the Great Crested Newts. A picture of the area is shown in Fig. 11.22. The buildings discernible in the centre of the picture are a row of existing semi-detached houses (five pairs) that will be kept in the development. They are of a very basic design and were probably built for lower-level colliery officials in the first part of the twentieth century.

Fig. 11.21. An artist's impression of a semi-detached pair for the Telford Millennium Community.

Fig. 11.22. The East Ketley site for the Telford Millennium Community before building had started. The cottages in the centre left of the photo were very likely built for colliery workers. They will be retained in the millennium development (photo 2006).

Concluding remarks

This chapter has addressed the plight of the semi-detached house

over the period 1990 to 2006. Unfortunately, official statistics no longer list the number of houses completed annually in the main categories: terraced, semi-detached, detached. The available statistics have changed their counting base to show the number of dwellings built with two, three or four bedrooms, etc. A review of recent sales literature from major estate builders indicates that approximately 30 per cent of the building sites include semi-detached houses, but the number of semis on these sites varies widely, from maybe ten to 30 per cent. If these figures can be trusted it means that less than ten per cent of the houses being built today are semi-detached. This is a dramatic fall from the inter-war boom years, where up towards 50 per cent of the houses being built were semi-detached, but the sharp decline has nevertheless been abated; statistics from around 1990 showed just slightly more than ten per cent being built annually. It is too early to assess whether the level of semis being built today has stabilized, or if there has been a slight growth over the past few years.

With regard to the architecture and style of the buildings erected around the turn of the millennium, the word 'unimaginative' about sums up the situation. The mock-Georgian and Scandinavian styles of the previous decades have continued, and even mock-Tudor has made a renewed impact on modern estate homes. The only significant change to the type of housing being built is the revival of the three-storey house in terraces, semis and detached properties. This has sometimes been the only way to provide spacious houses on developments where Government regulations have dictated high density housing. All too often, however, the results have been tall, austere houses that sit uncomfortably in their surroundings. One reason is, possibly, that although attention in many modern estates has been given to communal areas of landscaping and lawns, the houses themselves stand with their front façades more or less on the street; the luxury of a front garden that allows the house its privacy and the tenants to mark out their personal space has been denied most houses being built today.

Not all is discouraging, however. In this chapter, the section on Semis With A Difference showed a number of very non-traditional semi-detached houses, some with three storeys, that are both imaginative and exciting. The possibility of seeing a Modernist Revival was briefly debated. It is up to the potential purchaser, to the mortgage lender and to the planning authorities to decide if we are becoming courageous enough to leave the safe haven of established middle-class values.

References

1   Valerie Kam and Linda Sheridan, 1994. Quoted in David Rudlin and Nicholas Falk, *Building the 21st Century Home*, Architectural Press, Oxford 1999, p.69.

2   Office of the Deputy Prime Minister, *Planning Policy Guidance 3:Housing*, www.odpm.gov.uk, 2000.

3   RIBA, *Practice Bulletin – No.310*, 'Listening to the House Builders', 21 July 2005.

4   David Christopher, *British Culture, an Introduction*, Routledge, London and New York, 1999, p. 198.

5   Alain de Botton, 'The Special and the Ordinary', in *RIBA Journal*, February 2005, pp.26-27.

6   David Rudlin & Nicholas Falk, *Building the 21st Century Home*, Architectural Press, Oxford 1999, p.114.

7   Sarah Lonsdale, 'The Young Pretenders', in *The Sunday Telegraph, House and Home*, July 11, 2004, p.3.

8   E.L. Blackburne and E.F.S.Arch, *Suburban and Rural Architecture*, James Hagger, London 1867.

9   Bryant Homes, promotional material 2002.

10 Allison, promotional material 2004.

11 Beverley West, *The Changing Face of Housing in Britain*, UMIST, Manchester 1999, p.83.

12 Sergison Bates Architects, www.designforhomes.org, 2005.

13 Author not named, 'Stunning semis', in Planahome, Customer Publishing Ltd, Gomshall 2003, pp.126-27.

14 Bree Day Partnership, www.architect.co.uk, 2006.

15 Countrywide Properties, promotional material, 2005.

16 Contemporary Homes, a special issue produced by *Homebuilding & Renovating Magazine*, Ascent Publishing, Bromsgrove 2005.

17 *Ibid.* p.156.

18 Miller Homes, promotional material, 2005.

19 Telford Eye Newsletter, www.englishpartnerships.co.uk, 2004.

20 *Ibid.*

12

Suburban renaissance and the status of the semi-detached house today

"A lot of young professional couples who were previously based in the London area are opting out of the city and into a more suburban lifestyle"
The Times, February 2006

The quote above from a supplement to *The Times* in February 2006 hints at a possible change of attitude among younger people to today's highly celebrated urban life style. An URBED (Urban and Economical Development) report from 2004 commented: "A continuing 'urban exodus' combined with strong opposition to development in the country is likely to put the suburbs under increasing pressure" [1].

City living and urban regeneration or urban renaissance have been in the forefront of media attention for several years. Sections of the inner city (see Fig. 5.1) have in many cases been either renovated, or pulled down to make access for new apartment buildings. In either case the purpose has been to regenerate the city and create sustainable homes (a somewhat over-worked expression favoured by politicians and councillors) to attract a new generation of predominantly middle-class and upper middle-class city dwellers. In this, the efforts seem to have been successful.

Over-emphasis on inner-city regeneration has, however, left suburban areas sadly neglected. Only more recently has attention been turned to the suburbs. It has been recognised that the suburbs were the forgotten dimension of urban policies and that an urban renaissance could only work if also suburban problems were addressed and resolved. A partnership was created in 2002 to focus attention on the suburbs and to suggest solutions to revitalise suburban communities if and when necessary. The Partnership comprises a group of local councils, regional assemblies and the Civic Trust who have acknowledged that many suburbs have lost some of the qualities that made them so attractive to previous generations; the In Suburbia Partnership recognises that guidance and planning will be required for suburbs to survive and prosper – in short, that a suburban renaissance is called for. [5]

Public opinion, and certainly elitist opinion, has always been dismissive of the suburbs. William Howell, one of the architects of several high-rise blocks of flats built in the nineteen fifties at Roehampton, south London, stated in an interview in 1972 that "we don't want to rush out and live in horrid little suburbs and semi-detached houses"[1] and when questioned why the architects despised the suburban dream so, he answered: "We felt that it discarded the positive things from the city and got very little in exchange. We saw this in terms of the fact that we wouldn't want to go and live there because everything from bright lights to the art galleries, the continental restaurants, in short, 'life', the thing one goes to the city for – it didn't seem to be happening out in the suburbs" [2]. The argument is at best weak, failing as it does to recognise that the impetus to live in the suburbs is exactly to escape from the 'bright lights' of the city and to at least feel that you are closer to the green hills and the elusive cottage in the country. In 1935, J.B. Priestley in *The Beauty of Britain* wrote that there is "a great deal to be said for the suburbs: nearly all Englishmen are at heart country gentlemen" – a sentiment that still seems to hold true [3]. In 2004, Kate Fox wrote in *Watching the English*: "… the principle will be clear: the English all want to live in their own private little box with their own private little green bit" [4].

In this context, it is appropriate to remind ourselves of some of the statistics that address the way in which we have chosen to live in

---

1. The Roehampton flats and other massive high-rise developments in major cities in England were highly admired by the architectural community at the time. Unfortunately, many of these high-rise communities were a social failure, and in the seventies several blocks suffered the ignominy of being demolished with explosives.

12

this country. First of all, recent statistics show that nine per cent of us live in city centres, six per cent in villages and open country, 42 per cent in twentieth century suburbs, 23 per cent in a suburban/urban environment and 20 per cent in a suburban/rural environment, see Fig. 12.1. On the face of it a staggering 85 per cent live in either what we previously have called the outer suburbs, in the inner suburbs or in suburbia – in small, suburban-like estates on the edges of villages or townships. It looks as though suburban dwelling has a strong following.

It is interesting that large estates such as those created in Britain's new towns after the Second World War and those estates now being built in the Millennium Communities were never designated suburbs. The word suburb did not appear in the planning documents and official reports of the new town developments (see Chapter 10), nor does it appear in the official literature on Millennium Communities. The term Millennium Villages seems to be generally acceptable, as is Millennium Cities, but not Millennium Suburbs. This can only be because of the bad press suburban dwelling and suburban architecture has been subjected to for the past 100 years or so. One of the major efforts of the In Suburbia Partnership will be to ensure that the public perception, and maybe especially the media

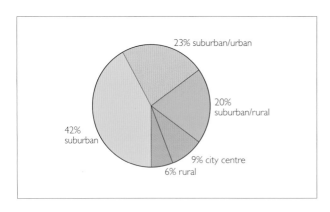

Fig. 12.1. Population distribution in England. Based on *In Suburbia* publication, 2005 [5].

perception of suburbs becomes a positive one. A senior policy officer from English Heritage told *The Guardian* newspaper: "There is a perception that the suburbs are not as fashionable as inner-city areas … there is a danger that the character of the suburbs will be overlooked" [6].

Suburbs are normally thought of as being robust communities, but they are less so today than when they were first built. Changing patterns of work, shopping and leisure have transformed them to a point where many will need help if they are to recapture some of their former attractiveness, see Fig. 12.2. Today, suburban high streets have lost their role as a place where you would go shopping on a Saturday morning and exchange gossip with shopkeepers and neighbours. Where you previously would find your local grocer, butcher, bank and bookshop, you now find take-aways, betting shops, cafes, hairdressing salons and boarded-up shops, see Fig. 12.3. It is not a question of turning back the clock, but a question of how to re-invent the high street to make it an interesting and appealing place to go to. The efforts of local authorities and the initiatives of associations such as the In Suburbia Partnership to champion a regeneration of suburban communities are very timely.

There are several factors that have brought about the decline of suburbs, but probably the most significant single cause is the dramatic rise in car ownership since the nineteen sixties. Firstly, the presence of one or more cars per household made many homeowners transform their front gardens into concrete parking spaces, as builders of semi-detached suburbia quite understandably had not built their estates with car ownership in mind, except in more affluent areas. Secondly, widespread car ownership means that suburbanites can travel to superstores on the edges of towns, where they can buy a week's supply of pet foods, price-cut beer, soft drinks and crisps and other household necessities more cheaply than in high street corner shops. One-stop shopping at superstores has taken over the role previously dominated by high street shopping parades. Many local stores on the high streets have already lost out to the supermarket chains and it seems inevitable that more will follow.

Another factor that has influenced the decline of high street shopping is the decrease in household sizes. According to Rogers and Power, household size has decreased from four persons per household in 1931 to 2.2 persons per household in 1991 [7]. The consequence is that there are just not enough people in the suburbs today for local retailers to make a living. Unless more people move into the suburbs and are offered high quality shopping and service locally, high street shops will continue to go out of business and banks will close their branches.

Fig. 12.2. High street in the nineteen thirties. Unidentified photo. It might be the high street of a market town or it could be the shopping parade of a suburban community.

Fig. 12.3. Photograph of a 2006 suburban high street showing a typical mixture of local services.

Bus services have already lost out to the motorcar and will continue to do so, with less frequent services now offered and the possible closure of some routes.

The plight of the semi-detached house is equally illustrative. Its history has been chartered in the chapters of this book from the late seventeenth century and into the new millennium. It has been accused of being jerry-built, it has been ridiculed in writings and in cartoons, it has been given insulting nick-names and the numbers being built annually have fallen over the past 50 years – but it is still the preferred dwelling in this country. Government statistics from 2003 showed that one third of us live in semi-detached houses, see Fig. 1.2. Land prices and building regulations have contributed to the decline of the semi-detached house, as has the changing structure of society. The three- or four-bedroomed semi is definitely a family-oriented dwelling. Now, however, the traditional family pattern is on the decline and more and more people are living on their own. The number of single-person households has increased over the past 30 years by ten per cent, so that it now stands at close to 30 per cent, which goes a long way to explain the current attention bestowed upon living in a flat in an urban environment. On a positive note, more and more people are working from home, thanks to the communications leap created by personal computers, laptops and easy access to the internet. This means that many more young entrepreneurs starting out in business will look towards moving into a house with space for one or two small offices. In this respect the traditional semi-detached house is a real option.

Notwithstanding the social and legislative changes we are seeing today, the semi-detached house is so much a part of English suburban life that it would be impossible to imagine our society without their familiar presence. They are just so resilient and enduringly popular. There are many good reasons why semi-detached houses enjoy the regard of broad swathes of English society, from working class to upper middle class. Some have already been mentioned in foregoing chapters, but the following list of positive attributes is a reminder of why we find so many:

1. They save land compared with detached houses.
2. They are cheaper to build than detached houses because they share a party wall.
3. There is easy access to the back of the house compared with a terraced house.

4. Being close to neighbours gives a feeling of security compared with a detached house.
5. They represent a financially attractive compromise between a terraced house and a detached house.
6. The front elevation is often unified to give the onlooker the impression that the house is detached – a status indicator.

Underlying the arguments above is the latent assumption that the owner or occupier has aspirations regarding his or her preferred type of dwelling. It is not without reason that we in this country, more than in most, talk about a property ladder. For many, and certainly for young couples and families, the starting rung of the ladder is an affordable terraced property; from here, you may advance to a semi-detached house and, ultimately, to a detached house in a 'good' area.[2]

The arguments listed above are logical enough, but they do not explain why the English seem to be the only nation in Europe that has such a preponderance of semis.[3] While semi-detached houses are not unknown on the Continent, they represent only a small proportion of the residences available. In fact, flats will, in general, make up the bulk of the dwellings. For young couples and single persons starting out in their careers, a flat is the natural first choice of accommodation. The next step can be a terrace house or, just as likely a small, detached property in a suburb.

The history of the semi-detached house in other countries is poorly documented and it would be presumptuous at this stage to propose weighty explanations for the significant differences between the number of semi-detached houses in this country and elsewhere. One can speculate that the Englishman's relationship with the semi may be part of a highly structured class system, an in-bred desire to 'keep up with the Joneses,' and what might be called the English national character. It is an interesting cultural phenomenon, which still awaits a consensus and the consideration of, for example, social anthropologists.

A final comment on the type and style of semi-detached houses being built today is in order.

First of all, as we have seen in Chapter 11, the trend over the past few years has been to build semi-detached houses in three storeys. This allows the builder who is restricted to small plot sizes to offer

---

2. These days, areas worth considering can be identified by their postcode.
3. When asked why the English have such an affinity to the semi-detached house, one person replied to me: "Well, we've always lived in them, haven't we?"

12

buyers a fairly generous house size in terms of number of rooms and floor area. It is, in a sense, a return to Georgian times, where the architects of limited plot sizes resorted to building upwards; this was in order to accommodate the required number of rooms – see the many examples in Chapter 2. It is basically a sound idea, and although it represents a significant breakaway from the conservative buyer's concept of a semi-detached house, it is quite likely to become a popular building type. The problem, if any, may be purely visual. Some of these house designs have been criticized as resembling slices out of a low-rise apartment block.

Secondly, the designs being offered to the house-buying public are still mostly a pastiche. Tarbuck's lament in the mid-nineteenth century regarding 'copyism' is evidently as applicable today as it was more than 150 years ago (the quotation is given in Chapter 3 of this book). Some styles are careful reproductions of Victorian villas (Fig. 11.3), some continue the Tudorbethan tradition of the inter-war period (Fig. 11.4) and most are just unashamedly eclectic and mildly boring (Figs. 11.5 to 11.8). There are, however, some quite different and much more interesting semi-detached houses being built, although still small in number, see Figs. 11.10 to 11.17. A 2006 estate development on the banks of the Grand Union Canal shows a successful compromise between the traditional and the enterprising, as shown in Fig. 12.4. Hopefully, more and more speculative builders will feel encouraged to move away from the present stock-of-trade building styles towards the more adventurous.

Fig. 12.4. An example of a new development of semi-detached houses on the Grand Union Canal north of London [8]. The houses are in three stories and represent a compromise between the traditional and the adventurous.

References

1   URBED (Urban and Economic Development Group), Neighbourhood Revival, www.urbed.com 2004.

2   Quoted in Paul Oliver et al., *Dunroamin*, The Suburban Semi and its Enemies, Barrie & Jenkins, London 1982, p.19 and p.21.

3   J.B. Priestley, *The Beauty of Britain*, 1935.

4   Kate Fox, *Watching the English*, Hodder and Stoughton, London 2004, p.111.

5   Hampshire County Council, *In Suburbia*, publication by Hampshire County Council 2002, p.4.

6   Matt Weaver, *The Guardian*, September 28, 2005.

7   Richard Rogers and Anne Power, *Cities for a Small Country*, Faber and Faber, London 2000, p.39.

8   Fairview New Homes Ltd, promotional literature for Kings Langley development 2006.

Appendix 1

Schematic of periods and architectural styles

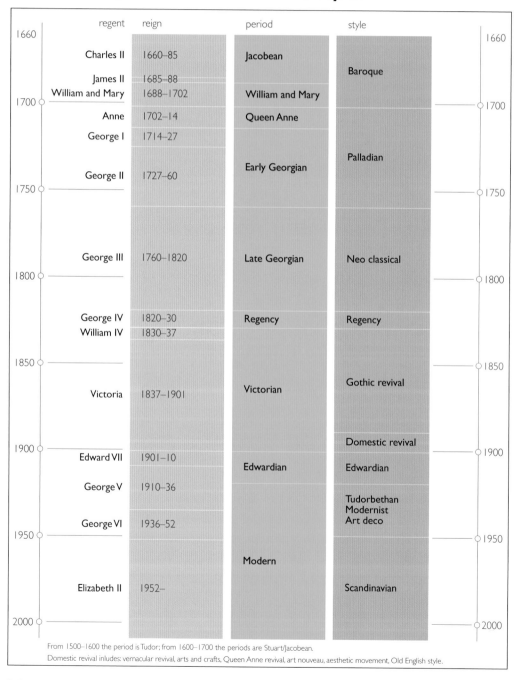

	regent	reign	period	style	
1660					1660
	Charles II	1660–85	Jacobean	Baroque	
	James II	1685–88			
	William and Mary	1688–1702	William and Mary		
1700	Anne	1702–14	Queen Anne		1700
	George I	1714–27		Palladian	
	George II	1727–60	Early Georgian		
1750					1750
	George III	1760–1820	Late Georgian	Neo classical	
1800					1800
	George IV	1820–30	Regency	Regency	
	William IV	1830–37			
1850					1850
	Victoria	1837–1901	Victorian	Gothic revival	
1900				Domestic revival	1900
	Edward VII	1901–10	Edwardian	Edwardian	
	George V	1910–36		Tudorbethan Modernist Art deco	
	George VI	1936–52			
1950			Modern		1950
	Elizabeth II	1952–		Scandinavian	
2000					2000

From 1500–1600 the period is Tudor; from 1600–1700 the periods are Stuart/Jacobean.
Domestic revival inludes: vernacular revival, arts and crafts, Queen Anne revival, art nouveau, aesthetic movement, Old English style.

Appendix 2

Neo-Georgian semis and speculative bungalows in the inter-war period

NEO-GEORGIAN SEMIS

It has been mentioned several times that the middle-class home owners of the inter-war period were loath to consider neo-Georgian developments because of their strong association with council housing and the lower classes. The speculative builders knew this and very few ventured to build in the neo-Georgian style. The situation changed after the Second World War, but in the nineteen twenties and thirties the number of speculatively built semis in this style was quite insignificant, and because of this they have not been included in the classes of universal semis. One rare example is shown in the advertisement in Fig. 1, itself quite a handsome house, but far removed from the prevailing romantic tastes of middle-class buyers.

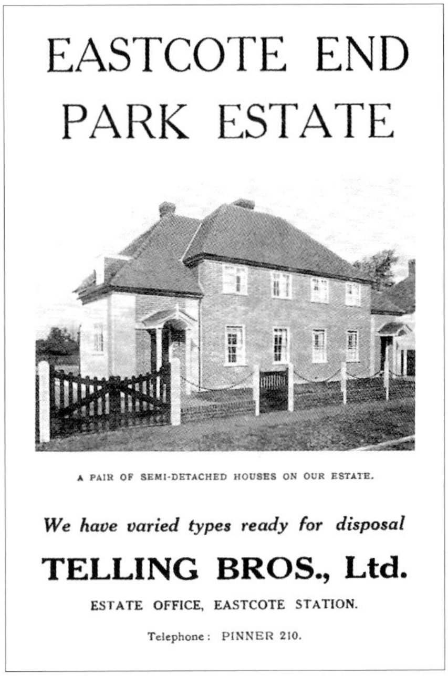

THE SPECULATIVE BUNGALOW

The inter-war period saw a surge not only of houses built in the mould of the universal semi, but also of bungalows. This single-storey dwelling originated in India. The word itself derives from the Indian word 'bangla' meaning from Bengal, now Bangladesh. The middle-class British who went out to administer the British Raj in the nineteenth century found the spacious and well-ventilated low buildings suited to their tastes. The bungalow was first introduced in England in a seaside resort for the wealthy in the mid-Victorian period, and it obtained instant social recognition.

By the end of the century the bungalow spread inland, mainly in south-east England, and started sliding down the social scale to cater for the aspirations of business men working in London and looking for a permanent or holiday home within commuting distance of the City. In the early part of the twentieth century, the bungalow became fashionable among the artistically inclined and the Arts and Crafts style was successfully combined with the bungalow form. Large estates of bungalows began to appear and the critics were quick

EASTCOTE END PARK ESTATE

A PAIR OF SEMI-DETACHED HOUSES ON OUR ESTATE.

We have varied types ready for disposal

TELLING BROS., Ltd.

ESTATE OFFICE, EASTCOTE STATION.

Telephone: PINNER 210.

Fig. 1. Advertisement from the 1924 edition of Metro-Land showing a speculatively built semi-detached house in the neo-Georgian style. This was quite exceptional for the period because of the council house image evoked by the style.

Fig. 2. Tudorbethan semi-detached bungalow, 1934 advertisement for New Ideal Homestead.

to coin the term 'bungaloid growth' that according to one writer in 1928 "constitutes England's most disfiguring disease, having, from sporadic beginning, now become our premier epidemic" [1]. Although the original glee of being able to retreat to solitude, nature and a healthy environment still remained, the more conservative and ever prudish middle classes were concerned about the social levelling and freedom of life, and not least by the stories circulating in the popular press of loose morals on the bungalow estates.

The bungalow was essentially a detached type of dwelling, and it is uncertain when the first semi-detached bungalows were built, but it is a fact that they became popular between the wars. One reason for the popularity was that people were able to see for themselves that their heroes from the silver screen lived in such single-storey homes. The glamour of Hollywood did much to allay the fears of the middle classes regarding the social acceptability of the bungalow. The builders were able to transfer all the elements of their two-storey semis onto the bungalows, Tudorbethan and non-Tudorbethan.

Fig. 3. Semi-detached bungalow with unifying hipped roof over the bays [2].

Figs. 2 and 3 illustrate just two examples of nineteen thirties semi-detached bungalows, a cottage with dominating bays and mock-Tudor gables, and one with a unifying hipped roof over the two centre bays. This roof, as well as the main hipped roof, has a small gablet.[1]

---

1. The architectural term for the main roof is a gambrel roof.

References

1   John Burnett, *A Social History of Housing 1815-1970*, Methuen, Newton Abbot 1978, p.265.

2   Greg Stevenson, *The 1930s Home*, Shire Publications, Princes Risborough 2000, p.14.

Bibliography

Abercrombie, Patrick, 'Modern Town Planning in England', in *The Town Planning Review*, I, No.2, 1910.

Abercrombie, Patrick, *Greater London Plan*, HMSO, London 1944.

Anonymous, 'The Systematic Study of Town Planning', in *The Builder*, 95, December 12, 1908.

Anonymous, 'Progress at Coventry', in *Garden Cities and Town Planning Magazine*, 11, 1912.

Anonymous, 'Listening to the House Builders', in RIBA Practice Bulletin, 21 July 2005.

Anonymous, 'Stunning semis', in *Planahome*, 2003.

Atkinson, T.D. *English Architecture*, 9th edition, Methuen & Co Ltd, London 1928.

Barker, F. *Greenwich and Blackheath Past*, Historical Publications Ltd, London 1993.

Barley, M.W. *The English Farmhouse and Cottage*, Alan Sutton, Gloucester 1987.

Barrett, Helena and Phillips, John, *Suburban Style*, Macdonald & Co (Publishers), London 1987.

Bates, Sergison, www.designforhomes.org, 2005.

Bayer, P. *Art Deco Architecture*, Thames & Hudson, London 1992.

Beevers R, *The Garden City Utopia*, Olivia Press, Abingdon 1988, p165.

Benton, Charlotte et.al. (editors), *Art Deco 1910-1939*, V&A Publications, London 2003.

Berry, F. *Housing: The Great British Failure*, 1974.

Bertram, Anthony, *Design*, Penguin Books, Harmondsworth 1938.

Betjeman, John, *Ghastly Good Taste*, first published 1933, reprinted by Century, London 1986.

Betjeman, John, Slough, poem 1937, reprinted in *Collected Poems* by John Murray (Publishers), London 2003.

Bird, Eric L. 'Your new house', in *The Daily Mail Ideal Home Book*, London 1947-48.

Blackburne, E.L. and Arch, E.F.S.A. *Suburban and Rural Architecture*, James Hagger, London 1867.

Botton, Alain de, 'The special and the ordinary', in *RIBA Journal*, February 2005.

Bowen, Elizabeth, *Attractive Modern Homes*, first published 1941. Reprinted in the *Collected Stories of Elizabeth Bowen*, Penguin, London 1983.

Bree Day Partnership, www.architect.co.uk, 2006.

Brookhouse, S. *The Artisan's Quarter*, The Hampstead Garden Suburb Residents Association, Hampstead 1998.

Brown, Richard, *Domestic Architecture*, 1842.

Brunskill, R.W. *Vernacular Architecture*, 2nd edition, Faber and Faber, London 1978.

Building News, 16 November 1877.

Burnett, John, *A Social History of Housing 1815-1970*, Methuen, Newton Abbot 1978.

Central Housing Advisory Committee, *The Design of Dwellings*, (The Dudley Report), HMSO, London 1944.

Cherry ,Bridget and Pevsner, Nikolaus, *The Buildings of England, London 2: South*, Penguin Books, London 1983.

Cherry, Bridget and Pevsner, Nikolaus, *The Buildings of England, London 3: North West*, Penguin Books, London 1998.

Cherry, Bridget and Pevsner, Nikolaus, *The Buildings of England, London 4: North*, Penguin Books, London 1998.

Chitty, M. *Discovering Historic Wavertree*, The Wavertree Society, Liverpool 1999

Christopher, D. *British Culture*, Routledge, London and New York 1999.

Clark, Kenneth, *The Gothic Revival*, 3rd edition, John Murray, London 1962.

Cosh, Mary, *The Squares of Islington – Part II*, Islington Archaeology & History Society 1993.

Contemporary Homes, a special issue produced by Homebuilding and Renovating Magazine, Ascent Publishing, Bromsgrove 2005.

CPRE, *Building in Cheshire*, Council for the Preservation of Rural England, 1939.

Cranfield, I. *Art Deco House Style*, David & Charles, Newton Abbot 2001.

Daniel, Rebecca, and Brandwood, Geoff, editors, *Ruskin and Architecture*, Spire Books Ltd, Reading 2003.

Davies, C. *The Prefabricated Home*, Reaktion Books Ltd, London 2005.

Davison, T.R. *Port Sunlight – a Record of its Artistic and Pictorial Aspect*, BT Batsford, London 1916.

Dickens, Charles, *Great Expectations*, first published 1861, Penguin Books, 1979.

Eden, Emily, *The Semi-detached House*, 1859.

Edwards, Arthur, *The Design of Suburbia*, Pembridge Press, London 1981.

Ellis, Sarah, *The Women of England: Their Social Duties and Domestic Habits*, 1839.

Flanders, Judith, *The Victorian House*, Harper Perennial, London 2003.

Foster, R.F.W.B. Yeats, *A Life*, Oxford University Press, Oxford 1997.

Fox, Kate, *Watching the English*, Hodder, London 2005.

Gardner, Jean, *Houses of the Art Deco Years*, Braiswick, Felixstowe 2004.

Girouard, M. *Sweetness and Light: The Queen Anne Movement 1860-1900*, Yale University Press, New Haven and London 1977.

Gloag, John, *The Englishman's Castle*, Eyre & Spottiswoode, London 1944.

Gloag, John, *Victorian Comfort*, Adam and Charles Black, London 1961.

Glazier, R. *A Manual of Historic Ornament*.

Gough Maps 41 G4, Bodleian Library, Oxford.

Greysmith, B. *Tracing the History of your House*, Hodder & Stoughton, London 1994.

Grossmith, G. and W. *The Diary of a Nobody*, first published in book form 1892, edition consulted published by Penguin Books, London 1999.

Guild, Robin, *The Complete Victorian House Book*, Sidgwick & Jackson, London 1989.

Guillery, John, *The Small House in Eighteenth-Century London*, Yale University Press, New Haven and London 2004.

Halsey, J. and Webb, J. *Twentieth-Century British Social Trends*, MacMillan Press, London 2000.

Hanson, J. 'Selling the dream', in *Architects Journal*, 15 April 1992.

Harrison, Michael, *Bournville: Model Village to Garden Suburb*, Phillimore, Chichester 1999.

Hicks, J. and Allen, G. *A Century of Change: Trends in UK Statistics since 1900*, Research Paper 99/111, House of Commons Library, 21 December 1999.

Hillier, B. *Art Deco of the 20s and 30s*, London and New York, 1968.

Hines, C. *Art Deco London*, Park House Press, Twickenham 2003.

Hubbard, E. and Shippobottom, M. *A Guide to Port Sunlight Village*, Liverpool University Press, Liverpool 1988.

Hughes, T.H. and Lamborn, E.A.G. *Towns and Town Planning, Ancient and Modern*, Clarendon Press, Oxford 1923.

In Suburbia Partnership, *In Suburbia, Delivering Sustainable Communities*, Hampshire County Council 2002.

Iredale, David and Barrett, John, *Discovering your Old House*, Shire Publications Ltd, Princes Risborough, 2002.

Jackson, Alan A. *Semi-detached London*, 2nd edition, Wild Swan Publications Ltd, Didcot 1991.

Jackson, F. *Sir Raymond Unwin: Architect, Planner and Visionary*, Zwemmer, London 1985.

Jensen, Finn, 'Mine's a half', in *Period House*, Essential Publishing, Colchester November 2003.

Kerr, Robert, *The Gentleman's House*, John Murray, London 1871.

Lancaster, Osborne, *A Cartoon History of Architecture*, John Murray, London 1975.

Lawrence, R.R. and Chris, T. *The Period House-Style, Detail & Decoration 1774-1914*, Weidenfeld & Nicholson, London 1996.

Leach, Maria, *The Wicked Wit of Oscar Wilde*, Michael O'Mara Publishing Limited, London 2004.

Lewis, D. *The Illustrated History of Liverpool Suburbs*, Breedon Books, Derby 2003.

Local Government Board, *Housing Manual*, HMSO, London 1919.

Long, Helen, *The Edwardian House*, Manchester University Press, Manchester 1993.

Long, Helen, *Victorian Houses and their details*, Architectural Press, Oxford 2002.

Lonsdale, Sarah, 'The young pretenders', in *The Sunday Telegraph, House and Home*, July 11, 2004.

Loudon, John Claudius, *Encyclopedia of Cottage, Farm and Villa Architecture*, Longmans, London 1833.

Mansbridge, Michael, *John Nash, A Complete Catalogue*, Phaidon Press Limited, London 2004.

Metro-Land, 1924, facsimile edition, Southbank Publishing, London 2004.

Miller, Mervyn, *Letchworth, the first Garden City*, Phillimore, Chichester 1989.

Miller, Mervyn and Gray, A. Stuart, *Hampstead Garden Suburb*, Phillimore Chichester 1992.

Ministry of Health, *Housing Manual*, HMSO, London 1944.

Ministry of Health, *Housing Manual*, HMSO, London 1949.

Ministry of Housing and Local Government, *Homes for today & tomorrow*, (The Parker-Morris Report), HMSO, London 1961.

MoDA, *Little Palaces, House and Home in the Inter-war Suburbs*, Middlesex University Press, Barnet 2003.

Muthesius, Stefan, *The English Terraced House*, Yale University Press, New Haven 1982.

Nelson, John, *History of Islington*, 1811.

Office of the Deputy Prime Minister, *Planning Policy Guidance 3: Housing*, www.odpm.gov.uk, 2000.

Oliver, Paul et.al. *Dunroamin, The Suburban Semi and its Enemies*, Barrie & Jenkins, London 1981.

Orwell, George, *Keep the Aspidistra Flying*, Penguin Books, London 2000, first published 1936.

Orwell, George, *Coming up for Air*, Secker & Warburg, London 1954.

Overseas Filmgroup Inc. *Keep the Aspidistra Flying*, film adapted from George Orwell's novel, shown on BBC2 1997.

Oxford English Reference Dictionary, 2nd edition, Oxford University Press, Oxford 1996.

Pain, William, *The Builders' Companion*, London 1762.

Penguin Reference, Dictionary of Architecture & Landscape Architecture, 5th edition, Penguin Books, London 1999.

Philpott, H.B. *Modern Cottages, Villas and Bungalows*, John Dicks, London 1908.

Powers, Alan, *Modern: The Modern Movement in Britain*, Merrell, London 2005.

Priestley, J.B. *The Beauty of Britain*, 1935.

Pugin, Augustus Welby, *The True Principles of Pointed or Christian Architecture*, John Weale, London 1841.

Prizeman, John, *Houses of Britain: The Outside View*, Quiller Press, London 2003.

Quiney, A. *House and Home: A History of the small English House*, BBC, London 1986.

Rasmussen, Steen Eiler, *London: the Unique City*, 1961.

Richards, J.M. 'Failure of the new towns', in *Architectural Review*, 114, 1953.

Richards, J.M. 'Live architecture, 1951', in *The Daily Mail Ideal Home Book, The Daily Mail Home Exhibition Department of Associated Newspapers Ltd*, London 1950-51.

Richardson, C.J. *The Englishman's Home from a Cottage to a Mansion*, London 1870.

Ritchie, B. *The Good Builder*, the John Laing Story, James & James, London 1997.

Rocque, John, *Plan of the Cities of London and Westminster and Borough of Southwark*, London 1746.

Rogers, Richard and Power, Anne, *Cities for a small country*, Faber and Faber, London 2000.

Rudlin, David and Falk, Nicholas, *Building the 21st Century Home*, Architectural Press, Oxford 1999.

Ruskin, John, *The Seven Lamps of Architecture*, first published 1849, edition consulted published by George Allen & Sons, London 1907.

Ruskin, John, *The Stones of Venice*, first published 1851-53, edition consulted in three volumes published by George Routledge & Sons, London c.1900.

Ruskin, John, letter 29, in *Fors Clavigera*, 1873.

Saint, Andrew et al. *London Suburbs*, Merrell Holberton Publishers, London 1999.

Sheeran, George, *Good Houses Built of Stone*, Allanwood Books, Pudsey 1986.

Short, J. *Housing in Britain*, Methuen & Co Ltd, London 1982.

Soisson, Louis de and Kenyon, A.W.M. *Site Planning in Practice at Welwyn Garden City*, Ernest Benn Limited, London 1927.

Stevenson, Greg, *The 1930s Home*, Shire Publications, Princes Risborough 2000.

Summerson, John, *Architecture in Britain 1530-1830*, Yale University Press, 9th edition, New Haven and London 1993.

Summerson, John, *Georgian London*, First published 1945, Yale University Press, New Haven and London 2003.

Tarbuck, E.L. *The Builder's Practical Director*, Hagger, London 1855-8.

Telford Eye Newsletter; www.englishpartnerships.co.uk, 2004.

Trendall, E.W. *Original Designs for Cottages and Villas in the Grecian, Gothic and Italian Styles of Architecture*, London 1831.

Unwin, Raymond, *Town Planning in Practice*, 2nd edition, T. Fisher Unwin, London 1911.

URBED (Urban and Economical Development Group), *Neighbourhood Revival*, www.urbed.com, 2004.

Wade, C. *The Streets of Hampstead*, Campden History Society, 2000.

Walter, Tudor, *Housing Manual on the Preparation of State-aided Housing Schemes, Report of the Committee on Building Construction and Dwellings for the Working Classes*, HMSO, London 1919.

Weaver, Matt, in *The Guardian*, September 28, 2005.

West, B. *The Changing Face of Housing in Britain*, UMIST, Manchester 1999.

Whitehouse, J.H. 'Bournville: A Study in Housing Reform', in *The Studio*, XXIV, No.105, December 1901.

Wilkinson, C. *Liverpool from the Air*, The Bluecoat Press, Liverpool 1999.

Wilmott, P. and Young, M. *Family and Class in a London Suburb*, Routledge and Kegan Paul, London 1957.

Woodforde, John, *The Truth about Cottages*, Routledge & Kegan Paul, London 1969.

Wright, H.M. *Small Houses £500-£2,500*, 2nd edition, The Architectural Press, London 1946.

Yorke, F.R.S. *The Modern House in England*, 3rd edition, The Architectural Press, London 1948.

OTHER GREAT BOOKS
FROM OVOLO PUBLISHING

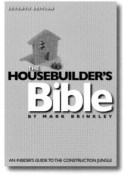

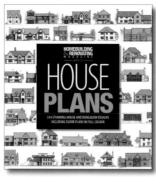

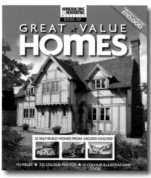

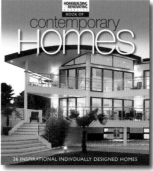

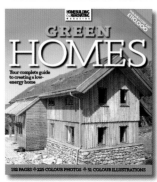

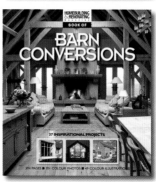

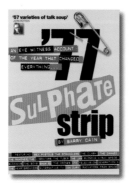

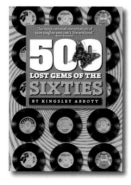

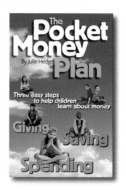

www.ovolobooks.co.uk